POPE FRANCIS AS MORAL LEADER

POPE FRANCIS AS MORAL LEADER

Ethicist, Discerner, Communicator, and Advocate for Social Justice

THOMAS MASSARO, SJ

Paulist Press
New York / Mahwah, NJ

Cover image by Mazur/cbcew.org.uk
Cover design by Sharyn Banks
Book design by Lynn Else

Library of Congress Cataloging-in-Publication Data
Names: Massaro, Thomas, 1961– author.
Title: Pope Francis as moral leader : ethicist, discerner, communicator, and advocate for social justice / Thomas Massaro.
Description: New York : Paulist Press, [2023] | Includes bibliographical references and index. | Summary: "This work describes and analyzes the contribution of Pope Francis as an ethicist, a practitioner of discernment, a skilled communicator, and a strong advocate for social justice on the global stage"—Provided by publisher.
Identifiers: LCCN 2023001722 (print) | LCCN 2023001723 (ebook) | ISBN 9780809156634 (paperback) | ISBN 9780809188246 (ebook)
Subjects: LCSH: Francis, Pope, 1936---Ethics. | Christian leadership—Catholic Church. | Social justice—Religious aspects—Catholic Church. | Church and social problems—Catholic Church.
Classification: LCC BX1378.7 .M3768 2023 (print) | LCC BX1378.7 (ebook) | DDC 282.092—dc23/eng/20230616
LC record available at https://lccn.loc.gov/2023001722
LC ebook record available at https://lccn.loc.gov/2023001723

ISBN 978-0-8091-5663-4 (paperback)
ISBN 978-0-8091-8824-6 (e-book)

Published by Paulist Press
997 Macarthur Boulevard
Mahwah, New Jersey 07430
www.paulistpress.com

Printed and bound in the
United States of America

To my parents, Joseph Massaro and Nancy DiNardi Massaro,
and Jorge Mario Bergoglio

CONTENTS

ACKNOWLEDGMENTS

I AM GRATEFUL TO the many people and institutions that have generously supported me in producing this volume. Though too many to count, the institutions certainly include the university communities that have provided the time and resources that allowed me to study and teach, over several decades now, the topics covered in this study: Catholic social teaching, leadership, church history, ethics, communications, spirituality, and the social sciences. A special word of thanks goes to Fordham University, my current employer and home, for its generous faculty fellowship and research support arrangements.

The Society of Jesus also qualifies as an institution that has supported me, but of course it is much more than that. Both the future Pope Francis and I were drawn to enter the Jesuits for many reasons, but above all because its mission and social justice commitments open unique opportunities to serve the people of God. I am eternally indebted to my brother Jesuits, to the USA East Province of the Society of Jesus, and to my current community, the Spellman Hall Jesuit Community at Fordham, for so much support and encouragement.

Finally, I am grateful to my family for nurturing and supporting me in innumerable ways at every juncture of my life, including during the writing of this book. No one could imaginably write a book on moral leadership without being surrounded by strong exemplars of ethical living, and I have certainly been blessed with many within my own family of origin. Each of my four sisters—Carla, Tana, Mari-Celeste, and Regina—have displayed splendid leadership qualities in raising amazing children and in their respective careers. My parents, Nancy and the late Joseph Massaro, not only valued but daily practiced outstanding principles of morality that shaped me and my siblings in significant ways. Interestingly, the life courses of my parents (Catholic children and grandchildren of immigrants from Italy to the New World, born in the 1930s in large cities of the Western hemisphere) bear striking similarities to that of Pope Francis. If there was something in their early life experience that led Joseph Massaro, Nancy DiNardi Massaro, and Jorge Mario Bergoglio to walk in such commendable ways of ethical leadership, I hope we can bottle that ingredient and distribute it widely. To these three moral leaders I dedicate this book.

INTRODUCTION

The Meaning of Moral Leadership

OPINIONS WILL NATURALLY vary. When asked about the most significant contributions of Pope Francis, some respondents will volunteer specific accomplishments, such as reforming the Roman Curia or reorganizing the Vatican Bank or diversifying the membership of the College of Cardinals, or perhaps publishing an encyclical letter that finally focused the Catholic Church's attention squarely on the environmental crisis. Other observers of Francis may propose as his greatest accomplishment not such a specific initiative but rather the enactment of some broader priorities. These might include his relentless advocacy for refugees, his longstanding rhetorical battle against clericalism, his attention to the many challenges facing family life today, or his ongoing focus on promoting virtues like mercy and practices like evangelization and dialogue—both within the church and among world religions.

Concerns and Accomplishments

There is, of course, no wrong answer to this inquiry. The papal achievements of Francis are many, as are legitimate perspectives on their ranking and relative importance, but notice how the items that might be selected to top any such list fall into two categories. First, many of them are primarily matters regarding the internal life of the Roman Catholic Church. Upon the election of Francis as pope in March of 2013, a consensus formed that the Cardinal-electors had selected this Jesuit archbishop of Buenos Aires, Argentina, largely because of his reputation for excellent organizational management and church renewal. In the wake of innumerable scandals that had dragged on for years, the worldwide church clearly needed to "get its house in order" and Cardinal Jorge Mario Bergoglio was perceived as the right man for this enormous job of reform and revitalization. He received an overwhelming mandate to tackle these longstanding internal problems within Catholicism.

Second, other prominent items on anyone's list of chief accomplishments in the papacy of Francis fall into the category of outward-directed initiatives, as the church seeks to engage the wider world. Though not specifically addressing the internal life of the church itself, these social concerns regarding such matters as peacemaking and global economic justice reflect the self-understanding of the Christian community as an agent of positive social change and prioritizing outreach to marginalized people of all faiths. While every recent pope has taken up the mission of social justice with insight and energy, Francis has excelled in his pursuit of an agenda of global social concern and advocacy for the most vulnerable.

Contributing as he has in word and deed to the social teachings of the Catholic Church, Francis embodies the public face of the church, as it turns its attention to what are often termed *ad extra* involvements. These outward-directed energies complement any pope's *ad intra* concerns, to cite the converse Latin phrase describing internal church affairs. As much as political heads of state must deal with both domestic matters and foreign policy, popes find themselves splitting their attention between these two parts of their job description. Of course, these two components of the huge portfolio that popes routinely manage are not so hermetically sealed as this summary description might suggest; papal decisions on internal matters invariably hold profound implications for world affairs and vice versa.

Principles of Leadership

A key word we have yet to employ is *leadership*. If this has become too much of a buzzword for the comfort of some, it is probably because of the immense (and uneven in quality) literature on leadership that has come primarily out of the business community in recent decades. Corporate executives—and the entrepreneurs, boards of directors, and investors who employ them—are always on the lookout for the optimal package of skills, personal qualities, temperament, and instincts that will produce commercial success. An entire industry focuses on identifying and developing the optimal mix of risk-taking innovation and organizational maintenance that will maximize profits or, in the case of nonprofit organizations that tread a parallel path, advance the mission as fully as possible. Besides innumerable books, articles, and workshops on these and related topics, a proliferation of MBA programs focusing on "best practices" in executive leadership are now joined by PhD programs on leadership in business contexts and beyond.

It is doubtful that Pope Francis has read any of the abundant leadership literature or taken much notice of these trends in business management training. It would be amusing to imagine his reaction to the typical portrayal of the ideal corporate executive that emanates from this veritable industry of books, videos, workshops, and degree programs. While he might dismiss some of its content, such as the frequent commendation of ruthlessness in seeking a competitive edge, there are many themes he might well affirm, including perhaps the emphasis on "thinking outside the box" and boldness in innovation. It is easy to predict that Francis would discover an affinity for the model of "servant leadership" that Robert K. Greenleaf developed as far back as the 1970s as a promising trajectory for all manner of success.

Of course, there is a vast gulf between a business enterprise and any religious community. The challenges faced and the goals embraced by leaders in each context are starkly different, even if some points of parallel can be identified. One prominent author who treats this intersection with great insight is Chris Lowney, a former Jesuit and highly accomplished business executive who has studied Catholic institutions in general, and the leadership of Pope Francis more specifically, in detail.

Just a few months after Francis assumed the papacy (his election was announced with great fanfare on March 13, 2013), Lowney published the volume *Pope Francis: Why He Leads the Way He Leads.*[1] What most accounts for the remarkably rapid publication of this book (it appeared in print well before the end of 2013) is that Lowney had for decades been studying management practices and the lessons that are transferable between the worlds of business and religious organizations, such as the Society of Jesus. His bestselling *Heroic Leadership: Best Practices from a 450-Year-Old Company that Changed the World* (2003)[2] drew noteworthy parallels between the leadership principles enacted by the Jesuit order as it built up its impressive footprint of influence over centuries of service to the faith, on one hand, and the practices of many highly successful corporations in the landscape of the contemporary global economy, on the other hand.

Styles and Strategies of Leadership

While the lessons outlined by Lowney defy easy summary, it is fair to say that the core points of similarity involve the ways that organizations, whether religious or for-profit, benefit greatly from conscious attention to eliciting authentic motivation of their personnel, particularly in ways that emphasize mission-orientation and broad service, as opposed to crass self-aggrandizement in a narrow sense. While religious organizations readily describe this overarching vision as a part of their operative spirituality, secular organizations—for-profits or even nonprofits such as schools—face a steeper challenge in developing explicit mission statements or implicit self-understandings that communicate the ideals of service that propel their efforts. A skilled servant-leader in either context, one who appeals to high ideals with authenticity and credibility in the pursuit of a laudable organizational mission, can really make a critical difference.

Does not this profile of a motivational leader describe Pope Francis? While eager to avoid falling into uncritical hagiography in describing the accomplishments of Francis, it seems fair to provide a highly positive account of the leadership qualities of the first pope from the southern or western hemispheres. Any objective observer would recognize how Francis brought a rich spirituality of service and many fresh perspectives to the papacy, and it is undoubtedly a valuable exercise to examine the nature of his leadership. Obviously, none of this analysis supports the claim that the pre-Francis Catholic Church, in its nearly two-thousand-year history, entirely lacked what Francis has contributed. Popes and other leaders, of course, have brought remarkable skills and virtues to the exercise of ecclesial authority as teachers, pastors, and administrators. The task ahead is simply to describe and assess the distinctive and noteworthy contributions of this one universal pastor. The following chapters pursue that task in a manner that is at once appreciative of Francis and still on the lookout for various shortcomings and deficits in his leadership. Like all leaders, Francis displays strengths and weaknesses; identifying and analyzing both sides of the coin will provide insight into crucial dynamics of leadership in the contemporary church and the wider world.

One of the clearest lessons on display—again, both in the business management literature and in the experience of church leadership—is that the most effective leaders do not settle for the simple agenda of consolidating all power in themselves. They resist the temptation, even when such a path might appear within their grasp, of arranging to concentrate all authority at the top of the "command and control" pyramid (whether in the CEO suite or in the office of the papacy). The superior alternative is to create a collaborative institutional culture that favors collective decision-making and distributing authority quite broadly. This is not simply a matter of prudent delegation of tasks by sheer necessity, but rather of credibly communicating respect, admiration, and trust in all members of the organization to contribute to a collective enterprise, in which all have a stake and therefore proper leadership roles.

The priority placed upon broad empowerment across an organization applies to businesses and religious communities—as a "best practice" that often encounters considerable resistance on the way to enactment. Indeed, a more recent book by Chris Lowney is *Everyone Leads: How to Revitalize the Catholic Church* (2017),[3] which appeared about four years into the papacy of Francis. Not coincidentally, Lowney's book endorses the practice of shared responsibility for Catholic life to be exercised at all levels of the church, as there is no place in a vibrant religion for "backbenchers." Lowney expresses his highest appreciation for those initiatives of Francis that have enhanced consultative structures and invited broad participation. Indeed, the global synodal process, treated briefly in the middle chapters of this present volume, would not be announced until four years after Lowney's *Everyone Leads* had gone to the printer, but clearly supports his contentions. While there is ample place for top-down innovations and leadership within the organizational pyramid, the true vitality of any religious community is evident at the grassroots, and valuable changes frequently unfold through bottom-up practices. Both Francis and Lowney display acute awareness of these insights into the nature of leadership, including its constraints and its potential for great contributions to all types of organizations.

Key Dynamics of Papal Moral Leadership

It is important to call attention at the very outset of this study to a key term in this book's title: the adjective *moral*. Only a fraction of organizational leadership is properly described as moral leadership, or even self-consciously aspires to be so in any meaningful way. This is not to demean or diminish the roles of corporate or political leaders, among others, but does commend certain features of religious leadership, in general, and papal leadership, in particular. Even on a strictly empirical level, it is undeniable that millions of people look to a reigning pope as a special moral exemplar or even as a personal role model—

someone who is expected to live out Christian ethical principles both consistently and instructively.

While it is unrealistic to expect a pope, or anyone else for that matter, to be perfect in every way, it is vital for the worldwide leader and universal pastor of well over a billion Catholics to embody certain key qualities. The obvious traits include being a man of prayer and having a closeness to God, being honest and truthful in his dealings, and displaying consistent integrity of character. To fall short of such expectations would constitute a scandal—a stumbling block hindering the religious life of a substantial portion of the faithful who will be disappointed by these shortcomings of the leader they long to trust. Because the pope also exercises the supreme teaching office (as a key figure in the doctrinal authority of the whole church, a notion captured by the Latin word *magisterium*), the potential forfeiture of trust by a disappointing (or even scandalous) pontiff constitutes a threat to the credibility of church teaching and the attractiveness of the entire religion.

Many further personal qualities crucial for a pope to display could be cited and treated here, but perhaps the most inclusive and overarching one has already been mentioned: service. While, as noted above, the leader of any organization rightly speaks frequently about and acts transparently in service to the core mission of the organization, popes as moral leaders do well to signal especially clearly and frequently how all efforts to steer the church are above all acts of service. Indeed, one of the most revered of all the traditional papal titles continues to be "servant of the servants of God." More than just a semantic flourish (sometimes teasingly dubbed an act of papal one-downs-manship), this title well captures a legitimate aspiration and expectation of the office; just as Jesus founded the church on acts of profound service possessing decisive salvific significance, popes understand their office primarily in terms of universal service to the faithful. Whatever prerogatives they exercise are legitimated by this solemn duty in the role of servant of all.

By opening the lens to include these insights into the theology of the papacy, this section is of course placing some distance between the ordinary analysis of leadership (the judgments that may apply, for example, to a politician or corporate executive) and what applies specifically to a religious leader like a pope. To continue this line of analysis further, and to sustain this shift of focus from leadership skills, in general, to prerequisites for religious leaders, specifically, it is worthwhile considering a word that does not surface often in business training programs on leadership: vulnerability. While it may seem counterintuitive to include in a treatment of the public-facing role of leadership such a personal quality—and one generally associated with weakness rather than the strength that most leaders are so eager to project—vulnerability turns out to be an inescapable dimension of life. On a human level, dedicating oneself to a cause or an institution immediately renders oneself somewhat vulnerable. The more you give as a leader, the more capable you are of finding yourself hurt in some way—through disappointment or betrayed hopes or even with the broken heart of unrequited love and dedication. The literature pertaining to Christian ministry is replete with such observations.[4] It makes sense that popes, whose assumption of high ecclesiastical office constitutes a total self-giving in every imaginable way, have to grapple mightily with the reality of their own vulnerability.

There are numerous ways in which Pope Francis bears the marks of a vulnerability built into his papal ministry. This vulnerability to suffering contains multiple dimensions, from taking on the burdens of office that surely includes loneliness to the inevitability of physical suffering. Because the office generally falls to rather senior men and comes with no actual term limit, the aging of popes proceeds most evidently and publicly while in office. St. John Paul II's struggle with Parkinson's disease in the final years of his papacy, culminating in his agonizing death in April of 2005, bore witness to his heroic dedication. In the case of Francis, a certain physical decline became evident just as the COVID-19 pandemic was beginning to subside. He underwent major intestinal surgery in the summer of 2021, followed by struggles with painful sciatica and knee ligament conditions that at first hobbled him and then caused him to start using a wheelchair openly during public appearances after May 5, 2022. He was forced to cancel a long-anticipated papal journey (originally scheduled for July 2–7, 2022) to Congo and South Sudan with just three weeks prior notice, prompting a heartfelt and elaborate public apology on his part to the Catholic communities of those two struggling countries that had been eagerly awaiting his visits.[5] Certainly, further developments regarding the inevitably declining health of Francis will most likely unfold.

Personal Qualities and Vocational Commitments

Displaying and managing vulnerability so forthrightly is certainly relevant to this analysis of moral leadership, but it is important to categorize it correctly—not so much as a leadership skill per se, but rather as a matter of personal temperament and even as an ethical and vocational obligation. Religious leadership has a way of foregrounding personal qualities in this special way. While business leaders may score some points among their employees, and politicians may garner some votes with similar displays of sincere devotion and even personal sacrifice for a cause or organization, it is religious leadership that can claim that such personal dedication is an intrinsic dimension of the role that has fallen to them. Dedicated pastors never abandon their flocks. Providing the key difference at play here is, of course, reference to the divine. Vocations to religious service are understood as emanating from God alone and include a solemn duty to respond with ultimate devotion and commitment. What is perceived as temporary and contingent service in other walks of life takes on an added layer of seriousness. What might be identified as a commendable "best practice" in other walks of life becomes a matter of serious vocational discernment and solemn obligation among religious professional and especially high-level leaders.

We could easily offer a litany of similar insights about related qualities with the same bottom line. For example, while a business or political leader might indeed benefit from displaying commendable listening skills or an ability to suppress proclivities toward arrogance, the stakes seem higher for religious leaders on both these counts. Here, any failure to practice excellent empathetic listening or any indulgence in the temptation to disregard the perspective of others may precipitously disqualify one from office, for it suggests an incomplete devotion to God who requires an unimpeachable response to divine initiatives.

Furthermore, positions of leadership in for-profit corporations or in public office tend to be temporary, featuring an often-rapid churn of holders of these posts, in contrast to the lifelong commitments widely expected of religious professionals. While a priest, campus minister, hospital chaplain, religious educator, or any other religious leader may move from place to place with some frequency, recall that popes generally remain in office for life, amplifying these marks of vulnerability in service of a sacred vocation that imposes unique demands on those called and selected to serve. In short, with no disrespect for the dedication of leaders in all positions and walks of life, the stakes regarding moral leadership of popes like Francis are higher than they are for these other leaders, religious or otherwise.

If taken too far, the above insights might suggest that there is no place in papal moral leadership for any of the skills and qualities associated with secular leadership. Such a dualistic characterization would not be accurate, as the phenomenon of secular servant-leadership attests and as papal history readily demonstrates. Popes can indeed "lean in" as tough administrators and firm negotiators, displaying many of the same goal-directed aspects of leadership routinely reflected by their assertive secular counterparts, including CEOs and heads of state—roles played by popes in our times, at least by analogy. These qualities supplement the "softer qualities" and spiritual priorities to be explored throughout the following chapters. Of course, each pope places his own personal stamp on his papacy, selecting distinctive priorities and strategies by which to pursue them—all in a style that will never be replicated.

A Statement on Leadership

Less than a week into his papacy, Francis revealed a great deal about the priorities, strategies, and style that characterize the leadership he would exercise throughout his subsequent years in office. He scheduled the celebration of his first ceremonial public Mass as pope (known formally as the Mass for the Inauguration of the Petrine Ministry) outdoors in St. Peter's Square on a consequential date: March 19, the Solemnity of St. Joseph, the earthly father of Jesus. His homily on that high-profile occasion focused on the distinctive role of St. Joseph in salvation history, emphasizing his generous service in protecting the Holy Family, including the Blessed Virgin Mary and the young Jesus, from all threats of harm. He appealed to the huge congregation (estimated to have reached 200,000 people) arrayed across the cobblestone landscape of the Vatican's largest square to consider the deepest nature of the power that he was assuming as a newly installed pope. Instructively, Francis urged his listeners to take to heart the example of St. Joseph. Perhaps the top soundbite repeated in press accounts of the occasion was: "Let us never forget that authentic power is service...the lowly, concrete and faithful service that marked Saint Joseph."[6]

Francis immediately applies the lesson to himself, affirming that the pope himself "must be inspired by" this brand of humble service. It is no challenge to read between the lines here and conclude that, for Francis, servant-leadership is the proper approach to authority in all parts and levels of the church he had just been chosen to lead. If power is for service, then there is no place for crassly imposing one's will and dominating others excessively. If the church is truly, as is claimed, built upon the love of God and neighbor, then the proper principles of its operation are incompatible with an ethos of domination, self-aggrandizement, or careerism. To clarify his points as the homily moved toward its conclusion, Francis posed two provocative questions: "How does Joseph exercise his role as protector?" and "How does Joseph respond to his calling to be protector of Mary, Jesus, and the Church?" He answers his own questions with a litany of virtues:

"a capacity for concern, for compassion, for genuine openness to others, for love." Emerging at the summit of his list was the quality of "great tenderness," which, he adds, "is not the virtue of the weak but rather a sign of strength....We must not be afraid of goodness, of tenderness."

This appeal to a countercultural style of church governance and operations is remarkable. Indeed, it does not, in itself, answer all the relevant questions regarding the extent of legitimate exercise of ecclesial authority or the full meaning of the restraint and sensitivity Francis is commending. Nevertheless, this inaugural homily of Francis contains a programmatic statement regarding his intentions for his papacy, and especially for the style of leadership he planned from the outset to enact.[7] Colloquially, papal observers received an early indication of "what makes Francis tick." The following chapters will unpack many of the implications of the preferred style of Francis as evident in his words and actions in the course of his papacy. As noted at the outset, papal actions hold implications for the inner life of the church (the *ad intra* considerations) as well as relations between the church and wider world (the *ad extra*), including the social justice advocacy that has experienced solid renewal in the papacy of Francis.

The Path Ahead

Each of the following four chapters makes a specific contribution to this portrayal of the ethical priorities of Francis and his exercise of moral leadership. While space does not allow comprehensive coverage of every imaginable item of relevance, my wager is that the reader will emerge with a solid appreciation for the major approaches and most important achievements of Francis relating to his moral leadership.

Chapter 1 is "Francis, the Ethicist," which explores the content and origin of the overall moral vision of Francis for the contemporary church. The significance of many of the internal church reforms enacted by Francis comes into sharper focus when viewed as components of an overall evangelizing agenda inspired by the Second Vatican Council and aimed at key ethical values such as greater inclusion, participation, and accountability in the life of the church. Chapter 2 is "Francis, the Discerner," which examines elements of Ignatian spirituality from which Francis draws in conducting fruitful communal discernments. Two case studies, demonstrating how Francis convened two worldwide synods of bishops on the topics of family life and pastoral challenges in the Pan-Amazon region, illustrate the style and substance of the pope's spiritual leadership. Chapter 3 focuses on "Francis, the Communicator," which follows Pope Francis as he engages diverse audiences and interlocutors through words and deeds and in six intriguing case studies. Not only does he display the leadership quality of effective communication but actively seeks out opportunities to bring his message of social concern and reconciliation to challenging settings in bold and innovative ways. Chapter 4 focuses on "Francis, Advocate for Social Justice," which investigates both the content and the style of the social teachings of the pope—the place where church leadership most directly meets the world beyond the boundaries of the church itself. Here, we will have occasion to view the distinctive ways that Francis employs a structural analysis of human institutions in promoting such values as peacebuilding, economic justice, and the integrity of the natural environment. Together, these four components of the words and actions of Pope Francis offer a comprehensive picture of his moral leadership.

The volume closes with a brief concluding section that brings together the findings of the four chapters and considers how each of the topics contribute to the mission of the church according to the contours that Francis has quite deliberately shaped. While the conclusion will offer some tentative assessments of the overall ethical significance of the papacy of Francis, it is important to highlight the limitations (and even the perils) built into any study such as this one, which ventures to address events that are still unfolding. Historians are prudent to remind us that reliable accounts and mature evaluations of any public figure, much less one occupying such a complex global role as

Pope Francis, must await the passage of adequate time to gain valuable perspective on the significance of that figure.

Obviously, it will require decades before comprehensive judgments may be reached with any degree of confidence regarding the merits and significance of any specific achievement or involvement of Francis. Even the passage of a century will not likely witness a definitive consensus about the merits and lasting significance of many of the things this pope has said, done, or accomplished. For now, we will have to settle for partial judgments and limited perspectives. Nevertheless, our confidence that the present study is worthwhile is supported by the insight that Francis has consistently crafted his ethical approach and undertaken his moral initiatives in a remarkably deliberate way, lending much value to any effort to reach certain tentative judgments regarding his ethical leadership.

CHAPTER 1

FRANCIS, THE ETHICIST

THIS CHAPTER CONSIDERS the moral leadership of Pope Francis and will have some twists and turns in the road that may surprise (or even disappoint) some readers. While we will certainly emerge by the end of this chapter with a clear picture of the moral vision and ethical priorities that Francis has displayed as pope and teacher, we may need initially to recalibrate certain of our expectations. Specifically, this chapter presents a portrait of Pope Francis that diverges somewhat from customary notions of what counts as an ethical contribution. Although his pursuit of his deepest moral commitments sets him apart in certain ways, his papal leadership has consistently focused on what he perceives to be the most pressing needs of the church.

This chapter begins by examining why and how Francis challenges some of the inherited notions of papal ethical leadership, and then describes the new directions and ethical initiatives he has undertaken to address the current needs of the worldwide church. The central wager here is that, by appreciating the distinctive perspective that Francis brings to his moral appeals for the church to pursue a renewed mission in our challenging age, readers will understand and endorse the fresh approach he brings to a pressing moral agenda appropriate for today.

The Contours and Contributions of Moral Theology

Moral theology is the subfield of Catholic theology that addresses the behavioral implications of faith. Although this branch of theology began with a rather narrow mission, as a body of advice compiled in service to confessional practice (as priests sought to determine appropriate penances for sinners based on the gravity of sins and to offer counsel for amending their ways), its set of concerns has broadened remarkably in recent centuries. By consulting the wisdom of divine revelation found in Sacred Scripture, as well as the riches of two millennia of Christian theological thought, the fruits of human reason and ongoing experience of the faithful as they interact with the secular world, the church's moral teachings now provide guidance to anyone discerning proper courses of action amid the complex circumstances that we all face each day.

Whether considering the fields of bioethics, social ethics, or the many varieties of professional ethics (such as political, legal, or technological ethics), we tend to consult the advice of trained experts for guidance in sorting out the lines between right and wrong. Such efforts assist us in informing our consciences regarding what actions are allowable or morally objectionable as we exercise our God-given moral freedom. In short, when faced with pressing moral decisions in our lives, we are never alone or without resources in determining our moral obligations and ethical commitments. The discipline of moral theology is our companion, available for ongoing guidance and instruction.

It is surely unnecessary to devote much space here to justifying the prominent place long played by religious voices in moral debates. From the beginnings of human history, religion has been recognized as a key locus where each generation takes up the deepest questions of human existence: What is the good life? How do we grapple with the central sources of meaning as we seek to conduct a life featuring both personal integrity and social responsibility? To what ultimate destiny are our lives oriented, and what moral obligations flow from these properly construed ends? In every age, religious voices, traditions, authorities, and communities have made prominent contributions to all these moral inquiries. Through the practices of teaching and preaching as well as maintaining written records of received ethical wisdom, religious leaders consistently shed abundant light on what it means to form and follow a conscience oriented to moral truth.

Few if any religious figures rival popes as leaders to whom many millions of faithful adherents have, for centuries now, looked for ethical guidance. While every pope is conscious of his status as heir to and guardian of a rich tradition of moral reflection, each successive pope naturally projects his own distinctive profile of moral leadership. The opportunities for providing such leadership are many and varied. Some are routinely built into the papal calendar, such as frequent opportunities for preaching and delivering regularly scheduled addresses to diplomats and many other professional groups, or on annual occasions such as the World Day of Peace or the World Day of Migration, to cite just two examples. Other such opportunities involve somewhat more deliberate papal decision-making regarding the promotion of ethical priorities, including the selection of the pope's travel itineraries, the convoking of extraordinary synods, or the convening of new types of meetings that send a moral message, for example, Francis's World Meetings of Popular Movements. Later chapters will describe several of Francis's strategic choices in these areas, as we explore how he has shaped his papal ministry as discerner, communicator, and advocate for social justice.

Another major ethical tool employed by popes is the publication of authoritative teaching documents on moral issues and concepts. Indeed, when many close observers of the church's moral theology consider the content of papal ethical leadership, the preferred starting point is the body of encyclicals, apostolic letters and exhortations that explicitly take up pivotal issues regarding morality. Pope John Paul II was especially outstanding in publishing many such documents that provided detailed guidance on morality. Of the fourteen encyclical letters promulgated during his twenty-six-and-a-half-year papacy, several weighed in at considerable length on such moral questions as the sanctity of life and proper methods of decision-making. The two most prominent of these encyclicals are *Veritatis Splendor* ("The Splendor of the Truth," published in 1993 and bearing the subtitle "Regarding Certain Fundamental Questions of the Church's Moral Teaching") and *Evangelium Vitae* ("The Gospel of Life, published in 1995 and bearing the subtitle "On the Value and Inviolability of Human Life"). Each is almost a book-length scholarly treatment of substantive issues relating to moral values and obligations, including norms and methodologies for reaching appropriate decisions and optimal strategies for implementing them.

St. John Paul's project in these two encyclicals, as well as many other papal writings, such as his three social encyclicals,[1] matches quite closely traditional expectations regarding how moral theology proceeds and how a given pope makes a valuable contribution to ethics. Indeed, the Polish pope's way of proceeding reflects broader received perceptions regarding the objectives of any ethicist, namely, to take up controversial questions and to provide clear resolution through prudent analysis and careful moral reasoning from initial premises to firm, detailed conclusions. By the end of the papacies of John Paul II and Benedict XVI (his successor and the immediate predecessor of Francis) who contributed further to the church's moral teachings along the same general lines, Catholics enjoyed the benefits of impressive moral guidance on many issues.

Moral Teachings in a New Key

Enter Pope Francis. The remainder of this chapter hinges upon two key observations that reflect the twin poles of continuity (in the substance of moral teachings) and innovation (in their evangelical focus and the style by which they are presented). The first highly important thing to report is that the Argentinian pope has done nothing whatsoever to repudiate, overturn, disavow, recant, or even distance himself from the moral teachings of the Polish or German popes who preceded him.[2] On the contrary, Francis has gone out of his way on many occasions—one of which is recounted below—to praise the moral teachings of his immediate predecessors, and has declared that there is no need to repeat this established body of doctrine. John Paul and Benedict provided insightful accounts, still fully valid these several years later, of how persons act in laudable ways displaying ethical consistency and how practical moral reason proceeds in line with a well-formed conscience. Francis readily affirms these descriptions and evaluations, along with the moral truths and judgments identified by his two predecessors and detailed in their moral teachings.

The second important thing to report is that the ethical leadership of Francis has proceeded in a rather different key. While there is perhaps some danger in overdrawing the differences in style, it is indisputable that the Francis papacy has challenged the church to view the moral life through a renewed lens. Yes, Francis presents as a moral leader who is consciously exercising his role as the Catholic Church's chief theological instructor; it is just that he embraces his role in his own distinctive way, one that emphasizes actions and gestures more than printed or spoken words in isolation. While he has (as of mid-2023) published three encyclical letters and five apostolic exhortations that contain at least some ethical content, the tone of these documents is very different from the scholarly writings of John Paul II and Benedict XVI. His papal teaching documents are far more spiritual, pastoral, and devotional in nature and contain far less didactic content regarding moral judgments, for example, rarely presenting firm or detailed conclusions about the liceity of specific types of human behavior.

One place where Francis clearly reveals the moral agenda animating his written teachings appears in the second chapter of his apostolic exhortation *Amoris Laetitia* ("On Love in the Family," published in April of 2016), that presents the fruits of two worldwide synods on family life. Early in that wide-ranging chapter titled "The Experiences and Challenges of Families," Francis reflects on the overall project of papal teachings on this sensitive topic:

> We have long thought that simply by stressing doctrinal, bioethical and moral issues, without encouraging openness to grace, we were providing sufficient support to families, strengthening their marriage bond and giving meaning to marital life. We find it difficult to present marriage more as a dynamic path to personal development and fulfillment than as a lifelong burden. We also find it hard to make room for the consciences of the faithful, who very often respond as best they can to the Gospel amid their limitations, and are capable of carrying out their own discernment in complex situations. We have been called to form consciences, not to replace them.[3]

This passage signals an openness to the role of human experience and a pastoral sensitivity to the needs of suffering people that is typical of Francis. It reflects a key evangelical priority of the Jesuit pope. While the church and its tradition of moral teaching has much to offer the contemporary world, a prior task is to connect with individuals and families and to enter fully into the challenges they face. As the noteworthy turn of phrase in the final line of this passage indicates, Francis is eager to invite members of families to develop and inform their personal consciences, as opposed to confronting them with settled moral conclusions and imposing on them judgments that may be received as abrupt and unwelcome.

The drawing of moral lines amid quandaries in contemporary life has simply not been a significant feature of the ethical agenda of Pope Francis. While he does on occasion point out morally objectionable stances and positions (for example, an entire chapter in his 2018 apostolic exhortation, *Gaudete et Exsultate*, denounces the errors of contemporary Gnosticism and Pelagianism along lines of analysis he provides), he is generally averse to applying moral purity tests or conducting what might be labeled "heresy-hunting" of any sort. The guidance he provides rarely if ever involves extended arguments from premises to precise moral conclusions, as his predecessors sometimes do when they address matters of ethical judgment and register their approval or disapproval of particular methods of moral reasoning.[4] In short, the pope who spontaneously asked, "Who am I to judge?" in response to an inquiry about the treatment of homosexual persons, does not hold the standardization of moral methodologies and inflexible conclusions among his top priorities.

Having established what Francis is *not* seeking to accomplish in his moral theology leadership, we might ask: What then *is* he especially keen to do, and what does that agenda look like? One obvious response is the forming and respecting of the consciences of the faithful, as noted in the above citation from *Amoris Laetitia*. Furthermore, it is fair to say that what has instead occupied most of the attention of Francis in his writings and public addresses has involved the central dynamics of evangelization: how the church may more effectively reach out to those in need, making the gospel message attractive, and assisting the marginalized as they attempt to live out the gospel amid the challenges of today's bewildering world. This chapter concludes with descriptions of a half dozen initiatives of Francis that embody this priority.

For Francis, then, the connection between ethics and evangelization is vital, and the church must do its utmost to maintain it. He identifies as supremely moral whatever serves this central Christian task, mission, and agenda. When historians in future eras reflect upon the papacy of Francis to assess the ethical contribution of the first pope from the Global South, they will surely highlight not some set of detailed moral prescriptions or precise recommendations for ethical behavior, but a more general challenge that Francis poses to believers to orient their lives more wholeheartedly to the demands of the gospel. The most ardent desire of Francis is to serve as a catalyst for a renewed spiritual encounter of the faithful with the God who proclaims and offers that gospel message to all.

Key Moral Concerns

Perhaps the best place to glimpse the contours of these ethical priorities of Pope Francis is with a set of remarks he made on this very topic early in his papacy. The first extended interview that Francis granted took place during his first summer as pope (to be exact, in three sessions during late August of 2013). The text of the wide-ranging interview was published simultaneously the next month by several Jesuit journals and translated into the multiple languages employed by that loose consortium, with America Media in New York serving the English-speaking audience.[5] The conversations were conducted, recorded, and redacted by Rev. Antonio Spadaro, SJ, editor-in-chief of the Rome-based *La Civiltà Cattolica*, whose final version (in the original Italian) was quickly approved for release by the Holy See.

Slightly past the halfway point of the interview, Fr. Spadaro asks the pope to address several specific ethical challenges facing the Catholic faithful and to comment on the pastoral tools and approaches appropriate to dealing with people in moral distress. The extended response of Francis certainly merits this full citation:

> We cannot dwell only on issues related to abortion, gay marriage and the use of contraceptive methods. This is not possible. I have not spoken much about these things, and I have been reprimanded for that. But when we speak about these issues, we have to talk about them in context. The teaching of the church, for that matter, is clear and I am a son of the church, but it is not necessary to talk about these issues all the time.
>
> The dogmatic and moral teachings of the Church are not all equivalent. The Church's pastoral ministry cannot be obsessed with the transmission of a disjointed multitude of doctrines to be imposed insistently. Proclamation in a missionary style focuses on the essentials, on the necessary things: this is also what fascinates and attracts more, what makes the heart burn, as it did for the disciples at Emmaus. We have to find a new balance; otherwise even the moral edifice of the Church is likely to fall like a house of cards, losing the freshness and fragrance of the gospel. The proposal of the gospel must be more simple, profound, radiant. It is from this proposition that the moral consequences then flow.[6]

Even before Fr. Spadaro can exercise the interviewer's prerogative of introducing the next topic, Francis hastens to elaborate these points in another paragraph that applies this statement of his moral priorities to the task of preaching, always one of the pope's favorite topics. Francis identifies the chief objective of effective preaching as connecting to the listener, presenting "the proclamation of salvation" in a first and most crucial moment, even before the more formal "catechesis" and the "drawing even of a moral consequence" can proceed. Indeed, he takes this opportunity to specify what he sees as so often going wrong in evangelization, concluding his coverage of this topic with the lament: "But the proclamation of the saving love of God comes before moral and religious imperatives. Today sometimes it seems that the opposite order is prevailing."[7]

Throughout this section of the much longer interview, Francis sprinkles his coverage of these delicate pastoral and moral matters with certain noteworthy key words. Organized according to three important parts of speech, they include: verbs like "accompanying with mercy" and "welcoming," at one point adding the vivid image of "keeping the church doors open" to all; nouns like "proclamation" and "proximity" that capture what, for Francis, a pastor must maintain with the people; and adjectives like the aforementioned "missionary," describing the style of church activity as it intersects with the modern world.[8] What emerges is the image of a pope who is committed, above all, to creating the necessary conditions for the proclamation of the gospel, presenting with energy and credibility the life, teachings, kenotic death, and resurrection of Jesus Christ. This is the core of the church's constant teaching and its efforts to evangelize. The entire papacy of Francis is oriented toward supporting and promoting these wellsprings of living the moral life in the contemporary world. While subtracting nothing from the astute moral analysis of his predecessors, he has focused his efforts on the fundamentals of the church's ministry: closeness to God, zeal for the kingdom of God, and attracting souls by displaying the tender love and mercy of the gospel message.

Regarding Moral Judgments and Relativism

This reframing of the church's central moral mission by Francis has not met with universal approval. Critics fret over a range of objections. Some are as simple as the fear of relinquishing or neglecting a well-established system of moral analysis and customary disciplines. Another may be the possibility of confusing the faithful by presenting new priorities and thus causing scandal by introducing potential doctrinal ambiguities. As this charge runs, even though Francis has not actually inserted any specific innovations into the church's moral teachings, even the perception of change involving accustomed approaches to ethics shakes the foundations of the faith of some church members, and thereby weakens the entire community. It is no secret that many detractors of Francis have sharply questioned the wisdom of his priorities and leadership of the church.[9] Documenting these developments, a 2020 book about Francis by veteran British religion journalist Christopher Lamb includes a twenty-page, 100-item appendix titled "A Timeline of Opposition," chronicling incidents in the unfolding panoply of resistance to the reform agenda of Pope Francis.[10]

Perhaps the most prominent objection to the style of moral leadership exerted by Francis concerns the potential risk of lapsing into relativism. The specter of ethical relativism involves the error of disavowing all moral absolutes and surrendering to a normlessness that no longer recognizes fixed values and standards of moral judgment. The strongest version of this criticism proposes that, in adopting a more open-ended approach to ethical determinations, the church under Francis is abandoning a valuable tradition of clear moral judgments, as well as the methodologies that produce them, that has guided the faithful for centuries. Indeed, Roman Catholicism is often identified as the primary "carrier" of moral absolutes—grounded in the natural law tradition it upholds—in a contemporary intellectual milieu that is not well disposed toward affirming absolute truths of any sort. Could it really be that Francis is undermining this valuable heritage from the very top of the church hierarchy?

In a sense, this accusatory question has already been answered above, with the recognition that Francis has repeatedly reaffirmed the inherited moral teachings of the church, including specifically those of his immediate predecessors. Indeed, in several places within his own authoritative writings—specifically in his 2015 encyclical, *Laudato Si'*,[11] and his 2013 apostolic exhortation, *Evangelii Gaudium*—Francis has himself warned about the dangers of relativism, addressing with great insight the importance of affirming objective truths and sound ethical principles, and even explicitly denouncing the "culture of relativism."[12] It would obviously be false to characterize Francis as in any way overturning or even downplaying this valuable normative tradition of Roman Catholicism.

However, there are also more nuanced and less sweeping versions of this concern about a supposedly "creeping relativism" being countenanced by Francis. Some observers express concern that, in presenting a more pastorally focused, less judgmental face of the Catholic Church, Francis is somehow watering down the content of inherited moral teachings, even if in a subtle way. Not surprisingly, the incident most often cited to support this version of the charge of a "relativistic Francis" occurred on the first transoceanic flight of his papacy. On July 29, 2013, while returning from World Youth Day in Brazil, Francis conducted the first of his now famous back-of-the-airplane press conferences. This inaugural airborne interchange with journalists assigned to the Vatican was particularly wide-ranging, lasting a full eighty minutes. In response to a reporter's question about gay Catholics—the full line of inquiry eventually included questions about the existence of a gay lobby within the church, and whether gay clergy are allowable—Pope Francis offered this oft-quoted sound bite: "If a person is gay and seeks God and has a good will, who am I to judge?"[13]

This rhetorical question launched a storm of controversy. Could it be that the new leader of over a billion Catholics had just embraced a stance of utter relativism, jettisoning centuries of carefully delineated moral teachings on sexuality? Many important and obvious points about this sentence of Francis come into focus when we consider the context of the pope's statement, and especially what was not being said. Certainly, the plain sense of the words of Francis on that occasion does not imply a blanket refusal ever to judge any aspect of any person's moral conduct, a position that would reflect a pure stance of moral relativism. Indeed, on that occasion, Francis reiterated a longstanding distinction within church teaching: that homosexual activity is morally wrong, but that a same-sex orientation is not in itself sinful. Explicitly invoking his reliance on existing church doctrine, Francis hastened to add that the *Catechism of the Catholic Church* explains all of this very well, as it does, quite clearly.[14] The careful observer of this episode can easily detect the twin themes developed in this chapter: the continuity with traditional church moral teachings that Francis preserves, but also a change in tone and style favoring a more consistently pastoral face of the church's presence in contemporary society—one that makes possible a more inclusive and effective evangelization.

In the end, merely venturing the question "Who am I to judge?" does not constitute an act of capitulation to utter relativism or disavowing all moral determinations and analysis. What it does potentially accomplish, very much in line with the evident hopes of Francis, is to reach out with mercy and empathetic understanding to believers who identify as homosexual, or any variety of nonconforming sexual orientations or gender identities. It is, of course, the case that no one should face rejection or suffer discrimination because of their sexual orientation; this is neither an innovation in Catholic teachings nor contrary to the central precepts of any religion that dares to proclaim a God of universal love for all creatures. If the church's message regarding God's love for all, regardless of personal qualities or ascribed markers of social recognition (that is, of race, caste, gender, and so on) had somehow remained ambiguous in previous eras, Francis signaled his eagerness to extend a hand of unambiguous acceptance and compassionate concern for all. Such gestures serve at once as eloquent ethical statements and sound pastoral strategy.

More generally, an outstanding feature of Francis's moral leadership is his commitment to addressing and overcoming any sense of disappointment or even alienation on the part of believers who may feel betrayed by the church for various reasons. The church's shortcomings include past and present failures to listen to those in special need, a persistent hesitancy to reach out across humanly constructed social boundaries, and a perduring rigidity that causes pain, even if unintended, among those who continue to feel excluded from the beloved community founded by Jesus Christ. As with all agendas of interpersonal, institutional, or social reconciliation, church leaders seeking such healing must be attentive to both the *past* (in the interest of promoting honesty about what has gone wrong to damage relationships) and the *present* (in a sincere effort to reverse those injustices and propose a better course). Each part of the world features its own landscape of such challenges, as the Catholic Church's involvements with local cultures have taken many forms and produced a wide variety of regrettable interactions over many centuries.

These ethical aspirations of Francis are evident in his attempts to set in motion many initiatives aimed at healing such as confronting the scourge of clergy sexual abuse or addressing persistent structural distortions of colonialism in which the church has been complicit, through his communications with Indigenous peoples (in Canada and elsewhere) grappling with the legacy of abusive church-run residential schools that harmed thousands of youngsters and contributed to the suppression of native cultures, and other areas where past injustices cry out for restoration. Even uttering sincere words of apology for past wrongs, which of course in isolation do not change actual material conditions, holds great significance in ethical terms. No leader will achieve a perfect record in such efforts at healing and restitution, but sincere efforts to rectify past wrongs hold great ethical value and do not go unnoticed. To do less would be to betray the command of Jesus to the church to establish a distinctive community of perfect love. Even if it will never be fully realized in human history, this moral aspiration rightly commands the attention of every church leader. Pope Francis's efforts to reach out to many varieties of suffering people indicate his commitment to such an agenda of reconciliation.

Three Wellsprings of the Ethical Commitments

The preceding sections portray Francis as a church leader pursuing a particularly urgent ethical agenda—one that includes the task of overcoming the marginalization of many and discovering creative ways for the church to reach out to millions with credibility and sensitivity congruent with the gospel. Further insight into this agenda of ethical leadership will come from considering some of the major factors why Francis has come to embrace this specific set of objectives. Of course, it would be simplistic, and potentially reductionistic in the psychological sense of the word, to imagine that even a detailed examination of his biography would reveal everything we might hope to understand about his personal and professional motivations. Ultimately, only Francis knows fully the mind of Francis, but it is nevertheless helpful to acknowledge at least the following three factors that emerge as relevant causal factors influencing his ethical agenda as pope.

First, Francis comes to us from a distinctive geographical and social background that unquestionably shapes many of his moral concerns and approaches. His homeland of Argentina lies at the literal periphery of the globe. At the time of his birth in 1936, his family of origin were recent immigrants from rural Italy, struggling to adapt to a new country, language, and culture amid a global economic depression that had seriously damaged the Bergoglio family's financial prospects (the family's fledgling business was ruined early in the depression). While it is somewhat perilous to ascribe too tight a linkage between the early life experiences and the later ethical commitments and policy positions of any public figure, it is no idle speculation in this case. When Francis agreed to offer a recorded TED talk in 2017, he spoke frankly about the vulnerability that pervaded his entire childhood and how that enduring recognition of human frailty has sensitized him to the plight of all those "who are left with nothing…the discarded people," and especially global refugees. Connecting the dots between his early social location and the ethical agenda of inclusion, universal concern, and solidarity that characterizes the later Francis is relatively easy to do. Francis twice repeats in his TED talk the question: "Why them and not me?" when referring to the millions of ever more desperate refugees and other marginalized people in today's less hospitable environment.[15] It would be difficult to imagine a clearer example of a public figure expressing the familiar, yet perennially poignant sentiment, "There but for the grace of God go I."

Second, the future pope's many years of religious formation and ministerial life as a Jesuit certainly exerted strong influences that confirmed and clarified these same moral commitments. From the age of twenty-one (at which point he entered the Jesuit novitiate in Argentina) until fifty-five (when he was named auxiliary bishop of Buenos Aires), Bergoglio lived in Jesuit communities and received his ministerial assignments from Jesuit superiors. To this day, he frequently references the profound ways that Jesuit life and Ignatian spirituality shape his priorities and perspectives on human society. It would be easy to compile a long list of themes within the spiritual heritage shared by Jesuits that have most evidently influenced the approach of Francis: an orientation to practical service of the church in response to God's gracious gifts to us; acknowledgement of one's sinfulness and innate unworthiness before the divine; an ardent concern for both the spiritual and material well-being of our fellow pilgrims on earth; selfless devotion to the greater glory of God; and commitment to "the service of faith and the promotion of justice."[16]

Some of these phrases have become buzzwords, even clichés, within the circles of Jesuit education and Ignatian spirituality. The last item on that list will forever be associated with Superior General Pedro Arrupe, a Spanish Jesuit whom the future Pope Francis greatly admired and who spearheaded a revival of social justice ministries within the Society of Jesus that blossomed during Bergoglio's years of formation and early priesthood. The apostolic energies and initiatives unleashed by Arrupe inspired the young Fr. Bergoglio, over a quarter-century Arrupe's junior, to commit himself to maintaining a feverish schedule of pastoral involvements focused on the poor, including visiting parishioners of very modest means in their ramshackle neighborhoods all over Buenos Aires, a practice he maintained for decades, even as cardinal archbishop of the metropolis. His clientele included many recent immigrants who arrived in Argentina from poorer regions of South America, further keeping him in touch with the distress experienced by so many downtrodden "people on the move."

To be clear, many Argentinian Jesuits demonstrated just as much exemplary apostolic zeal as Bergoglio. Indeed, in the years he served as a novice director, formation house rector, and provincial superior, Fr. Bergoglio encouraged (some would say cajoled) many of his Jesuit confreres to muster similar levels of energy in conducting pastoral visits and other demanding ministries, well beyond their usual work assignments. One further point of comparison is quite telling: Francis is the exceptional pope (at least in recent centuries) whose résumé includes extensive and prolonged ministerial contact with the marginalized. Setting Francis apart from the great majority of popes since the Renaissance era is his record of commitment to extending material charity and sensitive pastoral care to thousands facing such challenges as poverty, addiction, domestic abuse, broken households, and gang violence. In all this, Francis's Jesuit heritage paints this key contribution with a distinctive hue. One of the noteworthy fruits of the *Spiritual Exercises of Saint Ignatius Loyola* is the "eliciting of holy desires," and serving these hard-pressed people in their dire need as a worthy minister of the gospel certainly emerged as a key desire that shaped the ministry of Fr. (and later Bishop and Cardinal) Bergoglio. Nothing looms larger in the constellation of ethical priorities of Pope Francis.

Third, another relevant factor contributing to the sensitivity of Francis to matters of inclusion and service of the marginalized has to do with the sheer chronology of his life. While the previous two considerations each made some reference to generational dimensions of the influences on Francis, this third item relates to the most significant ecclesiastical event within Catholicism in recent centuries: the convening of the Second Vatican Council. Running as they did from 1962 until 1965, the four sessions of Vatican II unfolded in the middle span of Bergoglio's dozen years of Jesuit formation (he entered the Jesuit novitiate in 1958 and was ordained a priest in 1969). Like other seminarians of his cohort throughout the world, the future pope came of age at a momentous time in church history. He would have been studying the texts of major Vatican II constitutions and decrees in his theology classes, likely soaking up the excitement of his professors over the fresh perspectives offered in these new documents.

While no simple summary description of the content of the sixteen major documents of the Second Vatican Council is possible, one undeniable observation is that the council fathers issued a strong message of inclusion and outreach to the modern world in all its complexity and pluralism. This is especially true of the content of the 1965 documents *Gaudium et Spes* ("Pastoral Constitution on the Church in the Modern World") and *Dignitatis Humanae* ("Declaration of Religious Liberty"). A message of inclusion and benevolent openness certainly runs through further documents such as the constitutions on the sacred liturgy (*Sacrosanctum Concilium*) and on the church (*Lumen Gentium*), as well as the decree on the laity (*Apostolicum Actuositatem*) and the declaration on the relation of the church to non-Christian religions (*Nostra Aetate*).

To point out that the future Pope Francis enthusiastically took to heart these messages regarding a more open church, one newly rededicated to inclusion within and beyond its ranks, in no way questions the commitment of his two immediate predecessors to the teachings and values, indeed, even to the spirit, of Vatican II. To the contrary, it is noteworthy that both the future John Paul II (as a young bishop from Kraków, Poland) and the future Benedict XVI (as a theological consultant) were present at the council as active and valuable participants. Each helped to shape the proceedings and the resulting documents, and each, in turn, was shaped by them.

However, it may be possible to make an even stronger claim about the influence of Vatican II on Pope Francis. He is, after all, the first pope to be ordained a priest after the conclusion of the council. Its groundbreaking documents formed an important part of the curriculum of priestly preparation that he followed, and he clearly admired the council's fervent calls to social justice, an inclusive participatory church, and the universal call to holiness. As a further example, his desire to maintain fidelity to the vision of Vatican II has shaped his positions and actions on liturgical practice, including his courageous promulgation of the 2021 document *Traditionis Custodes* ("Guardians of the Tradition"), which consolidates and updates the liturgical reforms set in motion by the council.[17]

Historians have quipped that it takes a full century to implement a church council. If so, Francis seems impatient with that timeline, or at least eager to speed along the progress, as his papacy has clearly endorsed and pursued the priorities of the Second Vatican Council. Interestingly, Francis became pope at nearly the halfway point to a full century after the close of the council (that is, nearly forty-eight years elapsed between December 8, 1965, and March 13, 2013), at a time when many Vatican observers expressed frustration that the energies of Vatican II appeared to be stalled, or even fading, and were perhaps in need of a boost. It is important to clarify that we are speaking here not about matters of doctrinal definitions or even developments regarding church practices (such as liturgy) or disciplines (such as norms for fasting and penances), but primarily about apostolic energy and style—precisely those items treated above. The contributions of Pope Francis to progress in the implementation of Vatican II will ultimately be measured in the renewal of energies toward a more participatory, inclusive, and evangelical church. The remainder of this chapter reviews a modest selection of evidence for this claim, as we seek further insight into his ethical agenda and moral leadership.

Dynamics of Moral Leadership in the Papacy of Francis

Having reviewed the constellation of motivations and influences that shaped Francis and his commitment to a distinctive style of moral leadership, the time has arrived to draw linkages between the ethical priorities of Francis and the specific initiatives he has undertaken in his papacy. Even before surveying some of the actual efforts and accomplishments within the papacy of Francis, however, it is necessary to acknowledge a set of caveats relating to the very nature of leadership and its exercise in complex organizations. Even the most powerful and dedicated leaders are subject to constraints, resistance, and delays that sometimes frustrate their intentions and slow the momentum of attempted reforms. That Pope Francis has faced complications and setbacks in achieving much of his agenda should come as no surprise.

An analogy between the papacy and civil government may shed some light here. In democracies, voters are familiar with the perennial gap between the ambitious campaign promises pledged by candidates and what they deliver once in office, whether as executives or members of legislative assemblies. Putting aside all cynicism about how and why candidates for public office decide on their platforms and packages of promised initiatives, it is important to recognize the daunting hurdles that stand in the way of readily translating good-faith campaign pledges into effective results. Progress toward a set of defined goals is often maddeningly gradual, as it takes time and effort to build a workable governing consensus and assemble the requisite administrative support around any proposed agenda of reform, no matter how meritorious or appealing. Given bureaucratic inertia and sheer administrative complexity, whether in church or civil governance, no one achieves his or her governing objectives suddenly and completely.

The familiar political maxim "You campaign in poetry but govern in prose" captures some of these observations about the inevitable constraints faced even by the most visionary public figures. No leader can govern simply by personal fiat, not even a pope (whose power is essentially monarchical, though by no means absolute within church governance structures). Adopting realistic expectations regarding the timelines and extent of church reforms achieved by this or any other pope prevents us from growing unduly disappointed when confronted by the inevitable delays and resistance that may cause setbacks and demand compromises. Longtime Vatican watchers are acutely aware that, while most people fix their eyes on stopwatches, daily planners, or at most, monthly calendars, the church still measures the duration of time in terms of centuries. To modify the usual secular expectations regarding the pace of change in the church is not so much to make excuses for Francis or any other reform-minded pope, but simply to recognize the unique characteristics of the world's oldest continuous large-scale institution.

Another necessary preliminary note relates to the "outsider status" of Francis. Unlike many previous popes, he had no history of serving the church's central bureaucracy, either in the Roman Curia, as his immediate predecessor Benedict XVI had done for decades as prefect of the powerful Congregation for the Doctrine of the Faith, or in the Vatican's diplomatic corps, as several nineteenth- and twentieth-century popes had done in the course of their ecclesiastical careers. Indeed, spending almost his entire life and career in Argentina had placed Bergoglio as far away from the corridors of centralized church power as one can imagine. While he had been a somewhat frequent visitor to Rome—in the 1970s, as a Jesuit provincial superior attending mandatory meetings and, for the twenty years before his election in 2013, as a bishop and eventually a cardinal making regular *ad limina* visits to various curial offices—he was still quite removed from "the Roman scene."

An intriguing question is to what extent the future pope's remoteness from ecclesiastical power centers was an advantage or disadvantage, both regarding the papal election that brought Francis into office or the prospects for achieving his agenda once he was installed as pope. On the first count, it is no secret that

Cardinal Bergoglio's status as an outsider constituted at least part of his appeal to his fellow electors in March of 2013, as broad perceptions of the desirability of significant change generated support for "a fresh face," as it had in 1978 with the election of John Paul II.[18] A similarly complicated question is how his status as a Jesuit affected his appeal (recall that no Jesuit had ever been pope, and nearly two centuries had passed since the 1831 election of the last pope from any religious order: the Camaldolese monk who became Gregory XVI). On the second count, it is of course true that any newcomer to an established bureaucracy, indeed, an entire culture and way of proceeding, will require some lead time before acquiring adeptness at operating the administrative machinery required for effective governance, even once a qualified and talented support staff has been assembled (an accomplishment that may also require considerable time). These are just a few of the most obvious dynamics that have affected the ability of Pope Francis to translate his ethical priorities into effective action once he had assumed the papacy.

The Landscape of Moral Leadership

A current expression in colloquial English introduces the valuable distinction between "talking the talk" and "walking the walk." It captures the insight that it is one thing to give eloquent lip service to certain values to which you might subscribe, and another thing to pursue and enact those values with concrete and effective actions. St. Ignatius Loyola captured this same insight five hundred years ago in the words of the "Contemplation to Attain Divine Love," which appears toward the end of his *Spiritual Exercises*: "Love ought to show itself more in deeds than in words."[19] From his many decades of engaging in daily prayer and regular religious retreats guided by this spiritual handbook, Pope Francis is thoroughly familiar with this version of the distinction. It comes as second nature to him to strive strenuously to put into practice the ethical values he professes and to demonstrate his moral commitments in concrete and consistent acts of leadership.

Heads of large organizations customarily divide their attention between internal and external tasks and decisions. Just as a head of state routinely distinguishes between domestic affairs and foreign policy, the responsibilities of a religious leader like Pope Francis are divided (though perhaps not always so sharply) between internal church management, on one hand, and external social relations, including that religious body's social teachings and various matters relating to political advocacy and even international diplomacy, on the other hand. Of course, each level displays its own challenges and requires distinctive but inevitably overlapping sets of skills. Even when the values underlying papal positions and priorities on internal and external affairs might be identical, the specific ways of proceeding will display differences. For purposes of conceptual clarity, this present study postpones consideration of how Pope Francis manages his "external portfolio" until the final chapter, which examines the pope's social justice advocacy and peacebuilding efforts.

The remainder of the current chapter takes up the narrower task of describing some of the concrete ways that Francis has enacted his core ethical priorities and values within the internal life of the church. While space does not allow comprehensive coverage and extensive supporting evidence regarding the full range of internal church reforms and initiatives flowing from Francis, even the brief accounts that follow will provide enough of the "flavor" of his papacy to support this key observation. Francis has indeed exerted practical moral leadership in ways that align tightly with the ethical priorities he espouses. The remarkable consistency between his words and actions allows any objective observer to conclude that this is a pope who, in a clever hybrid phrase, "walks the talk."

The next section of this chapter treats six church reforms that have unfolded under the leadership of Pope Francis. While this list is by no means exhaustive, it does highlight a half-dozen of the most prominent areas in the life of the church and its operations that have witnessed highly impressive reshaping during the papacy of Francis. There are two ways of framing the significance of these items. On the one hand, each discrete item on this list obviously contains great value in itself, for each constitutes great progress regarding how the church conducts itself. On the other hand, however, even beyond the specifics of improved organizational structures and procedures lies a deeper significance. Each set of changes pursued and enacted by Francis represents an impressive commitment to an ethically superior way of proceeding that sends a powerful message about the longer trajectory of expectations regarding the church. In other words, these reforms taken together achieve far more than the sum of their parts.

Expressions of Moral Leadership in the Church

Each of the following six items is a promissory note issued in recent years by the church's current pope that the future will be different from the past. These six areas of reform are imagined and proposed not as quick fixes with a limited lifespan, but rather as expressions of permanent commitments that will not be allowed to expire. Of course, while Francis cannot control the decisions of future popes or the courses of action to be pursued by church leaders after him, he is initiating changed patterns of church conduct that, at least under favorable conditions, will constitute sustainable markers of ongoing progress. With the support and cooperation of his successors, Francis is playing the lead role in inaugurating a new kind of church, one featuring the distinctive marks of his ethical priorities and commitments.

Pope Francis has undertaken many initiatives to instill more thoroughly in church structures and practices the moral priorities he espouses. While no brief treatment of these developments will be complete, this listing of these six major items from his papacy provides a strong start.

Responses to the Crisis of Clergy Sexual Abuse

On May 7, 2019, Francis promulgated the apostolic letter *Vos Estis Lux Mundi* ("You Are the Light of the World"), which constituted the worldwide church's most comprehensive response to address the crisis of clergy sexual abuse and cover-ups that has rocked the Catholic world for decades. The text of the document minces no words in calling out the gravity of instances of "crimes of sexual abuse" against minors and other vulnerable people that clearly horrify Francis.[20] Its nineteen articles provide a legal framework for universal compliance with norms that include procedures for scrutiny, oversight, mandated reporting, investigations to be conducted of all credible accusations, and the imposition of penalties, such as the permanent removal of proven offenders from ministry. It was supplemented two years later with the promulgation of the apostolic constitution *Pascite Gregem Dei* ("Tend God's Flock") introducing a thorough revision of the penal disciplines relating to clergy malfeasance contained in Book VI of the Code of Canon Law.[21] As evidence of the solemn importance of these legal changes, note that not since its initial appearance in 1983 had the current compendium of church law been altered in such a major way.

The promulgation of these two documents, along with sets of related pastoral guidelines, is the culmination of decades of effort by church officials to "get it right" in response to the need to assure accountability and justice on the crucial matter of the protection of children from sexual abuse. The administration of Francis, as well as those of John Paul II and Benedict XVI before him, had endured much (often well-founded) criticism for the delays, fits and starts, half-measures, and uneven responses that long characterized previous efforts. Half a dozen years into his own papacy, Francis was most evidently extremely eager to reverse the gruesome record of sexual mistreatment, lax enforcement, and unconscionable loopholes that plagued previous rounds of response to the ongoing crisis. While no set of revised church laws and procedures will establish adequate responses to and reparations for the pain and lost innocence on the part of the victims, the invocation here of the values of honesty, openness, humility, repentance, sincere contrition, and good-faith efforts at restitution hold the promise of at last getting beyond the angry defensiveness that long blocked the path to true accountability in these painful scandals.

The gruesome crimes of sex abuse involve individual perpetrators, but, of course, also large institutions and complicit structures that allowed these patterns of misconduct to persist for generations. Reform, of course, does not happen overnight. Genuine change depends upon both concrete norms, such as these new regulations provide, and a thorough transformation of culture, including an end to attitudes that tolerated immoral conduct, such as the scourge of clericalism (excessive deference to priests and deacons) that enabled and perpetuated so many abuses. No church document or regulation provides a silver bullet to resolve the longstanding problems of clergy sexual abuse, but concrete measures can be effective if they are received favorably and enforced broadly in all jurisdictions—both across geographical entities such as dioceses and throughout all the religious orders and congregations—of the Catholic world.

Reform of Church Financial Management

The area of church finances emerged early in the papacy of Francis as demanding attention and urgent reform. Revelations of financial irregularities during previous papacies—the most infamous being the Banco Ambrosiano scandal that implicated American archbishop Paul Marcinkus in the early 1980s—had alerted Francis to the need for a thorough review and restructuring of how the Holy See manages its assets, annual budgets, and accounting practices. By the end of 2014, just the second year of his papacy, Francis had engaged an impressive coterie of international consultants and independent auditing firms to conduct a comprehensive review of the financial operations and balance sheets of the Vatican. The initial reviews culminated in the establishment of a new office called the Secretariat of the Economy, headed initially by Cardinal George Pell of Australia and a new oversight agency, a mixed body initially comprised of eight cardinals and seven lay experts, called the Council for the Economy. New controls were imposed on the assets and accounts of the

Vatican Bank (formally known as the Institute for the Works of Religion).[22] Further reforms and restructuring continued to unfold as part of the comprehensive reform of the Roman Curia (to be described below).

Financial assets and cash flow are of course hardly the first things one associates with the Catholic Church, nor should they be. Indeed, in the grand scheme of things, the annual budget of all Vatican operations combined is quite small (at under a billion dollars, easily dwarfed by the municipal budget of any sizable city), as most assets and activities of the Catholic Church belong to local dioceses scattered throughout the world, to which a pope has no claim and over which he exerts no control. Nevertheless, Francis is rightly concerned to demonstrate his commitment to financial propriety and consistent support for best practices in stewardship of all church resources he does manage. Even the perception of suspected financial irregularities, not to mention outright corruption or misdirection of church funds, is potentially very damaging to the credibility and moral authority of the church. Francis has thus signaled his firm intention to tolerate no financial mismanagement at all, just as he has pressed the priority of eliminating sexual abuse by church personnel.

Francis himself gives every indication of living a frugal life, displaying an impressive personal history of foreswearing luxuries and preferring to direct all surplus resources to the needs of the poor. He provides a valuable example to the organization he leads to practice thrift and avoid waste, so that it can better fulfill its mission of charitable generosity. But more than this, managing those finances over which he exerts a measure of control affords Pope Francis a high-profile opportunity to "walk the talk" regarding key values such as accountability, transparency, and social responsibility. Perhaps not coincidentally, these and related values have in recent years gained recognition as hallmarks of laudable practices within the governance of private and public corporations around the world. If the corporate culture of for-profit firms can support these values and motivate considerable efforts to achieve these aspirations, then the leader of a worldwide faith community is surely right to challenge the institution he heads to embody these ideals in its own modest financial operations. Indeed, Francis promulgated a flurry of papal documents and initiatives in 2020 and 2021[23] (perhaps in response to credible allegations of embezzlement and fraud involving a handful of suspicious Vatican real estate investment ventures) that enforced new requirements regarding financial transparency and accountability, summing up the new ethical demands the pope has imposed on Vatican officials at all levels regarding these very priorities.[24]

Reorganization of the Roman Curia

Francis completed a comprehensive reform of the entire Roman Curia with the promulgation of the apostolic constitution *Praedicate Evangelium* ("Preach the Gospel") on March 19, 2022. This stunning accomplishment completes a process of organizational restructuring that had eluded Vatican leaders for well over a generation, and represents the completion of a maddeningly slow process of study and reform proposals that had been stuck in neutral since the 1980s.[25] Among the features of the reorganization of the many dicasteries—there are now sixteen, down from twenty-one, and with newly standardized nomenclature—that comprise the Roman Curia are provisions that open up to the laity numerous new opportunities for leadership in key church offices. For the first time, nonordained Catholics, including members of women's religious congregations, are eligible for appointment as prefects and secretaries, that is, the top positions, of Vatican dicasteries.

Emerging from the details of precisely how the new constitution overhauls and realigns various offices within the church's central bureaucracy are several trademark leadership priorities of Francis. Hard to miss, since it appears in the very title and repeatedly in the preamble of the fifty-plus page document, is a renewed emphasis on the task of evangelization—including the reminder that all Christians, not just ordained clerics, rightly share fully in the church's evangelizing mission of service to humanity. In an interview on June 5, 2022, shortly after the reforms went into effect, Francis summarized the purpose of the new constitution as to "better harmonize the present exercise of the Curia's service with the path of evangelization."[26] A closely related priority, also prominent in the preamble of *Praedicate Evangelium*, is captured in the phrases "collegial unity" and "missionary communion," which entail establishing "a synodal church marked by reciprocal listening whereby everyone has something to learn…all listening to each other and all listening to the Holy Spirit."[27] The next chapter examines these themes of synodality and discernment in some detail, as key dimensions of the leadership of Francis.

Clearly animating the reform is the pastoral orientation of Francis himself. Understanding his mandate—dating from deliberations of the 2013 conclave of cardinals that elected him—to include enforcing accountability upon a church bureaucracy that had grown alarmingly self-referential and often obstructionist, Francis here challenges the culture and style by which the curia routinely proceeds. Particularly striking is the third section of *Praedicate Evangelium*, which has been perceived as something of a rebuke to priest-functionaries in the curia who may have forgotten the purpose of their work in Rome. That section stipulating "general norms" features five articles under the heading "The Pastoral Nature of the Work of the Curia." Section 3, article 6 contains a norm that reads: "Along with the service provided in the Roman Curia, clerics should also attend to the care of souls whenever possible and without prejudice to their work in the office."

This provocative guideline presents as folksy and scolding; one can almost hear an avuncular Francis summoning those priests preoccupied with shuffling paperwork all day to imitate him in "getting out of the office once in a while" to encounter the people of God firsthand, and even perhaps to attract new believers. After all, if the Roman Curia exists to be of service to the mission of the church, its daily operations should reflect this commitment in a more direct way than has hitherto been achieved. The priority of direct, gospel-inspired pastoral service imbues all the leadership activities of Francis, and managing the central administrative bureaucracy is no exception. Only time will tell what fruits this reform of the curia will bear, but its favorable initial reception in Catholic circles around the world already suggests that this set of institutional reforms may be a true game changer, closing the perceived gap between the pastoral vision of Vatican II and the routine operations of the Roman Curia.[28]

Leadership Roles for Women in the Church

Any consideration of topics relating to progress regarding the role of women in the church must begin with the admission that the Roman Catholic Church has a long way to go to achieve gender justice in its operations. No pope will change the culture of discrimination and even misogyny that has devalued the contributions of women over the centuries and limited the leadership opportunities for over half the members of the worldwide church overnight. Even if we bracket entirely the question of the continued denial of priestly ordination to women (Pope Francis has repeatedly taken off the table the possibility of change on that specific topic), numerous injustices and indignities are routinely perpetrated against women seeking fair treatment in church-sponsored institutions around the world.

Opinions will naturally vary depending on the perspective of any given observer, but it seems indisputable that Francis has done more to advance the empowerment of women in the Catholic Church than any previous pontiff. While he remains very much a person of his age and culture of origin, fully capable of gaffes, tone deafness, and blind spots regarding gender roles and social expectations, his track record of supporting women's progress may pleasantly surprise the casual observer who looks into the matter. On many occasions in his writings and public addresses,[29] Francis has encouraged his listeners to recognize the vital role that women already routinely play in the life of the church. Surprisingly often has he called attention to the rightful demands of women for full recognition of their dignity as persons and as valuable members of the faith community. While the pace of change is surely judged by many too slow for full comfort, we can point to many encouraging concrete developments along these lines during his papacy. Some of these items fit into the category of "things that thankfully did not happen," such as the termination of various investigations into the work of female theologians who were under suspicion when he came into office, or challenges to the governance authority of women's religious congregations that were pending in the papacy that preceded his but have since expired.

On the more positive side, Francis has appointed more women to the International Theological Commission than any previous pope, expanding to unprecedented levels the representation of highly qualified women on that important church body. He has promoted laywomen and women religious to the highest ranks of professional leadership in several Vatican offices and even in the top dicasteries of the Roman Curia.[30] By appointing many women to key positions, not just as consultants as before, but now as full participating members and even presiding officers within several dicasteries, Francis has acted quickly upon the new protocols of the 2022 apostolic constitution *Praedicate Evangelium* that make nonordained persons newly eligible for many top positions.[31] The appointment of three women, in July of 2022, to serve on the Dicastery for Bishops, the body that selects candidates for bishoprics around the world, was heralded as a breakthrough that few Vatican watchers anticipated.[32]

Francis has also opened certain liturgical roles to women that were formerly reserved to men. Specifically, in 2021, he altered Canon 230 to make women eligible for the "instituted ministries of lector and acolyte" (formerly called minor orders). On January 23, 2022, he even presided over the festive liturgy in Rome at which some of the first candidates for these positions were solemnly instituted. Also in 2021, he established a newly instituted lay ministry: that of catechist, a role long held by millions of women around the world and now finally eligible for formal ecclesial recognition.[33] Admittedly, skeptics may judge these expanded opportunities for service newly opened to women to be mere "consolation prizes" that in no way compensate for the denial of priestly or even diaconal ordination to women. Then again, however, it may at least be said that Francis is also the first pope to authorize a commission to study the history of the female diaconate, which might turn out to be the first step toward opening the eligibility of further church offices to over half of humanity—and surely more than half of the church's active membership.

Welcoming Members of the LGBTQ Community

The strides that Francis has made toward fuller recognition of the rightful place of women in the church may seem modest to those impatient for more sweeping change, but at least two things about these recent changes will be undeniable even to skeptics. First, the measures Francis has championed regarding women are oriented toward themes of Vatican II that lie at the core of his leadership agenda: a commitment to the inclusion of all; ever greater openness to welcoming the previously excluded; and extending new opportunities for the full participation of the marginalized. Second, the progressive steps Francis has already taken may hold great potential for appealing to the moral imagination of many observers who find in current reforms the bases for even further progress toward a more welcoming church. As time unfolds, the germinating seeds of broader inclusion may yield further fruits in ways that present observers can hardly imagine. Change rarely comes all at once. An agenda that appears modest and incomplete at one moment may turn out to be decisively important in the longer term, provided a promising trajectory can be maintained.

These same priorities and dynamics apply to another community struggling for justice and recognition in the Catholic Church: members of LGBTQ communities. No one could blame members of these communities of sexual identity for feeling left out of Catholic life. Church personnel and programming have largely treated them as nonpersons at best, and indeed have often made them victims of scapegoating and objects of suspicion because of the ways they differ from received social norms.

Rather than perpetuating the church's past patterns of ostracism and exclusion, Pope Francis has offered numerous words and gestures of inclusion and understanding. Several incidents in the papacy of Francis stand out as emblematic of his desire to communicate a stance of openness to members of the LGBTQ community. We have already seen one: the controversial comments in July of 2013 during his first airborne press conference when Francis famously asked: "Who am I to judge?" In a tender pastoral moment in April of 2018, he told the openly homosexual Chilean abuse survivor Juan Carlos Cruz that "it does not matter that you are gay. God made you the way you are and He loves you the way you are and it does not matter to me. The pope loves you the way you are."[34] On several occasions, only some of which have been acknowledged publicly in official Vatican news accounts, Francis has extended pastoral care to gay or transgender people and even welcomed transgender individuals and small groups to the Vatican for private audiences.[35]

From time to time, Francis has demonstrated his support for church ministers who advocate for the LGBTQ community. On more than one occasion, Francis publicly commended with letters of encouragement James Martin, SJ, whose book *Building a Bridge* advocates for a church stance of enhanced openness to LGBTQ people and responsiveness to their pastoral needs.[36] Fr. Martin is just one of many priests and religious sisters (some affiliated with the Catholic outreach program in the United States called New Ways Ministry), who have worked to counter the discrimination, prejudice, and stigmatization that have prevented members of the LGBTQ community from overcoming marginalization and alienation from church circles.

It is important not to overstate the changed reception accorded to members of these sexually nonconforming communities within the church. Even top leaders sending some new signals about pastoral accompaniment and promoting inclusivity on certain occasions does not constitute a thorough revision of persistent moral judgments throughout an institution as large as the Catholic Church. The extent of even Francis's open acceptance seemed to reach a limit on March 15, 2021, when the

Vatican's Congregation for the Doctrine of the Faith released a directive (technically, a response to a doctrinal question that had been posed to it, one necessarily approved by Pope Francis) ruling that it is not acceptable for priests to bless same-sex couples or their civil unions.

The basis of this decision lies of course in the church's continued refusal to condone homosexual activity, which is still considered contrary to natural law and thus sinful according to formal Catholic teachings; the *Catechism* continues to label homosexual activity as intrinsically disordered. Francis himself explained the decision by repeating that it is not possible to bless sin.[37] Some observers immediately accused Francis of hypocrisy or at least of acting far out of character on this occasion, but the larger message on display in these events pertains to a perduring reality within the dynamics of Catholicism itself. Certain distinctions between pastoral practice and doctrinal teachings on these sensitive matters of sexuality remain in place, and future persistence of tensions regarding full acceptance of the LGBTQ community will come as no surprise to any close observer of the church in recent decades, even after the clarion call for broader inclusion issued by the Second Vatican Council.

Still, for all the ambiguities and mixed messages, it is safe to say that Francis displays more openness to the LGBTQ community than any previous pope. His deliberate decisions to model a stance of pastoral concern and acceptance, even within certain limits, is emblematic of his core leadership priorities.

Broadening Leadership across the Global Church

As a product of the Global South himself, Francis has demonstrated an ardent desire to promote the well-being of local churches in all parts of the world, especially in those regions and locales considered to be on the peripheries. An important priority for Francis is to offer support for local Catholic communities that lie far from the center of global political and economic power. To this end, one tool he has used to good effect is his prerogative to select the sites of papal travels. He has quite deliberately chosen itineraries that call attention to small and hard-pressed outposts of the church, often where Catholics find themselves in the minority and sometimes even targets of persecution or terrorist violence. These are special places where he can offer personal encouragement during his visits as well as draw global attention to concerns regarding social justice, peacebuilding, and local cultural challenges. Chapters 3 and 4 will return to the papal voyages of Francis as a component of his larger communication and advocacy strategies.

A more specific objective for Francis is to broaden the geographic scope of the top levels of church leadership and distribute authority more widely in the global church. If the previous era of an excessively Eurocentric Catholic Church is ever to end, a path must be cleared for transferring an increased share of ecclesial authority and visibility to the Global South, especially to Africa, Asia, and South America, where an emerging majority of Catholics make their homes. One way of advancing this objective involves the appointment of more cardinals (that is, the most senior clerics, who are almost always already bishops or archbishops before their elevation) in currently under-represented regions of the world. By promoting more diverse membership in the College of Cardinals, a pope like Francis can use his power today to promote a more equitable distribution of influence in the future.

At any given time, there are approximately 120 cardinal electors eligible (by virtue of being under the age of eighty) to participate in a papal conclave that would elect a papal successor.[38] Each year, a pope will announce his selections to fill new vacancies in the body of eligible cardinal electors, and then hold a consistory (a ceremony of induction) to create the new members of the College of Cardinals. The record shows that Pope Francis has been quite deliberate in favoring candidates who have made the College of Cardinals more geographically diverse than ever, and especially by increasing the representation of developing countries of the Global South. Under Francis, countries of the world that have never (or rarely) before had the honor of producing a cardinal gained this distinction: Burkina Faso, Bangladesh,

Tonga, Madagascar, Brunei, Nicaragua, Cape Verde, Singapore, Haiti, Angola, Myanmar, Ivory Coast, East Timor, Albania, Mongolia, Mozambique, Papua New Guinea, Rwanda, Paraguay, Iraq, the Central African Republic, Laos, Mali, Pakistan, and Malta, among others. The consistory held in August of 2022 produced a College of Cardinals with a startling new composition: for the first time, less than 40 percent of its members eligible to vote in the next papal conclave come from Europe.

Of course, any pope selecting new cardinals surely has numerous considerations in mind; the eventual election of a successor is just one factor as a pope alters the composition of the College of Cardinals to place his personal stamp on the shape of that influential body. While he certainly assesses potential candidates by how closely they share his views on numerous ecclesiastical and social matters, he also clearly favors selections that will achieve broader geographical representation.[39] Francis is also the first pope to assemble a Council of Cardinal Advisors (sometimes called the C8, but fluctuating membership has deprived it of a stable number). The rule of thumb for the composition of this inner circle of papal consultants is "one cardinal representative per continent," revealing yet another initiative of Francis that effectively distributes influence across all corners of the world.

Conclusion: Gauging Francis as an Ethicist

The above list of six ethical achievements of Francis is representative rather than exhaustive. An attentive observer may well identify further important items, or even judge other initiatives of Francis to be more significant than certain of these six. Later chapters in this book will indeed provide additional candidates to expand this list of the ethical accomplishments of Francis, as well as agenda items yet to be addressed and realized fully.

The main point is that these are indeed *ethical* initiatives and achievements, and as such constitute major moral contributions that Francis has chosen to offer the church as its leader. As noted at the outset of this chapter, some observers may be disappointed that Francis has not staked out more of a traditional papal profile in this area, perhaps by offering detailed guidance on discrete moral issues and questions as some previous popes have.

The distinctive brand of ethical leadership that Francis *does* choose to offer reflects the prophetic injunction "to get your own house in order." The achievement of this imperative requires leaders capable of adopting clear moral priorities and modeling consistent and accountable behavior in the major and even in the smaller matters of church management. Furthermore, Francis displays keen awareness that success in the church's mission to evangelize absolutely depends on its ability to embody a core of ethical principles—inclusiveness, justice, mercy, accountability, a participatory order—in its internal life; only then will the gospel proclaimed by the church be attractive to those encountered on the peripheries.

By thus prioritizing improved conditions for evangelization, the moral agenda of Francis largely sidesteps the wedge issues and litmus tests of orthodoxy that preoccupy "culture warriors," who rely on a predominantly legal model of ethics and emphasize the drawing of bright moral lines. In fact, the style of moral teaching and leadership exhibited by Francis bears a remarkable resemblance to the school of "virtue ethics" that has witnessed a revival in academic moral theology in recent decades. Virtue ethicists focus on the powerful role played by settled habits and qualities of personal character in shaping good behavior and moral growth over the course of our lifetimes, rather than on discrete decisions or mental judgments we might make at any one moment. They are fond of asking questions such as: What kind of people are we becoming over time through our actions? How may we cultivate patterns of thought and action that will build up the virtues and habituate responsible behavior? What concrete practices will enable us to improve the contours of our moral agency and the quality of our relationships?

Although Pope Francis has only on rare occasions, such as in *Evangelii Gaudium* (no. 37), *Laudato Si'* (no. 211), and *Gaudete et Exsultate* (no. 60),[40] given an extended treatment of the moral virtues in his writings, the resemblance between his ethical approach and the "turn to virtue" in recent moral theology has not escaped the notice of theologians. For example, Daniel J. Daly, in his monograph, *The Structures of Virtue and Vice*, dedicates half a chapter to what he terms "Francis's contextual virtue ethics."[41] He calls attention to the affinity between what Francis has said about the practical living out of the virtues of charity, mercy, and solidarity, on one hand, and the revival of virtue ethics in academic circles, on the other hand. Daly is just one of many close observers of Pope Francis who notice and describe the distinctive trajectory his papal leadership has provided to a church that is being challenged to supplement its previously rule-centered approach to moral theology with more personalistic and virtue-based messages about what it means to live a life of upstanding moral quality in the contemporary world.

Of course, Francis has not produced entire academic treatises on the ethical virtues or textbook treatments of any aspect of the moral life of Christians. His modus operandi, somewhat different from that of his predecessors, is to view moral challenges through a lens that is primarily pastoral and practical. While his perspective is not chiefly rule centered, his methodology retains a legitimate place for moral laws, with the stipulation that we discern in a deliberate way how moral laws and principles apply to the concrete circumstances in which we find ourselves. This allusion to the role of careful moral discernment provides a felicitous transition to the topic of the following chapter, which examines how Francis has modeled spiritual and ethical discernment in the creative moral leadership on display in his papal ministry.

CHAPTER 2

FRANCIS, THE DISCERNER

OBSERVERS OF ETHICAL leadership often identify two complementary components that are simultaneously at work: substance (what a leader does); and style (how those things are accomplished). The previous chapter examined the ethical priorities of Pope Francis through a sample of six items that comprise part of the substance of his papal leadership. Further glimpses of that substance, including achievements in the fields of social justice advocacy (chapter 4) and regarding the ethics of family life (later in this chapter), await us. First, this chapter considers certain matters of style.

Knowing Francis as a man of the church who is quite deliberate about his leadership choices, we gain much insight by noticing not just *what* he does but *how* he operates. What are the principles, procedures, and methods he employs as he sets about his papal agenda? Can we detect any patterns in how Francis proceeds, both in day-to-day activities and in the long-term trajectories of his papal initiatives?

These questions involving the style employed by Francis will occupy most of these central chapters of this book. Chapter 3, "Francis, the Communicator," will take up the communication strategy of Pope Francis, describing major features of the style with which he projects his messages to the church and the wider world. It calls attention primarily to the "outward-facing" dimension of the pope, while this current chapter examines his somewhat more "inward-facing" aspect and provides a glimpse of the principles of deliberation and decision-making that the pope, drawing on his Jesuit spiritual background, customarily follows.

It would be unwise, of course, to overstate this inner/outer divide, as discernment is rarely a strictly private act. Public figures who lead large organizations invariably end up modeling behavior, hopefully in admirable ways, for many others, even if they may imagine that they are only undertaking narrowly personal planning. A pope who undertakes the task of leading a worldwide church will soon find himself inspiring a global faith community eager to emulate an attractive exemplar of ethically accountable behavior. If Francis is perceived as practicing careful and responsible discernment, his style of decision-making will have a way of catching on in ways that may animate the lives of the many people whose eyes are focused on the pope and who follow his cues for conducting a commendable spiritual life.

Although spiritual discernment is a common theme in many faith traditions, religious discourse holds no monopoly on offering wisdom regarding discernment. Even secular approaches to these matters, such as the literature of business leadership, readily acknowledge the importance of careful deliberation that leads to prudent planning and sound decision-making at both the personal and institutional level. However, to speak of spiritual discernment, as Pope Francis often does, brings the conversation about shaping the future to an entirely different level. As we shall see in the following pages, in the context of religious perspectives and their attendant obligations, recognizing and then following proper paths to pursue are not just matters of figuring out how to achieve a self-determined set of optimal results—measured in ordinary ways that might involve quantifiable "bottom lines" of our own choosing.

Rather, for spiritual masters like Francis, the deepest goals of any discernment involve remaining faithful to moral principles that we ourselves do not set in isolation, but which ultimately reflect God's intentions rather than our own preferences. In decisions that will affect the life-course of an individual or even set a distinctive direction for the entire people of God, fidelity to our sense of vocation and to the divine plan of creation, as nearly as we can comprehend it, is a crucial dimension and criterion of discernment. In short, like all Christians, Francis is devoted to promoting God's purposes and plans, not his own.

Throughout this chapter, we will have the opportunity to explore the spiritual roots that influence the discernment style of Francis and then to observe the pope leading the church in complex multiyear communal discernment exercises involving two topics: (1) contemporary challenges to family life and (2) the well-being of the vital Amazon region of South America. While the first of these case studies will command somewhat more extensive coverage, each reveals important elements of the spirituality and discernment style of Pope Francis.

Overcoming Two Sources of (Potential) Reluctance

Importantly, there are two preliminary considerations regarding the moral leadership of Francis as it relates to discernment. Both involve some "reading between the lines" and perhaps a bit of guesswork, even for those who might consider themselves close observers of the pope. The bottom line of each of the following two claims is that Francis may exhibit some initial reluctance or even discomfort regarding how he executes discernment in the context of his papal office. Neither consideration is a genuine game changer, but each merits the attention of any close observer of moral leadership.

Aversion to Being Placed on an Ethical Pedestal

First, while the preceding paragraphs might make it sound as if Pope Francis gladly basks in the global limelight as "discerner-in-chief," there is good reason to doubt that he relishes this precise kind of attention. Certainly, any high official in the church is aware that many eyes may be fixed on him; over time, most leaders grow accustomed to, though still potentially uneasy with, the attention that inevitably comes their way. Even more than political officeholders or secular celebrities, religious leaders may feel a distinct burden that accompanies their status as a recognized ethical role model. Every aspect of their behavior is potentially under the microscope of public scrutiny.

This aversion to being placed on an ethical pedestal may go in two directions, each with its own sources of possible discomfort. On the one hand, a religious leader in the limelight is wise to practice vigilance against appearing as a hypocrite, because even the appearance of unethical behavior will bring not only personal embarrassment but lasting harm to the entire faith community. On the other hand, such a religious leader with a high public profile should never give the appearance of being presumptuous about his or her own moral achievements. While it may at times appear allowable to call attention to the supposedly meritorious example of moral behavior that one provides (St. Paul holds himself up as an example on occasion in the New Testament), it remains the case that no one likes a show-off. Inflated claims that others should always be emulating one's ethical example will surely backfire, producing resentment or worse. No human being should set himself or herself up as an ideal exemplar of moral consistency, as a practitioner of exceptionless good judgments or a flawless vessel of any virtue for that matter.

Anyone who has observed Pope Francis closely over the years will recognize a healthy reluctance to promote himself as perfect in any way. Refreshingly, he resists the temptation to hold himself up as an ideal model for others and is certainly not afraid to call attention to his own personal faults, even laughing about his own regrettable personality traits at times. He has started interviews with explicit recognition of his shortcomings, not shying away from placing front and center his constant awareness of his status as a sinner.[1] This is much to his credit, of course, and is never presented glibly but rather as a component of the profound spiritual tradition in which Pope Francis locates himself.

While Francis consistently demurs from holding himself up as the perfect role model, this is not the end of the story, for he also knows the enormous value of projecting positive qualities of leadership that are potentially helpful for others to imitate—or at least aspire to do. So, there remains a legitimate place for Francis to model in a deliberate way the skill at discernment that he has acquired. While he may be reticent to play the role of a "grandstander," neither would he want "to hide his lamp under a bushel" (see Jesus' admonition in Matt 5:15), especially if this would deprive the church of valuable guidance. As an experienced practitioner of spiritual discernment—one with proven success in encouraging others to examine their consciences, engage their minds, and stir their passions—Francis clearly has much to offer. For as long as the opportunity persists for him to reap good fruit by displaying the spiritual acumen he has acquired, we may expect him to continue his practice of tolerating the limelight of personal attention that he would otherwise prefer to shun. The two episodes of papal leadership in moral discernment described later in this chapter would not be possible otherwise.

To wit, Pope Francis is a master of the Jesuit tradition (described in some detail below) of mentoring others in principles and techniques of discernment. We understand his papal leadership more clearly when we acknowledge certain aspects of his biography. Before he became pope, he wrote frequently on topics of spirituality.[2] As a young priest, Bergoglio spent years as a superior working with young men in formation, offering his service as a spiritual director, as a teacher, and as a mentor in the spiritual life. This was in addition to the dozen years he spent in formation himself, learning the spiritual tradition of the Society of Jesus and familiarizing himself with the practices of individual and communal decision-making that date back to St. Ignatius of Loyola, the sixteenth-century founder of the Jesuits. In short, Francis has much to offer in the area of discernment, and like all Jesuits is eager to share this spiritual inheritance with all interested parties.

Reluctance to Invoke Papal Power to Excess

The second area where we might detect in Francis some initial reluctance to exert papal leadership as an authoritative discerner pertains to the evolving understanding of papal power itself. Comprehending this subtle point requires reflection on certain historical trends within Catholicism. The currently dominant model of nearly absolute papal authority over the church has not always held sway, nor is it unquestioned today. In assessing the evolution of papal prerogatives, church historians are quick to point out that until the eleventh century, the Bishop of Rome rarely aspired to exert much influence beyond his own diocese. Although claiming various titles associated with the status of recognized successor to St. Peter, the Bishop of Rome was long considered merely the first among equal holders of spiritual authority (that is, *primus inter pares* among the chief patriarchs of the church).

Much changed with the Gregorian Reforms, and specifically with the intervention of Pope Gregory VII (r. 1073–85) in the Investiture Controversy that proposed a model of popes as actors capable of challenging the power of secular rulers even to the point of deposing them. Although the maximalist versions of such claims to plenary papal power on the political scene have long since faded, within the realm of the church itself over the second millennium a "top-down and hierarchical mode" replaced the primarily "synodal and collegial mode" of the first ten Christian centuries. Historian John O'Malley, SJ, identifies Vatican I's definition of the doctrine of papal infallibility as the high point of what he terms "the papalization of the church."[3]

Remaining to be seen is to what extent the reforms of Vatican II provide definitive momentum toward a church featuring greater *collegiality* (shared authority among all bishops as authentic teachers of the faith) and *synodality* (a collaborative ethos featuring relationships of respectful consultation and co-responsibility among the entire "people of God"). Church historians are never surprised when several generations pass before the teachings of an ecumenical church council are fully implemented. Although all postconciliar popes affirmed the basic commitments of Vatican II in various ways, Francis represents the first holder of the papal office who speaks with great enthusiasm of his desire to enact synodality in the church's polity and to devolve a significant range of authority to more local levels, as we note below. Indeed, in his first months in office, Francis often expressed his preference to be referred to as "Bishop of Rome," rather than by other customary titles such as Supreme Pontiff, Vicar of Christ, or even simply pope.[4]

Why, then, does Francis continue, with so little obvious alteration, the previous patterns of papal power-wielding? What explains the ostensibly enthusiastic embrace of a wide variety of papal powers and prerogatives on the part of Francis? The explanation that follows represents a bit of guesswork and "reading between the lines," but does offer a coherent and plausible set of conjectures. We start by recalling the account of six major ethical accomplishments of Francis that appeared at the end of the previous chapter—items such as addressing head-on the church's sex abuse crisis, promulgating comprehensive reform of the church's financial management, restructuring the Roman Curia, opening new leadership roles for women in the church, and placing his own personal stamp on the geographical composition of the College of Cardinals. Even where definitive action took years to unfold completely, each of these initiatives bears the imprint of a confident leader with few scruples about applying potent measures to enact important changes.

On the surface, these activities surely suggest that Francis appears to have continued without abatement the patterns of previous popes, who have long employed, without hesitation, the full share of the ecclesial authority entrusted to them. Occasionally, Francis has even exceeded ordinary expectations regarding how popes use their disciplinary power, such as when he took the extremely rare step of submitting a powerful senior cardinal, Giovanni Angelo Becciu of Italy, to a public Vatican trial and ultimately stripping him entirely of the privileges of his status due to his evident role in financial misdeeds. Clearly, Francis is not a pope who shies away from exerting ecclesiastical muscle to get especially important things done. Like the old-fashioned Jesuit superior that he was for decades, he is fully capable of asserting robust religious authority when necessary for sufficiently weighty purposes.

That final thought about especially pressing purposes provides a crucial clue to resolving this seeming "Francis conundrum," whereby his words suggest a preference for disavowing some papal powers, but his actions display a willingness to continue using the full measure of that power. As noted earlier, only Francis possesses full knowledge of the mind of Francis, of course, but a plausible inference calls attention to extenuating circumstances that have forced his hand. Emergency situations have a way of constraining, or at least delaying, the set of actions we might prefer in an ideal world. It appears that the years of Francis's papacy have simply presented too many pressing challenges and serious crises calling for decisive action to justify pulling back from exercising customary papal prerogatives on so many important matters.

Although Francis might prefer to refrain from exercising some of the ordinary powers of the papacy and thus to model creative ways to disavow the application of unaccountable power, perhaps by delegating some of his inherited authority to lower levels of the church, he has continued to tailor prudent interventions to the contours of exigencies that simply cannot wait for resolution. The most urgent task for Francis is to follow the prophetic injunction to "set your house in order" by all justifiable means at his disposal. This has simply not been a propitious time for a reform-minded pope to cede substantial shares of authority and to entrust important reform initiatives to others at the local level. The strategic rationale at play here is not hard to decipher. A reform-minded leader at the top of any pyramid of authority must first provide the tools for forging ongoing progress and insuring future good order. The crucial need for timely measures that address these deep concerns has left too little room for a strategy of relinquishing, for now, many papal powers.

Once again, this is only one possible interpretation of the overall leadership strategy of Francis, but this educated guess regarding "What makes Francis tick?" does explain much about how he has fashioned his papal agenda, holding together means and ends in a distinctive way that "meets the moment" and responds to the challenges that his election mandated him to address. This plausible line of analysis certainly possesses ample explanatory power to reconcile a seeming gap between the long-term ethical goals Francis has articulated and the short-term strategies he has employed to manage pressing needs of the church during his papacy. If accurate, it portrays Francis as a somewhat reluctant wielder of the full powers of the papacy, but one who is nonetheless confident that the full-throated (if temporary) employ of his considerable authority will be justified by the ultimate results: the empowerment of those currently on the peripheries, even if it must come after a period of transition. With Francis, we may expect to see the emergence of a church that is better positioned to evangelize with energy and credibility because of the reforms that he has implemented, even if the process of enforcing certain changes necessarily delays the redistribution of power and authority in a more participatory church.

This section has invited us to perceive Francis, then, as a leader ultimately overcoming his initial reluctance to lead in certain ways (that is, by calling attention to his own expertise in the practice of discernment, and by invoking the fullness of papal power he inherited). Future historians will perhaps consider it the chief irony of Francis's papacy that he discerned the necessity of following these two lines of action, since they appear on the surface to delay the attainment of the very goals this temperamentally humble pope is most eager to achieve: the de-centering of power in the church. The remainder of this chapter will describe select initiatives of Francis that, in a real sense, already embody the principles of collegiality and synodality, and especially certain instances that display valuable principles of spiritual discernment.

Ignatian Principles of Discernment

St. Ignatius Loyola was not, of course, the first pioneer of Christian discernment, but his handbook of prayer called the

Spiritual Exercises is perhaps the text most cited as a source of valuable wisdom regarding this spiritual practice. Although the entirety of the *Exercises* is relevant to anyone facing decisions along the path of the Christian life, the text contains a discrete section squarely on this topic, bearing the title "Rules for the Discernment of Spirits" or "Guidelines for Perceiving the Movements Caused in the Soul," depending on one's preferred translation.[5] Readers are sometimes disappointed that the items covered by St. Ignatius in these pages (there are twenty-two items that cover somewhat less than ten pages in most printed versions) do not provide a comprehensive or tightly systematic method of decision-making, although the coverage of general principles of discernment and modes of concrete application do display a solid and appealing approach to facing up to uncertainties and resolving spiritual quandaries. Ignatius was most evidently seeking to provide a flexible set of guidelines that capture the highest priorities in any discernment process, though what he is explicitly describing here are the spiritual movements one may experience during a month-long religious retreat.

The value of the *Exercises* for the individual retreatant and, by extension, for collectivities such as a church in search of ethical clarity or broader spiritual guidance, hinges upon a handful of key assumptions behind the text of Ignatius. Among the chief assumptions are these four: (1) God is never distant from us, but rather is always active in the world, inviting and directing us to what is good for us; (2) all people have access to the promptings of the Lord if they are prayerfully attentive to the movements of the Holy Spirit in their interior lives; (3) emotions such as consolations and desolations, when properly interpreted, can be reliable guides to sound decisions (Ignatius favors the term *elections*); and (4) our ability to embrace the good and to reject what is evil hinges on prior acts of will to purify our motivations, discover the purposes for which we are created, accept our limited creaturely status, and receive the freely offered redemptive love of God revealed in Jesus Christ.

Even in noting these fundamentals of his approach to the spiritual life, it soon becomes obvious that Ignatius is far more comfortable than most contemporary people in speaking of such realities as mortal sin, grave temptations, and the power of evil (and specifically of the devil) in our world. His preference for such quaint-sounding notions as "testing the spirits" and "battling the enemy of human nature" may not always closely match our modern notions of what is going on within the decision-making process; nevertheless, these Ignatian motifs often place a refreshing spin on the perennial task of weighing the positive and negative sides of any human decision, especially regarding the imperative to avoid all forms of pride and self-deception.

Although these are just a few initial elements of Ignatian-style discernment, close observers of Pope Francis will easily recognize ample resonance with his way of approaching and speaking about the spiritual life. In his various homilies and public addresses, he does not shy away from appealing to such Ignatian-tinged notions as "the state of one's soul," the struggle for ever more profound self-knowledge, the joy and inner peace that are the fruits of cooperation with divine promptings, and even the effects of the work of the devil, especially when referring to the scourge of corruption in church circles.[6] Although living more than four hundred years apart, these two Jesuits display a markedly similar impatience for laziness, pride, vainglory, deceit, or self-serving behavior of any sort.[7] In speaking so often of the virtues of boldness and magnanimous willingness to make difficult sacrifices for the greater good, the pope even seems at times to adopt the preferred semi-military idiom of the founder of the Society of Jesus. In short, Francis displays a thoroughly Ignatian temperament—one that combines an affirming and attractive easy-goingness, capable of occasional bursts of open exuberance—with an ardent determination to challenge people to be their best selves, even when that may require a detour from the comfortable path of least resistance.

There is also a certain upfront practicality to all that Francis says about making choices between alternative courses of action—a proclivity that echoes the words that St. Ignatius wrote five centuries ago regarding the spiritual life. Neither Jesuit leader displays any interest in obfuscating or needlessly complexifying the central dynamics of the spiritual life. Although the literature of spiritual direction is sometimes accused of lapsing into baffling jargon or devolving into arcane obscurities, Pope Francis is fastidious about never confounding his listeners by employing technical terminology that would mystify what should remain ever clear and accessible: God's desire for their flourishing in this life and for their participation in eternal life at the end of time.[8] A key hallmark of the Ignatian heritage is its ability to communicate spiritual guidance in a direct way, and Francis is especially eager to leverage his mastery of the principles of discernment to share the riches of this tradition with all eager audiences.

Although it springs from these straightforward premises, sound spiritual decision-making also requires certain structures and conditions that support favorable outcomes. It requires strenuous work indeed to attain the interior spiritual freedom that allows an individual or a group to reach difficult decisions. The fruits of genuine discernments may entail considerable sacrifices, such as the renunciation of certain privileges and sources of personal or group security. What are some of these structures and conditions?

Gathering adequate information and conducting thoughtful weighing of various options is a precondition for any successful exercise in discernment, as there is no substitute for a careful analysis of the full range of relevant factors and potential courses of action. Another commonsense imperative in any sound deliberation is avoiding distractions that might sidetrack the central enterprise entirely; such diversions represent temptations that lure us away from the most urgent issues. An optimal process of deliberation will also settle on a felicitous balance of reason and emotion, each of which may contribute to good decisions but only when supplemented by the other. Spiritual masters know that all too often we reduce decisions to strictly rational determinations, neglecting the role of feelings and the human imagination entirely. Indeed, a willingness to acknowledge and honor the legitimate role of the emotions and affective responses in decision-making may be the single most prominent thing that sets spiritual discernment apart from ordinary deliberations, for example, in secular organizations like for-profit businesses. The fact that religious individuals and communities understand and gauge their decisions in terms of divine purposes, and even God's providential will for us and our world, makes an obvious difference in the frame of reference here.

The Ignatian spiritual tradition in particular accords a central place to consulting the emotions that will naturally inform any sound human decision. For example, Jesuit spirituality foregrounds the key importance of feelings of gratitude (for the freely given and unmerited graces of God) or anxiety (related to human sin) that arise while conducting the regular "consciousness examen" recommended by Ignatius and described in detail in the *Spiritual Exercises* (nos. 24ff.). Among the many factors that deserve to be consulted in the discernment process is the honest acknowledgment of what brings a sense of long-lasting peace to a given person (especially a retreatant or spiritual directee) in moments of prayer and reflection. Good decisions tend to build organically upon central facets of self-awareness, including the consolations and desolations treated above.

It is commonplace to recognize the Jesuit spiritual tradition as a potent force for transformation, on both the personal and social levels. Inspired by a religious vision that attunes them to the possibility of a better world, those touched by this spiritual heritage seek to make a positive difference at all levels of human society. Ignatius and Pope Francis provide particularly clear examples of figures whose lives were marked by profound interior transformations; both men describe pivotal moments when their early lives were interrupted by overwhelming experience of God's compassion and mercy. The fruit of the "internal reorientation" that each underwent eventually ripened into a strong outward-directed impetus toward social transformation, as each spearheaded remarkable apostolic initiatives through energetic leadership.

Undergirding the subsequent exertions of Ignatius, of Francis, or of any practitioner of the spirituality they exemplify is a confident hope that positive change is indeed possible—both in the interiority of our souls and in the external social order.

An activist spirituality thus holds implications for both the present earthly (inner-worldly) order and the supernatural (otherworldly) order. Making no concessions to fatalism or despair, these spiritual practitioners dare to become agents of transformation, assuming all the risks and liabilities that stalk those who hope for things unseen. Providing a foundation for the leadership of Francis is his evident confidence that well-conducted discernments will direct the church's energies in ways congruent with its divinely appointed missions of evangelization, with inclusive social concern and sensitive pastoral care for all members of the faith community.

Communal Discernment

The remainder of this chapter examines two especially revealing instances when the work of "Francis, the discerner" is on full display. We will have an opportunity to view specific ways in which the pope applies the fruits of Ignatian spirituality that formed him to tasks that require discernment affecting the life of the church and the wider world. It is important to note that each case study proceeds not on the level of the individual person (where most of the foregoing analysis of spiritual discernment has unfolded), but rather on the larger stages of social institutions (such as the church) and entire societies. This shift of scale requires that we adapt the spiritual principles governing ordinary personal discernment to the challenges of "communal discernment." This topic is a relatively new one in the literature of spirituality. Only in recent decades have large groups, often religious communities, begun to pioneer principles and procedures for reaching sound decision through structured deliberations, often referred to as "corporate discernment." Applying the best practices that have surfaced so far to the worldwide church is one of the more intriguing challenges taken up by Francis.

While individual discernment has focused almost exclusively on personal vocation and the "vertical" relationship of each person with God, a focus on communal discernment necessitates more attention to nurturing the "horizontal" relationships we maintain with other people. An obviously different set of requirements is in effect when responding to the promptings of our Creator, on the one hand, and the needs of fellow mortals with whom we interact, on the other hand.

Considering the implications for action when "things go wrong" in both types of relationships sheds further light on this contrast. The damaging, or even rupturing, of one's vertical relationship with God is what we call sin; the fraying of horizontal relationships involves such notions as injustice and the need for social healing. The remedies for each variety of dysfunction are also naturally quite different; correcting sin requires individual contrition and repentance, while addressing social injustice involves large-scale reconciliation such as a process of restorative justice. Appropriate to each situation are distinctive principles and dynamics of discernment. We will have the opportunity to view both the style and substance of Pope Francis's handling of several diverse challenges relating to communal discernment along these very lines.

Both case studies to be presented below involve meetings of the worldwide synod of bishops. A few preliminary words of explanation will assist our understanding of the workings of this unique church institution. Initiated by Pope Paul VI in the wake of the Second Vatican Council, the synods were established as a way of continuing the practice of collegiality (shared governance and consultation) experienced by the more than two thousand bishops from around the world who participated in the four sessions of the council (1962–65). Paul mandated a regular three-year cycle (some exceptions have been made to the ordinary spacing) of meetings in Rome at which a representative selection of the Catholic bishops throughout the world (typically in the vicinity of 250) has been joined by a smaller number of further voting members (such as major superiors of religious orders) and nonvoting consultants or invited observers in attendance. Synod topics have included broad themes (such as evangelization, missionary activity, youth, and family life), sacraments (such as penance and the Eucharist), and the challenges to the church in various regions of the world (such as Africa, Asia, the Americas, and most recently Amazonia).

To facilitate thoughtful preparation, preliminary theological study and fully consultative deliberation, the topics of each synod are determined several years in advance. The first few synods (most notably the one in 1971) produced their own freestanding final documents that were recognized as holding considerable doctrinal authority. The practice continues of compiling and publishing a *relatio synodi*, or public final report, the component items of which, drafted by a relator or small committee of redactors, are subject to a paragraph-by-paragraph vote of approval (a two-thirds majority of the voting delegates is required for each item to pass). However, within a decade the practice developed whereby the reigning pope issues an authoritative "post-synodal apostolic exhortation" interpreting the results of the deliberations on the central topics at hand. Those substantial and authoritative teaching documents have come to eclipse the actual meetings, prompting the complaint that popes sometimes seem to disregard the deliberations of the gathered delegates altogether, even though the pope typically attends the plenary sessions.

To contend (as we will in presenting the following two case studies) that a pope displays remarkable skills at discernment in directing a meeting of the worldwide synod of bishops is actually an extraordinary claim—one that may not be obvious at first encounter, but which may prove to be true upon closer inspection. Items that must be factored into any such judgment include the complexity of the synod process and especially the sheer duration of time required to complete the work of a synod. Though the actual meetings last only about three weeks, the onsite proceedings are the product of years of planning that requires coordination on many levels. Only those rare observers with inside access to the long and complex process of planning and executing a synod can accurately assess a given pope's influence on the proceedings. The judgments that follow regarding Francis's guidance of the discernment process are based on clues that emerge from the public record and written accounts of the synods to be covered.

Of course, popes delegate much of the work of preparing and running a worldwide synod to trusted advisors, including the staff of an entire Vatican office, called the General Secretariat of the Synod of Bishops, dedicated to these tasks. While it would be impossible for an outside observer to attribute any given decision or initiative regarding a synod to either the pope himself or any specific set of officials in this structure, it is safe to assume that the sitting pope assumes ultimate responsibility for supervising the overall process, and that he approves its major directions. With the assistance of this office, the pope oversees the development of preparatory materials relating to the chosen theme, including compiling the *instrumentum laboris*, an initial procedural document that reflects advance research and related proposals regarding the topic at hand. Further advance coordination extends to the level of national and regional episcopal conferences, where local deliberations identify the bishop-delegates and other representatives and consultants to the synod as it approaches.

Case Study #1: Two Synods on the Family

This section covers the events of the first three-year "synod cycle" in which Pope Francis fully participated, which culminated in the publication of his post-synodal apostolic exhortation, *Amoris Laetitita* (the literal wording of the Latin title is "the joy of love," but the usual English rendering is "On Love in the Family"), in April of 2016.[9] We have already had occasion to cite Francis's only previous apostolic exhortation *Evangelii Gaudium* ("The Joy of the Gospel"), which was published on November 24, 2013, just eight months after he took office. His predecessor, Benedict XVI, had presided over the October 2012 synod on the topic of evangelization but had left office early in 2013 without producing the expected teaching document, so it fell to Francis to issue an exhortation. The new pope took advantage of that opportunity to communicate his wide-ranging analysis of a topic close to his heart, and in the process produced a programmatic document on the mission of spreading the gospel that has guided his entire papacy. Interestingly, when it was released, *Evangelii Gaudium* (at 47,500 words in the English version) was the lengthiest papal teaching document ever; it now occupies second place behind the even longer *Amoris Laetitia* (at 60,000 words in English). Both are substantial multichapter books (on the same scale as this present volume) containing extended theological treatments of pivotal topics in the life of the global church.

The central focus of this section is specifically how Francis displayed exceptional discernment skills in guiding the process by which the synod of bishops treated family life. The most obvious place to start is by noting the sheer length, scale, and complexity of the deliberation process that Francis designed—a process that bears the personal imprint of this pope in many ways. As a disciple of the spiritual master, Ignatius of Loyola, who designed retreat experiences of a full thirty-days duration for individuals facing a potentially life-changing "election," Francis displayed his own high regard for the benefits of careful discernment and prolonged attention to weighty issues, however long the process might take. He thus insisted on a more extended and elaborate process for synod deliberations on such a sensitive topic as the challenges faced by families today.

Specifically, Francis judged that the single triennial synod meeting, already scheduled to meet in Rome, October 4–25, 2015, was inadequate for the extensive and profound deliberations he was hoping to conduct. To build in more time for the necessary reflection and consultation, Francis mandated the addition of a preliminary extraordinary synod meeting to be held one year earlier (October 5–19, 2014). Although not completely unprecedented (there had been two previous "extraordinary general assemblies of the worldwide synod" in the previous half-century), this unusual mandate communicated the desire of Francis to supervise a process featuring enhanced depth and seriousness of purpose. The first synod meeting was designated "The Pastoral Challenges of the Family in the Context of Evangelization," and the second was labeled "The Vocation and Mission of the Family in the Church and the Contemporary World." There was much (though obviously far from total) overlap between the 260 delegates to the 2014 meeting and the 318 delegates to the 2015 meeting; in both cases, bishops comprised the great majority of the voting delegates, but some married couples and additional laymen and laywomen attended as consultants.

Besides extending the deliberation process over a much longer span of time than usual, Francis took important steps in shaping the two synods in ways that revealed his commitment to a fresh style of discernment. To indicate his high regard for the opinion of rank-and-file members of the church—the theological term is *sensus fidelium*, or "the sense of the faithful"—in matters that touch their lives so intimately, Francis encouraged local jurisdictions (individual dioceses and even national episcopal conferences) to conduct opinion polling on a range of key issues regarding family life. As early as December of 2013, a sample thirty-nine-item survey instrument was circulated, with a wide variety of questions regarding how the church's teachings on marriage and family life are understood, valued, and practiced. Although anecdotal evidence suggests rather uneven distribution, collection, and reporting of data resulting from the survey process, many expressed their appreciation for this extraordinary gesture toward inclusion. Even though the survey instrument was received with mixed reviews, the mere effort to conduct such an ambitious inquiry into opinions among the people of God pointed to a greater-than-usual commitment to consulting a wider-than-usual segment of the laity around the world.

Francis also earned "style points" for his personal presence and comportment at the synod proceedings. By many accounts, he supervised the plenary sessions of both multiweek Rome meetings in an exemplary way, with evident attentiveness at all the sessions, whereas some previous popes had received media criticism for occasionally dozing off or appearing distracted with reading material at the presider's chair. Further demonstrating his commitment to listening carefully to the voices of many parties regarding family life, Francis even went well out of his way to attend the Eighth World Meeting of Families held in Philadelphia in late September of 2015. Note that this global church-sponsored meeting (scheduled with regularity every third year, whether the pope can attend or not) fell just two weeks before the second synod meeting in Rome on the same topic, and that Francis extended his stay in the United States for the express purpose of participating in this constructive and wide-ranging dialogue that was hosted, most appropriately, by the Catholic community in the "City of Brotherly Love."

Before turning to the substance of the proceedings and Francis's resulting teaching document, a final word is in order regarding Francis's discernment style as it was on display at the two synods. Each began with the customary initial oration by the pope to set the tone and expectations for the plenary sessions and working-group meetings. On each occasion, Francis used a revealing Greek word, *parrhesia*, which appears thirty-one times in the New Testament (see, for example, Acts 28:31 and Phlm 1:8). The word denotes a "bold or courageous freedom of speech." In thus encouraging the delegates to speak with frankness and candor—to reveal what was in their hearts, without concealment or obfuscation—Francis was clearly attempting to set these proceedings apart from the somewhat stagnant and *pro forma* quality of many previous synods of bishops.

Synod participants had long complained that synod speeches were extremely bland and predictable, with only rare insightful engagement of the preceding interventions or potentially controversial topics of relevance. Many of the speakers, it had been whispered, seemed more interesting in currying favor with the sitting pontiff than raising substantive points that might potentially challenge church practices. So, these "pep talks" of Francis breathed fresh air into the synods, inspiring delegates to take some risks and speak their mind on contentious issues such as how the church deals pastorally with homosexuality and premarital cohabitation. Refrain from tightly scripted monologues and ceremonial set pieces, Francis urged, but, by all means, venture to engage in genuine dialogue about sensitive issues. Everything would be on the table for meaningful dialogue.

Delegates seemed relieved and newly empowered. Just as the spiritual life of any individual grows healthier as fear is replaced by freedom, so the value of a communal discernment is greatly enhanced when speakers in a public assembly turn away from timidity and toward constructive authenticity of expression. Once again, Francis was serving as a role model for excellent discernment practices. Beyond these improvements in the overall spirit of the deliberations, veteran delegates also reported greater satisfaction even with the nuts-and-bolts procedures of these two synod meetings. According to news reports at the time, votes were tallied more rapidly, translations were available on an expedited basis, and interim committee reports were released with more transparency than at previous synods.[10] Whereas procedural delays and secretiveness had marred some earlier synods, the new era of synods supervised by Francis took on a new spirit of frank openness—a further meaning of the Greek word *parrhesia.*

Beyond those matters of *style* regarding how Francis conducted this worldwide communal discernment lies the *substance* of what the synod meetings discussed. The content of weeks of deliberations obviously resists easy summary, but, suffice it to say, a wide range of topics surfaced regarding the church's pastoral engagement with the needs of families. Reflecting the guidelines in the preparatory materials, the delegates grappled with sensitive matters relating to sexuality, marriage, and child-rearing. The delegates deserve praise for taking up the challenge of Francis to move beyond speaking in generalities and platitudes—a tendency that was recalled as a particular shortcoming of the 1980 synod of bishops, the last occasion when the theme of family was on the table in this global church forum. A review of the content of the 1981 post-synodal exhortation of John Paul II *Familiaris Consortio* ("The Role of the Christian Family in the Modern World") provides revealing insight into the tenor of those proceedings.

By all accounts, the deliberations in both the 2014 and 2015 synods "really did get down to the concrete" as the delegates surfaced and analyzed specific challenges to received notions of what it means to live a Christian family life amid such challenging contemporary conditions as evolving sexual mores and spiraling rates of divorce and out-of-wedlock births. Breaching the delicate topics that lay on the table before the participants naturally exposed certain differences of opinion, even sharp ones at times, among the delegates. Reporters covering the two synods sometimes clucked (as media covering the Vatican are wont to do, hungry as they are for storylines featuring conflict in the church) that Francis was receiving more irascible input than even he had bargained for. Perhaps he now regretted opening a Pandora's box of contentiousness, but there is ample reason for confidence that the pope ultimately was pleased with the long arc of the deliberations. He had received what he most hoped for: frankly expressed dialogical insight, gathered from around the world, regarding key pastoral issues. The sharing of wisdom from diverse sources, though by no means forming a unanimous consensus, positioned him well for his ensuing objectives going forward in this exercise of communal discernment.

The topline summary of the deliberations is that the church's inheritance of values and virtues that have long guided its reflection on family life was found worthy of reaffirmation. These include a set of sturdy familiar principles: the calling to lifelong sexual fidelity within monogamous heterosexual marriage; the permanence of the covenant of marriage; the God-given gift of human intimacy that becomes wonderfully fruitful in the transmission of life; the perduring importance of sincere commitments to assume the solemn parental duties of educating and nurturing children, including raising them in the faith starting with "the domestic church"; the impermissibility of procured abortion and artificial contraception; the priority of establishing stable and wholesome home environments where love is shared among the generations of each family. The task of strengthening families receives a positive start when each item is confirmed. Beyond that baseline, the synod discussed proposals for improving the church's pastoral response to extreme hardships experienced by families today, including domestic abuse, economic distress, addiction, and family breakup. Francis was not the only synod participant in the assembly hall who displayed the heart of a genuine pastor of souls.

All of these enduring family principles and new challenges take on distinctive faces in the many diverse cultures where the church operates and attempts to serve the faithful, so optimal pastoral engagement with families will naturally account for cultural adaptations from context to context. Many constructive suggestions for enhanced sensitivity in the church's response to families' needs appear in the final *relatio synodis* approved by a two-thirds vote of the 2015 synod delegates (as can be said of the parallel 2014 *relatio*), and Francis has eagerly acknowledged its immense contribution.[11] Not only has he recommended on many occasions that everyone read that synod document, but he himself cited those texts on many pages of his own 2016 post-synodal exhortation, *Amoris Laetitia*. Numerous paragraphs (see, for example, nos. 62, 82, and 242) of his exhortation begin with phrases such as, "As the Synod Fathers noted...." Indeed, 92 of Francis's 391 footnotes reference either the *relatio synodis* of 2014 (34) or of 2015 (58). Another fifty or so footnotes reference the writings of Pope John Paul II, particularly his teachings on family life.

The Publication of *Amoris Laetitia*

What guidance for family life, then, do we find in the nine chapters and 325 paragraphs of Francis's *Amoris Laetitia*? What is the nature of its advice? The document is clearly intended as a contribution to Christian formation and pastoral life, not as a place to work out speculative theology or new church doctrines (Francis disavows the notion that he was introducing any doctrinal innovations here). Indeed, *Amoris Laetitia* may best be understood as an extended exercise in discernment that comes from an experienced and sensitive pastor—someone informed by extensive study, consultation, and dialogue. Parts of the document—especially chapter 2, "The Experiences and Challenges of Families"—conduct perceptive social analysis regarding the cultural and economic forces that make family life a greater challenge in our age than any other. In its coverage of parental responsibilities in chapter 5 and elsewhere, Francis reveals that he is keenly aware of the dynamics of generational change and especially the ways that new technologies may disrupt family lives—hence his folksy but poignant plea in no. 278 to banish smartphones from family dining rooms. Other parts of the document offer elements of a comprehensive spirituality of marriage and the family (chapter 9), propose needed improvements to marriage preparation programs[12] (nos. 205–16 in chapter 6), and even supply some inspiring exegesis of 1 Corinthians 13, the lyrical New Testament chapter most selected by couples planning their church weddings (nos. 90–119 of chapter 4).

If in those upbeat sections of *Amoris Laetitia* we gain a glimpse of Francis the affirming pastor during good times, elsewhere we witness the heavy-hearted Francis pondering human fragility and real pain. Periodically throughout the document, he introduces notes of sobering realism, such as in his coverage of some of the all-too-common ordinary stresses of married life, including the inattentiveness of spouses to one another, habitual self-absorption, laziness, and other personality flaws (see nos. 120–30 of chapter 4). He offers recommendations to affected couples, including the practice of better communication skills and virtues like patience and forgiveness. Francis ups the ante in chapter 6 ("Some Pastoral Perspectives"), evidently drawing on his deep personal familiarity with families in deep crisis for innumerable reasons. Here, he takes up the most serious situations, lamenting the plight of those subjected to violence, addictions, and persistent unemployment—factors that often hasten the breakup of already stressed marriages. In surely the saddest sections of the document (nos. 241–52), he regrettably acknowledges that, in spite of best efforts, some marriages simply cannot be saved, and to ignore this would hold potentially serious consequences for the safety and security of mistreated spouses and children. In the wake of utter marital breakdown, separation and even civil divorce, ministers of the church are obliged to step up their efforts to accompany the former spouses, who, often through no fault of their own, find themselves in nearly impossible situations.

This is the point where Francis displays a further act of discerning care and mercy. Some of these former spouses eventually find themselves in intimate relationships with new partners, and in the absence of an official annulment granted by ecclesiastical authorities, the church routinely denies them a second sacramental marriage, as distinct from a civil marriage. Because the annulment process is long, expensive, and often literally impossible for many to navigate, millions of Catholic adults find themselves living in what are termed "irregular unions" and as a result canonically cut off from the sacraments, most notably the Eucharist. One of the prominent concerns that surfaced during the synod process is that the church, through inflexible application of canon law, has effectively abandoned these many hurting adults—people who hunger for holy communion and who would greatly benefit from reception of the sacraments.

Francis addressed these issues in chapter 8 of *Amoris Laeitita*, which bears the title "Accompanying, Discerning and Integrating Weakness." This is the chapter that has garnered by far the most attention, mostly because of the whiff of controversy raised by Francis's entertaining the possibility that, under certain circumstances and in close consultation with their local pastor, adults in this unfortunate situation may, even without the benefit of an annulment of their first marriage, be admitted to the Eucharist despite these ordinarily prohibiting circumstances. Francis was immediately and sharply criticized for supposedly violating the principle of the indissolubility of marriage, muddying the strictures of canon law regarding "irregular marriage situations" and thus "confusing the faithful."[13]

Of course, Francis was not intending to do any of these things of which he was accused, nor does the characterization of the pope as favoring a crass laxism ring true at all. In no way cavalierly abandoning the high standards regarding marital fidelity that the church has long affirmed, Francis was displaying ministerial sensitivity to the excluded, signaling pastoral flexibility and making prudential concessions to human frailty. The section titles of the first three parts of chapter 8 provide some of the flavor and tone of the approach Francis takes to these delicate matters: "The Discernment of Irregular Situation," "Gradualness in Pastoral Care," and "Mitigating Factors in Pastoral Discernment." The repeated appearances of phrases including the word *discernment*, here and throughout the entire document, are most noteworthy for present purposes. Opening the possibility of readmitting certain adults in difficult situations to the Eucharist is an achievement of a careful discerner, one who had consulted widely and listened deeply in advance of acting.

Guiding this discernment of Francis is his characteristic awareness that the moral life is more of an art (with a premium on the practice of prudence) than a science (featuring the inflexible application of a set of laws). At several points in chapter 8, he cites the work of St. Thomas Aquinas, whose theology is redolent with a commendable appreciation for the role of prudence in adjusting human behavioral adherence to legal obligations. In support of his overall approach to members of families in crisis, Francis insightfully appeals to the traditional Catholic principle of the primacy of a well-formed personal conscience since decisions of conscience are at the core of so many of the family issues treated in the synod process. Earlier in the document, Francis had reminded the reader, "We have been called to form consciences, not to replace them" (no. 37). By connecting norms and concrete situations, the human conscience, as the basis of all moral knowledge, plays a vital role in discernment and decision-making.

Furthermore, it is highly significant that Francis is careful here not to invoke his papal power to change any official church law or even to mandate any specific course of action in these situations. There is nothing heavy-handed about his approach; Francis is deliberately treading lightly on what he knows is delicate territory. Close inspection of chapter 8, and especially its footnotes,[14] reveals that he is merely signaling an openness to a wider range of local pastoral options to accompany people in such difficult cases. His guidance has the effect of empowering pastors to use their discretion—a principle already in effect anyway through "internal forum solutions" between parishioners and their pastors—in handling specific cases. In short, there is less novelty here than the pope's detractors fear or than media coverage would suggest.[15] Indeed, the guidance offered in chapter 8 may best be understood as an extension of Francis's initiative in 2015 (as part of the "Year of Mercy" that he conducted) to streamline the annulment process, making it less expensive and onerous for estranged couples in new relationships to return to the Eucharist with a clear conscience.[16] Now, readmission to holy communion would be out of reach to even fewer souls.[17]

The backlash against Francis proceeded, nonetheless. Even long after the publication of *Amoris Laetitia*, detractors continued to criticize Francis for supposedly harboring a predetermined hidden agenda from the start of the multiyear synod process, as if this extended worldwide discernment was a sham—a cover for his intention all along to loosen the conditions under which the divorced and civilly remarried may receive holy communion with papal approval. It is unfortunate that so much polarized discourse resulted from the pope's attempt to extend a hand of mercy and inclusion to family members in distress. Such criticisms rest on a decontextualized, narrow, and hardly credible construal of what was demonstrably a very broad agenda regarding family life today and the many challenges facing it. The harshest reactions also conflated two distinct roles that popes may play—that of teachers who instruct and that of gatekeepers who command and draw lines.[18] Telescoping these two roles erases the possibility of a pope who may lead the church creatively along the path of discernment.

In shaping the text of his post-synodal exhortation on family life, Francis returns often to the theme of joy. He repeatedly holds up and affirms the manifestations of joy that the family brings to us, and he even selected a title for the document that translates literally into English as "The Joy of Love." The vision of inclusive love that most people discover first in family life guides the discernment that Francis is eager to offer to the worldwide church, as it deepens its understanding of its constant mission to reach out to all. The subsequent case study, though briefer, reveals further commitments of Francis as he attempts to place his leadership and discernment skills at the service of the church.

Case Study #2: Synod on the Pan-Amazon Region

The next worldwide synod of bishops was dedicated to the theme "Young People, the Faith and Vocational Discernment." Although this 2018 meeting in Rome featured the word *discernment* in its title, the specific variety of discernment, personal and individual in nature, is not of direct interest for present purposes.[19] However, the following year, Francis hosted in Rome an additional gathering classified as a "Special Assembly of the Synod of Bishops for the Pan-Amazon Region." It met from October 6–27, 2019, and consisted of about 300 participants, of whom 182 were voting delegates, a majority of whom were bishops from Amazonia itself. The meeting featured the familiar elements of any synod of bishops: preparatory documents, including a formal *instrumentum laboris* that structured the proceedings, an opening address of the pope, a final document (*relatio*) prepared by a chief relator, the late Brazilian Cardinal Cláudio Hummes, and voted on by delegates, and of course a post-synodal apostolic exhortation from Pope Francis. The latter bore the Spanish title *Querida Amazonia* ("The Beloved Amazon") and was issued on February 2, 2020.[20]

Once again, the leadership and discernment skills of Francis were on full display, beginning with the selection of the topic and focus. The church had over recent decades convened a dozen such special assemblies organized along geographical lines; most recently, Benedict XVI had convened two such synods (on Africa and the Middle East) during his eight-year reign. A 2019 "synod profile document" explains that such special assemblies are "for matters that mostly concern one or more specific geographical regions."[21] At first glance, the Argentinian pope might have been perceived as opening himself up to accusations of favoritism in conducting a synod focusing on the needs of his native continent. However, the Amazonia region faces an array of pastoral and other challenges that distinguish it sharply from Argentina and other parts of South America. Its 34 million people inhabit parts of nine countries that form the greater Amazon River Basin, large swaths of which are nearly unreachable by paved or even unpaved roads.

Millions of the Catholics of this vast region (about the size of Australia) are Indigenous peoples, some of whom live in voluntary isolation, hesitant to engage economically or politically with Western culture. The Indigenous peoples often speak only languages unfamiliar to the priests who reach the "mission stations" nearest them only sporadically from their own distant bases of operation. One of the concerns that surfaced during the synod is that many communities of Catholics are deprived of the Eucharist and other sacraments because months go by between visits of overtaxed, circuit-riding priests who have great difficulty reaching their localities.

The commitment, then, of Francis to engage these highly distinctive regional concerns reflects his overall vision of "a church of encounter" that is dedicated to hearing all voices, no matter how costly and inconvenient it may be to engage those on the periphery. The valuable knowledge required to improve pastoral responses to people with distinctive needs surfaces only in the context of extended and respectful dialogue with many others, especially those whose voices have been systematically excluded in the past, such as the Indigenous peoples of the Amazon. The process of overcoming exclusion in this way may find that those "in the center" must unlearn what they thought they knew about the church and various cultures as well as their previous assessment of how these two entities interact. The needs of those who are "off the grid" in many ways make real demands upon a church heretofore dominated by the Global North, so that conducting the considerable effort to engage in constructive dialogue is a work of corporate discernment.

A chief contribution of Francis throughout the Pan-Amazon synod, then, was simply the way he modeled a commitment to surface and engage the full range of issues that challenge people of this region so unfamiliar to most people, even to some of the delegates, at least those who represented parts of the world beyond Latin America. To avoid repeating the previous coverage of the discernment style of Francis, the remainder of this section will focus on just three principles of exemplary discernment that were on display at this 2019 synod, which bore the intriguing title "The Amazon: New Paths for the Church and for an Integral Ecology."

1. Avoiding Distractions as a Principle of Discernment

First, although it would eventually cost him some support, Francis displayed his awareness that effective discernment requires sustained focus, and that the enemy of the requisite reflection is the ever-present threat of distractions. St. Ignatius, as noted above, encourages anyone expecting fruitful prayer to resist distractions, including the temptation of considering too many items at once—much in line with the more general insight that trying to accomplish too much at once can hinder any program of action.[22] The leadership of Pope Francis in the course of the synod on the Pan-Amazon region displayed his mastery of this insight, especially in the final stages leading to the publication of the post-synodal exhortation, which appeared just three short months after the conclusion of the synod sessions. The achievement worth noting concerns not just the speedy writing of *Querida Amazonia* but also what it contained—and did not contain.

By all accounts, the deliberations were especially animated—the participants hardly needed Francis's repeated encouragement to speak with *parrhesia*—and the delegates proposed many creative measures to address the urgent pastoral, cultural, and even ecological needs of the region. Among the 120 paragraphs of the final *relatio synodi* were startling proposals for two momentous changes in Catholic practice.[23] First, in somewhat veiled language, the delegates issued a recommendation that, for the purpose of meeting pressing pastoral needs, the church open new ministerial opportunities to women, hinting that they supported the establishment of a female diaconate. Near the end of a section, "The Time for Women's Presence," containing five full paragraphs (nos. 99–103) devoted to this topic came the novel request: "We ask that an instituted ministry of 'women community leadership' be created and recognized as part of meeting the changing demands of evangelization and care for communities."

Second, in plainer language, a paragraph (no. 111) that received the qualifying two-thirds vote (the precise count was 128–41)[24] proposed the priestly ordination of approved married male deacons (the Latin term is *viri probati*). Note that this is a recommendation that, if enacted by Francis and the wider church, would overturn the thousand-year-old discipline in the Latin Rite Church prohibiting married men from entering the priesthood.[25] The paragraph begins with an acknowledgment of the continued value of celibate priestly ministry, which it proposed to augment, not replace, but proceeds to document the hardships that prolonged lack of access to the sacraments exact upon so many communities in Amazonia, and so argues that the proposed dispensation from the priestly celibacy requirement is warranted "in order to sustain the life of the Christian community." News of this request, coming as it did from such a distinguished body of high church officials (mostly bishops), shook the Catholic world.

Neither of these recommendations, as popular as they were among the voting synod delegates, found their way into Francis's *Querida Amazonia*. Nor has the pope acted further upon these requests, although he did reconstitute a previous commission to study historical evidence relating to the work of deaconesses in the early centuries of the church. Naturally, the lack of papal approval and action has disappointed many. While Francis clearly takes the problems that motivated these requests seriously, especially the scarcity (indeed the near absence) of priests in some localities, his personal discernment did not affirm the same path to resolve the problem as the communal discernment conducted by the delegates as they sought answers to profound regional problems. In listening closely but not ceding to their request to meet the pastoral and sacramental needs in this way, Francis was once again exercising the papal prerogative as the ultimate church authority. What does this say about his leadership?

One could speculate along numerous lines of analysis. Some of those disappointed in the pope's refusal to change church practices in these two ways interpreted Francis as reverting to the stance of cautious conservatism he had assumed on occasion earlier in his life. Others judged Francis to be overreacting to the firestorm set off in 2016 by *Amoris Laetitia*, when traditionalists objected sharply to even the hint of a potential relaxation of one disciplinary practice of the church. It had been less than four years since Francis found himself embroiled in a near mutiny that included even several cardinals expressing severe reservations about the pastoral options that he had appeared to open. Some Vatican watchers imagined that he was either intimidated by the earlier fierce opposition to his relaxation of a church discipline or perhaps simply too weary of controversy to make a bold choice in early 2020 for changed practices regarding ministry.

An alternative interpretation, one with perhaps greater plausibility, involves the discernment principle relating to distractions we have been considering. In his own discernments, Francis had identified a set of priorities—ecological, pastoral, and cultural—that he was convinced took precedence over the reconfiguration and deployment of more ordained ministers in the region, as desirable in the short run as enhanced sacramental availability might be. In other words, if the Pan-Amazon Synod became the occasion when the Catholic Church broke the dam (the Spanish noun capturing the image of a surging river breaking its banks is *un desborde*, a word Francis interestingly used more than once in addressing the synod in October of 2019)[26] and approved the ordination of married priests, all other priorities and recommendations surfaced by the Amazonia Synod would quickly be eclipsed or even forgotten altogether by the global audience. All the headlines and media coverage would surely be about this momentous decision, which of course would hold repercussions for all parts of the world, even if Francis had opted to approve an experiment with limited geographic extent (applying to a circumscribed "missionary zone" as some imaginative commentators ventured). The distractions would take the form of ceaseless speculation about which other dominoes of church practice would be the next to fall. What might be good for one region in the short term and for specific reasons might not ultimately be the best thing for the church either in that region or globally.

The experienced discerner that he is, Francis appeared to have one eye on Amazonia, but the other eye on a larger picture—one that surely included a dose of global church politics but also featured multiple dimensions. Perhaps this desire to hold these many considerations in a prudential balance explains the words of Francis in his closing address to the synod "when he urged reporters not to focus on the who-won-what on 'minor disciplinary matters' but to 'take time to look at the diagnoses, which is the denser part, the part where the synod expressed itself best.'"[27] While it is easy to chide Francis for engaging in a vast understatement in dismissing potentially momentous church reforms as "minor disciplinary matters," it is also easy to follow the logic of his prioritization of issues. When Francis sat down shortly thereafter to draft *Querida Amazonia*, the urgent "diagnoses" regarding the cultural, social, and ecological perils facing this vulnerable region and its inhabitants would remain with him in the strongest possible way.

2. Social and Cultural Analysis in Service to Discernment

This is the precise juncture where the second of the three discernment principles on display in the Pan-Amazon Synod process comes to the fore. Even more than previous special synods on regional or continental topics, this synod was confronted with a clearly identifiable set of unique and urgent challenges. The structure of the *relatio* was organized according to a list of four areas of concern, couched in terms of "new paths of needed conversions" (pastoral, cultural, ecological, and synodal), whereas the pope's *Querida Amazonia* was structured according to four closely parallel "dreams" (social, cultural, ecological, and ecclesial). Both documents call for close study and careful analysis of each dimension of the challenges facing the region. Our collective responses will be only as strong as the data gathering and analysis that precedes it. The social sciences, natural sciences, cultural anthropology—all of the tools of academic and humanistic learning should be at the church's disposal as she discerns the way forward to a better future for the people and ecosystem of this region.

These commitments to well-informed social and cultural analysis are grounded in a theological methodology long employed in Catholic social teaching: the see-judge-act (in Spanish, *ver-juzgar-actuar*) paradigm. The method had surfaced in European social action circles in the early decades of the twentieth century and was even recommended explicitly in no. 236 of Pope John XXIII's 1961 social encyclical *Mater et Magistra* ("Christianity and Social Progress"). Like so many Jesuits around the world who came of age when he did, Francis approaches issues of social justice with this schema at top of mind. When he served as the final editor of the influential documents of the 2007 Aparecida Conference of the Latin American Bishops (CELAM), Bergoglio instinctively structured his redaction around the stages of the see-judge-act paradigm.

The social and cultural analysis that proceeds in church circles and appears to be "second nature" to Francis becomes an important resource not just for the church's institutional planning but indeed for its spirituality and discernment. If this does not seem immediately obvious, it is simply because of the perennial human tendency to bifurcate aspects of human experience that are actually closely connected. All of our decisions, as individuals and as a corporate body, depend on the gathering of accurate information, broad consultation, insightful analysis, and the overcoming of biases that threaten to distort our perspectives. To reach the point of making sound decisions (or "good elections" in Ignatian terminology) is to have successfully navigated a path that features both spiritual and analytic dimensions. All these considerations filled the mind of Francis as he participated in the Pan-Amazon Synod and, in ways that never had a chance of pleasing all interested parties, responded to the proposals of the delegates.

3. "Discerning Love" as a Final Resource

The Jesuit spiritual tradition features a Latin phrase, *discreta caritas*, that is highly relevant to any consideration of the discernment style of Pope Francis. Examining the notion of *discreta caritas* thus provides an especially appropriate way to conclude this chapter. This polyvalent phrase has been translated into English as "discerning love," "discriminating love," and even "enlightened or moderated charity." The adjective *discreta* shares evident common roots with the English words *discernment*, *discreet*, and *discriminating*; the semantic fields of all these related terms conjure up images of careful judgments being drawn, with a sense of balance and prudence. The connotation is that the mark of any sound discernment is a careful weighing of the potential results of a decision, mindful of the imperative to purify our motivations in advance of any action, and thus ridding our judgments of selfishness or disordered attachment. The high regard with which the Jesuit founder St. Ignatius held prudence and good balance is confirmed by the way he invokes this phrase in his spiritual writings, correspondence, and even juridical instructions.

However, we must not forget that the phrase *discreta caritas* also includes the word for love, which is both a virtue and an emotion that includes the element of ardor—a "warm" passion that might on the surface seem to contradict the "cool" virtue of prudence. No less an authority than a former Superior General of the Society of Jesus, Peter-Hans Kolvenbach, notes the tension evident in how Ignatius combined such terms, often in deliberately pregnant juxtaposition that served his purposes in providing spiritual guidance to many. Kolvenbach even calls attention to the appearance (see no. 754 of the Jesuit *Constitutions*, written by Ignatius himself) of the related phrase, *prudenta caritas*, which forms part of the founder's description of qualities displayed by the ideal religious superior.[28] Ignatius evidently found value in the creative tension implicit in a love that exhibits prudence. The same man who challenged his brother Jesuits to strive boldly and passionately for the *magis* (ever greater service of God and neighbor) also simultaneously recommended deliberateness in decision-making and careful discernment that is marked by balance and moderation. Demonstrating great apostolic energy is good; tempering such energies with prudent judgment is even more commendable.

The place where these two poles of spiritual discernment are reconciled, for Francis as for Ignatius, is in the very core of the spiritual life—in a God-centered vision of the universe and its purposes. Recall the Ignatian idiom that so often portrays the goal of spiritual discernment as responsiveness to the "good spirits." Our decisions will be good if they are characterized by the spiritual freedom that allows us to purify our motives, to avoid excess and distractions, and to respond to our vocation to serve God. No human is the ultimate author of his or her life; rather we are called to play our appointed role in furthering divine purposes for the world as far as we can discern them. Progress in the spiritual life consists of conforming our lives ever closer to the will of God.

When we examine the papal leadership of Francis through the lens of these elements of Ignatian spirituality, we gain new insight into the ingredients of his discernments, the arc of the process by which he reaches decisions, and even his exercise of the authority of his office. Even without assuming that each of his determinations reach perfect outcomes, we readily see *discreta caritas* on display. Consider how Francis exercised his papal agency in presiding over the synod on the Amazonia region. Contributing fully to the preparatory phases, participating attentively in the weeks-long proceedings, and receiving with evident graciousness the final recommendations of the delegates—all demonstrate the pope's commitment to this quite elaborate process of consultation and communal discernment. He manifestly pursued the Ignatian goal of deeper spiritual freedom, combined with the practical goal of gaining a heightened capacity to see clearly the profound needs of the region so as to evaluate prudently the options that lay before him. These are the motives of someone profoundly shaped by the magnanimous Ignatian temperament.

None of these acknowledgments will likely erase the disappointment of the delegates whose proposals for new ministerial arrangements for their hard-pressed region were ultimately not taken up by Pope Francis. While the concerns they articulated on behalf of the millions of underserved people of the Amazon region were received with respect and due consideration, the recommendations to approve the ordination of female deacons and noncelibate priests did not persuade Francis to approve the momentous changes requested. The merits of their proposals were ultimately outweighed by other priorities to which the pope responded in his eventual discernment. No matter how much Francis may have harbored certain desires to accede to their requests, his ultimate response was to deny the requests, at least for the time being.

Unless we appreciate the overall context of this exercise of papal decision-making, and especially the rootedness of Francis in Ignatian discernment, we might interpret this instance as just another episode in the long history of papal intransigence and obstructionism, when a pope wielded his power to effectively silence a marginalized group of people. In reality, Francis was showing no disrespect for the people of the Amazon region, nor was he turning a blind eye to the pressing pastoral and other needs he witnesses there, as the text of his subsequent document *Querida Amazonia* abundantly demonstrates. Although he supplied few hints regarding the bases for his decisions regarding ministries in those communities, there is no reason to imagine that Francis is in any way lacking in commitment to stand in solidarity with the millions of suffering people of that region.

Indeed, Francis stands ready to do all he can to protect these endangered people from the violence and exploitation that has long plagued their lands. While the cross-cutting priorities pressing on any pope are so numerous—such as the pursuit of several "goods" (or goals and objectives) that may conflict with one another along with the hard decisions that inevitably surface—no fair assessment of this pope's manifest commitments would question his love for the peoples of Amazonia and the high regard he has for preserving the ecosystem of the region, including the rain forests and the riverways themselves. Indeed, Francis frequently refers fondly to this vast section of his native continent as one of the "vital lungs" of planet earth.[29]

No leader is able to grant every request to use his or her available authority in particular ways, but the best leaders are those who conduct genuine discernments that display the hallmarks of *discreta caritas*, including prudence, balance, passion for causes, and deep love for the people affected by any given decision. In the two episodes examined in this chapter (the synods on family life and the Pan-Amazon region), Francis has modeled this for the Catholic Church, which he leads ably as its discerner-in-chief.

CHAPTER 3

FRANCIS, THE COMMUNICATOR

PRUDENT LEADERS ENGAGE in highly deliberate discernment (the topic of the previous chapter) before acting to advance an agenda of advocacy and constructive social change (the topic of the next chapter). But communication, the topic of this chapter, is an essential component of strong leadership in any field of endeavor, including religious leadership. There is never a bad time for a leader to make the extra effort to share thoughts, plans, and priorities with appropriate audiences. The task of crafting excellent communication is an ongoing challenge for leaders in all walks of life.

There is no single model for effective communication, even when considering only the spoken word (the topic of these next three paragraphs). Someone can convey information in a wide array of speaking styles and get the message across perfectly well—especially if the vocal style is carefully calibrated to the content and context. Think for a moment of all the world leaders, including American presidents, whom you may have heard over the years addressing an audience in venues large or small. Each has a favored oral and rhetorical strategy by which to deliver the messages that have been crafted for a given occasion. Some raise their voices, with pronounced forcefulness at selected high points to signal their conviction and heighten the sense of urgency. Others choose to speak in a more modulated way, perhaps even in a near whisper to get their message across, especially if the points they seek to make are subtle and nuanced in nature.

Recall the moniker frequently applied to President Ronald Reagan: he was dubbed "the great communicator" for his remarkable skill in reaching and persuading diverse audiences. He had been a screen actor for decades, after all, so perhaps he had a head start over other politicians whose instincts and experience may not lend themselves to such effectiveness in oral expression. There were times when Reagan chose to raise his voice in evident irritation or even anger, for example, during candidate debates or when challenging the Soviet leader Mikhail Gorbachev to "tear down this wall" on a famous 1987 visit to West Berlin. Other times, he deliberately dropped his voice to a soft whisper to convey a sense of closeness and easy familiarity with his listeners. Both techniques proved effective for this skilled communicator.

Pope Francis, too, displays great range in his vocal patterns. He is capable of captivating a large audience by projecting his voice to booming dimensions, but also of modulating his speaking style to assume an almost grandfatherly demeanor—easy to relate to, certainly nonthreatening, even halting in his speech patterns at times. On most occasions, Francis appears to favor the latter approach, to edge toward the side of approachability, cordiality, and affability. Even before large audiences on formal occasions, he somehow maintains an air of reserved informality, as if relating a personal story to close friends gathered around a kitchen table. He is authentic, self effacing, and "comfortable in his own skin," and those personal qualities of character come across as natural and effortless. Francis displays that rare ability to "read a room" with accuracy and to establish an immediate rapport of empathy even with new acquaintances. He also seems acutely aware of the venerable rhetorical principle that most listeners are eager to make a personal connection with an interlocutor first, before getting down to the business at hand. Speaking softly, leaving ample openings for spontaneous exchanges, and displaying genuine interest in the concerns of others are crucial stances for any religious leader, even one whose ethical agenda ultimately includes a good dose of persuasion regarding topics that may issue stern moral demands upon all within earshot.

The Medium and the Message

This chapter takes up many aspects of the communication style of Pope Francis beyond his vocal patterns or habitual mode of speaking, as important as they are for setting the tone of openness, empathy, and accessibility associated with the pope. Further elements of communication style are just as important: fluency in the language of symbolic gestures, the ability to read bodily cues of others, the intangibles of personal presence, and of course, careful attention to details. To communicate the full range of messages he has in mind successfully, a religious leader like Francis needs to engage in an especially great amount of highly deliberate advance planning. Such a leader needs to make multiple strategic decisions each day regarding communications, answering such questions as: To whom will I be speaking and in what context? Where will I travel to deliver my message and under what conditions? How will I shape the precise message to account for the full range of relevant factors and important relationships at stake in this instance of communication?

Because the answers to all such questions are so specific to the given situations at hand, the best procedure to follow in this chapter on "Francis, the communicator" is to examine several instances (six "case studies" will be presented below) when the pope placed his communication skills on display for all to see. The treatment of each case study includes description of the episode at hand and brief analysis of how Francis connected with the issues and personages he addressed. Rather than speculating at great length in generalities about the skills and strategies Francis customarily employs, it is preferable to allow these vivid episodes to speak by and large for themselves, reserving to the final few pages of this chapter the task of drawing out common threads that run through these case studies in successful communication.

However, one further "framing comment" is helpful here. Each instance of papal communications examined below represents a complex interplay of the twin dimensions of style and substance, or the medium and the message. The "what" and the "how" of communication run inextricably together. If Pope Francis intends, for example, to deliver a message of deep ethical concern regarding people affected by a great social injustice, he (as the messenger) must win a favorable hearing for that message by speaking with transparency, sincerity, and moral consistency. He needs to walk the tightrope of leveraging the warm-hearted and relatable persona that is authentically his, without appearing to be cultivating a certain image in a way that might be judged manipulative. While these qualities of personality may well be labeled elusive intangibles and resist being pinned down, they nonetheless emerge as preconditions for the credibility and effectiveness of any moral leader. Only a religious leader perceived as genuine and beyond reproach will exert the intended influence and inspire constructive changes in attitudes, culture, and practices.

Recall that this book's main concern is with moral leadership. By now, even before reaching chapter 4 covering many specifics of his social justice advocacy, we easily recognize Pope Francis as supporting certain things and opposing other things. For example, we know that he supports better treatment of refugees and policies favoring labor rights; he opposes environmental degradation, unbearable pressures placed on struggling families, and the scourge of indifference to marginalized peoples. As obvious as these conclusions seem, ponder for a moment this question: Precisely how do we come to know about each of these stances of Pope Francis?

There are two logical answers: his words and his deeds. In any given year, a pope may write or speak in public several million words. They are often powerful and insightful words, indeed, and most of them find their way onto the website of the Holy See or other Vatican outlets such as the Vatican News.[1]

A small fraction of these words, usually thoroughly filtered and sometimes distorted, will find their way into the religious or popular media, where an even smaller slice of the world's population will hear or read them—though most consumers of news will turn the printed page quickly or click elsewhere on the screen where they might appear. But truly hard to miss, even for the casual observer of religious news or public affairs, in general, are the rich symbolic gestures and actions—the visible deeds—that a pope undertakes, and that Francis has been especially skilled at executing. Think of the many papal photo opportunities that grab global attention on special occasions such as papal visits abroad; for each of them that any casual observer may notice throughout a year, there are many more episodes of effective nonverbal communication on the part of Francis. Perhaps more than any person on earth, because of the office he holds, the pope's mere presence at pivotal places and events speaks volumes.

Venturing into out-of-the-way places (even potentially dangerous ones) to support a peace process, meeting with victimized people to signal deep solidarity, convening large or innovative gatherings of diverse people, conducting riveting public ceremonies that have a way of capturing the zeitgeist, and daring to meet even with avowed enemies of Catholicism—all of these and others to be described below demonstrate the commitment of Francis to move beyond mere words to eloquent deeds of moral leadership. In choosing to communicate his positions through vivid symbolic gestures, extensive travel, even his very bodily presence itself, Francis is echoing a point captured by his own spiritual mentor, St. Ignatius, in a meditation that appears at the very culmination of the *Spiritual Exercises* (no. 230). The "Contemplation to Attain Divine Love" includes the affirmation: "Love ought to show itself in deeds over and above words."[2] As the case studies developed below illustrate, Francis has mastered the art of communicating religious messages through nonverbal means.

The available space allows us to treat only a small selection of the many instances during his papacy where Francis has engaged in extraordinary efforts to communicate his intended messages in service to God, the church and all of humanity. If there is a common theme that runs through these six diverse case studies, it is the building of bridges between people rather than walls—a motif that summarizes Francis's entire papacy, and an image that he himself invokes frequently. Even the formidable obstacles of clashing cultural understandings and language barriers do not prevent diverse members of a global audience from recognizing in his actions a consistency of style and substance, of medium and message, that transcends what may divide us at any given moment in human history.

Case Study #1: Displaying Solidarity with Refugees

The case studies presented below will not follow strictly chronological order, but this first one happens to have unfolded in the very opening months of the papacy of Francis, involving as it did his very first air travel after his election. On July 8, 2013, Francis undertook his first "apostolic journey" (to invoke standard Vatican terminology) to the small Italian island of Lampedusa. This speck of land in the Mediterranean between Libya and Sicily has been dubbed "the isle of tears" because it has found itself in recent years on a major migration route, with tragic results. Surrounded by choppy waters, Lampedusa had become a stopover point for refugees from many countries, mostly in North Africa and the Middle East, who were fleeing wars, persecution, gang violence, famine, and the effects of climate change in their homelands. In hopes of forging a better life in the more stable and prosperous nations of Europe, many thousands each year have been taking to rafts and boats of dubious seaworthiness to venture the precarious trip northward. By 2013, thousands had already drowned due to storms at sea and the inevitable shipwrecks, their lifeless bodies sometimes washing up on the shores of Lampedusa, which came to house thousands of displaced souls in makeshift refugee camps.

While the immediate physical needs of these refugees were being cared for by relief agencies funded by the local church and the Italian government, unbearable grief and anxiety about lost and separated family members ground down the spirits of those stranded on the island. The immigration status of those who survived beach landings was extremely uncertain, and resettlement policy had become a political football and wedge issue not only in Italy but across an increasingly xenophobic Europe. Legally and spiritually, in terms of humanitarian assistance and global publicity, these people stuck on Lampedusa and similar refugee transit points needed an advocate. Into this breach stepped Pope Francis.

Having already accomplished the hard work of persuading his advisors that this trip was worth the great effort, Francis arranged to preside at an outdoor Mass at the only suitable place on the island: the open-air "Arena" sports camp. His heartfelt homily on that occasion was a masterpiece of communication, clearly intended for a dual audience: the suffering refugees gathered there with him that day; and a global audience that had long averted their eyes from the tragedy of the contemporary migration crisis. To the first audience, he signaled his solidarity immediately, with phrases such as "I offer a sign of my closeness" and "The Church is at your side as you seek a more dignified life." To the second audience, he issued stirring words to "challenge our consciences lest the tragedy be repeated." Francis offered his diagnosis regarding the root cause of the unmet needs of refugees, namely, that "we have fallen into globalized indifference" that leads people throughout the world to shirk our individual and collective responsibility for "the misery of others." The pope attributed the persistent unmet needs of refugees not only to inadequate public policies but also to "the culture of comfort, which makes us think only of ourselves and makes us insensitive to the cries of other people."

To bolster his point about the shame of complicity in the process of victimization, Francis alluded to the Old Testament Book of Genesis, in which Cain, having killed his brother Abel, attempts to evade God's question, "Cain, where is your brother?" with the counterquestion, "Am I my brother's keeper?" Along with the parable of the Good Samaritan, which is also cited in this powerful yet brief homily, this is a key scriptural passage condemning the guilt of omission as well as commission, and establishing the moral obligations that human beings hold toward all their neighbors without exception. The implied answer is, of course, that we are all indeed our brother's keepers; dire threats to the well-being of anyone must not be met with indifference on our part. It was impatience with such indifference to moral duties to alleviate human suffering that drove Francis to Lampedusa in the first place.

A skilled communicator is ever aware of the multiple audiences listening in, so Francis concludes this homily by addressing, fittingly enough for a sacred liturgy, God watching from above. Naturally, the pope simultaneously tailored his prayer to the audiences in front of him and far away as well. Striking a note of lament, he looked up to heaven and implored, "Lord, in this liturgy, a penitential liturgy, we beg forgiveness for our indifference to so many of our brothers and sisters. Father, we ask your pardon for those who are complacent and closed amid comforts that have deadened their hearts; we beg your forgiveness for those who by their decisions on the global level have created situations that lead to these tragedies." Later, as Mass concluded, Francis expressed his further hopes that Lampedusa will be "a beacon that shines throughout the world, so that people will have the courage to welcome those in search for a better life."[3]

Thus far, only the actual words uttered by Francis on this occasion have been recounted, but beyond dispute is the eloquence and lasting impact of the nonverbal communication on display that day. While it is commendable that Francis verbally pledged solidarity with the refugees who no doubt feel that they are being warehoused in substandard conditions on the island, it is highly significant that he sat with dozens of refugee families in the cramped quarters of the makeshift messroom where they eat their meals in shifts, sharing the simple lunchtime fare served to all in the camp. Knowing that many of the residents awaiting resettlement elsewhere were still mourning loved ones killed, missing, or separated along the migrant way, Francis brought along a memorial wreath (made of flowers in the Vatican colors of white and gold) that he tossed from the deck of a small boat bobbing in the shallow water just off the island's shore. In another gesture of lament honoring the victims of shipwreck, he arranged to use Mass implements—a wooden chalice and other eucharistic vessels as well as a rough-hewn wooden altar—carved from parts of shipwrecked craft that had washed ashore on Lampedusa. These highly vivid ways of lamenting the victims surely spoke as powerfully to the surviving refugees as even the most well-chosen of the pope's words on that sad occasion.

A similar narrative could be related about the subsequent travels of Pope Francis to support displaced persons and to visit refugee camps in various parts of the world. Opportunities to express concern for the conditions faced by migrants and refugees arose during many of his voyages: to East Africa in November of 2015; to Myanmar in November of 2017; to Thailand in November of 2019; and perhaps most dramatically, to the Mexican border town of Ciudad Juárez in February of 2016 where Francis prayed under a gigantic cross set up just yards from the U.S. border where so much violence, suffering, and death has unfolded in recent years. On November 25, 2014, Francis's sole trip to France consisted exclusively of the four hours that he spent at the European Parliament in Strasbourg, pleading to the legislators to adopt more humane policies regarding migrants throughout Europe.

The closest parallel to Francis's Lampedusa visit is surely his journey to the Greek island of Lesbos, where, on April 16, 2016, the pope visited the sprawling Moria refugee camp to express his solidarity with thousands of refugees desperately awaiting resettlement—for similar reasons but in even harsher, more crowded conditions. Many were fleeing the civil strife in Syria, Iraq, and Afghanistan, and found their way to Lesbos hoping it would serve as a brief stopover point in transit, only to be stranded in this prison-like setting for months or years on end awaiting the processing of their asylum applications. Accompanied on Lesbos by his friend Ecumenical Patriarch Bartholomew of the Orthodox Church, Francis led another tearful public Mass, laid another floral funerary wreath ceremonially tossed into the waters of the Mediterranean that had claimed so many lives to drowning, and again shared simple meals with many stranded refugees. This time, the pope had arranged, with advance coordination with Italian immigration authorities, to bring back with him on the papal plane a dozen refugees—all members of Muslim families to be resettled in the safety of Rome. Not only was this extraordinary gesture of welcome praised widely in the global media, but it inspired Catholic parishes throughout Europe to emulate the largesse of Francis and sponsor refugees for resettlement. The pope's effort to communicate his priorities had succeeded with demonstrable effects. His return to Lesbos five years later (during a voyage in December of 2021 that included Cyprus, a nearby island housing similar encampments of refugees awaiting resettlement) further conveyed his commitment to publicizing the plight of refugees stranded in what are termed "transit countries."

Whenever Francis extends a hand of solidarity to refugees and migrants, the encounter has its own dynamics and effects. Each is a unique communicative act, combining words and symbolic gestures that are powerfully creative. In the aggregate, the words and deeds of Francis display two dimensions: they express internal emotions (such as lament, regret, sorrow, penitential intent, and resolve) and they achieve external results (bolstering the morale of the afflicted, providing needed encouragement to relief workers, hastening compassionate policy responses on the part of the powerful, among other possible outcomes).

Arguably, no dimension of the pope's efforts to support migrants and refugees is more significant than the simple fact of his recurring presence in these forsaken venues of such great hardship. Merely communicating that he cares enough to visit these forgotten places, this global figure sparks hope that a better life may not be too far distant for some of the most hard-pressed people of all. By sojourning "out to the peripheries" and shining the spotlight of global attention upon the plight of so many refugees desperate for relief, Francis is defining the meaning of solidarity and hope in today's sharply divided world far more eloquently than any encyclical or teaching document.

Case Study #2: Communicating with Young People

On a far more upbeat note than the foregoing case study, Pope Francis has invested considerable effort in communicating with young people throughout the world. Taking advantage of opportunities to participate in forums where youth gather in large numbers, the pope has demonstrated an uncanny ability to connect with young people on many levels—from the sheer joy of large celebratory gatherings to the sharing of serious concerns about the future in more intimate forums.

Francis's first opportunity to spend time with youth presented itself in his first months as pope: the World Youth Day held in Rio de Janeiro, Brazil, during the final week of July of 2013. A regular gathering (usually held every third year) that John Paul II had initiated in the 1980s to reinvigorate the church, World Youth Day has sometimes been called the "Catholic Woodstock" for the exuberant quality of its massive liturgies and vibrant communal spirit shared by young pilgrims drawn to the multiday religious experience from countries around the world. Approximately four million people attended the final Sunday liturgy on Copacabana Beach, which naturally featured themes related to youth and how they live out the faith. Although the pope's week in Brazil featured a crowded schedule that included visits to slums, hospitals, churches, and the offices of civic officials, the focus of his impressive energy during that trip was on the young pilgrims with whom he mingled freely. Austen Ivereigh's account of the week captures breathlessly the pope's interactions with the young attendees and their reception of him: "They loved his simplicity, his directness, his humility, his passion for social justice, his tireless capacity for vigorous hugging....They praised his well-aimed three-point speeches, his cozy references and his vivid metaphors; his cheeky, almost conspiratorial manner with the young; his humor and his candor."[4]

This is a remarkable testimonial to the high energy level and magnetic personality of a seventy-six-year-old man, who had just endured a thirteen-hour flight and yet sustained his vivaciousness and good humor in the course of dozens of appointments and speaking engagements over a seven-day span. Perhaps the radiance of Francis that week may be attributed to the positive chemistry he enjoys with members of the younger generation, whom he sees as signs of hope and whom they see as a wise and trustworthy grandfather-figure. Francis reprised his performance, with similarly glowing reviews, while attending subsequent World Youth Days in Kraków, Poland, in July of 2016 and in Panama in July of 2019.

Even before those two regularly scheduled events, Francis timed his first-ever visit to South Korea so that he could speak at another youth rally, when fifty thousand Christian youth assembled in the Daejeon World Cup Stadium, on August 15, 2014, for the sixth Asian Youth Day. On that occasion, Francis tailored his message to the specific needs of that industrializing nation, where youth are often unable to find jobs commensurate with their educational attainments and are too often relegated to menial work or precarious arrangements in the gig economy. Many find the resulting anxiety unbearable. It is no secret that South Korea has one of the world's highest rates of youth suicide, and the concern expressed that day by the pope reflects his awareness of the near despair faced by many of his listeners. During the Mass held in the stadium that day, he encouraged those young people to find in "the hope held out in the Gospel…the antidote to the spirit of despair that seems to grow like a cancer in societies which are outwardly affluent, yet often experience inner sadness and emptiness. Upon how many of our young has this despair taken its toll!" In the same homily, Francis also denounced "the allure of materialism…and the spirit of unbridled competition" associated with "inhumane economic models which create new forms of poverty and marginalize workers."[5] On other occasions during his stay in the country, he expressed concern about unenlightened public policies and unscrupulous employers who prey on the insecurities of young people—paying them too little for the strenuous work they perform and risking the onset of unbearable stress in young people that can prompt them to self-harm.

This expression of profound concern for young people supports the observation that Francis is highly sensitive to the special needs of youth. Further illustration of how Francis listens closely to young people was on full display on February 24, 2022, when, in a livestreamed forum, the pope spoke for two hours with just a few dozen college students from various universities in North and Latin America. In a structured interchange made possible through the magic of Zoom modality and simultaneous translation, Francis sat at a large table in his papal study in Rome and engaged in a wide-ranging dialogue about such issues as environmental sustainability, consumerism, immigration, nonviolence, and overcoming cultural divisions and political polarization. Francis seemed to relish the intimacy of the exchange, as just a handful of students at a time appeared on the screen he was viewing, and this arrangement facilitated a particularly satisfying spontaneous dialogue. He communicated especially strongly his eagerness for the youngsters to set the agenda and identify topics that were of particular interest to them and the aspirations of their generation. A high point of this interchange came when several students voiced concerns that the pope found so perceptive that he reached across the table for a pen and a blank pad of writing paper and, in a simple act probably unprecedented in papal history, proceeded to scribble copious notes to himself to capture his young interlocutors' thoughts.[6]

A more extended display of careful listening to the voices of young people took place in connection with the Synod on Youth, which Francis convened in October of 2018 in Rome according to the usual protocols for such worldwide synods of bishops, as outlined in chapter 2. The wide-ranging post-synodal exhortation, which Francis titled *Christus Vivit* ("Christ Is Alive: To Young People and to the Entire People of God") and published on March 25, 2019, captured numerous rich insights about the situation of young people today that Francis had heard in the course of the weeks-long synod proceedings and through other avenues of input, much of it coming from young people themselves from all parts of the world. The content and tone of the document reflect what we have already seen about Francis: when he is interacting with young people, he is especially keen to listen closely and communicate with all the empathy and understanding an elder can muster.

One high point of *Christus Vivit* is where Francis affirms, "I know that your young hearts want to build a better world," and proceeds "to encourage you in this effort" for "the young want to be protagonists of change....You are the ones who hold the future! Through you, the future enters into the world. I ask you to be protagonists of this transformation" (no. 174). Francis concludes this upbeat document with two stirring chapters treating the notions of vocation and discernment as they relate to youth. He takes pains to develop these important themes in direct, non-technical language—easily comprehensible to the young readers to whom he addresses the teaching document. This material engages the eager striving for meaning and holiness on the part of young people that arose from the synod deliberations; as such, it represents an expansion of certain themes Francis had introduced in his previous teaching document, the 2018 exhortation *Gaudete et Exsultate* ("Rejoice and Be Glad: On the Call to Holiness in Today's World"). Each of these documents afford Francis precisely the kind of opportunity he clearly cherishes: to apply his communication skills in listening closely to many people, including the youth he so loves, and to provide encouragement to live a life worthy of the gospel message wherever it leads.

Case Study #3: Communicating Social Concern on the Global Stage

This section examines, as instances of especially vivid and effective communication, a pair of events that were carefully planned and meticulously scripted by Francis and the papal staff. The first, on September 7, 2013, was an outdoor prayer vigil for peace in Syria, and the second, on March 27, 2020, was a prayer service to implore divine assistance as the coronavirus pandemic was descending upon the world. Though these two events were nearly seven years apart, they shared certain striking features in common. Each took place in St. Peter's Square, the central focal point within Vatican City. Each featured Pope Francis himself as the main presider and speaker (in the latter case, almost exclusively so). While neither was a sacrament of the Catholic Church in the strict sense, each featured liturgical dimensions—addressing God in prayer and being presented to a large global audience accessing the events through electronic media. Each unfolded at what may be considered a crisis or inflection point in recent history, as the world looked to a credible moral leader to provide encouragement and ethical guidance. In each case, Francis filled the pressing need for timely leadership and applied his well-honed communication skills to impressive effect. The details of each event reveal much about effective communication in words, symbols, and gestures.

A Prayer Vigil for Peace in Syria

A grinding civil war in Syria had already been raging for years when Francis was elected in March of 2013. An agonizingly large percentage of that Middle Eastern nation's population (topping twenty million at the start of the fighting) had already been displaced by the fighting, which had devolved into a deadly multiparty free-for-all dividing the nation into zones of influence controlled by armed factions. The ongoing carnage perpetrated by the government of Bashar al-Assad and various rival rebel groups was now joined by ISIS forces—technically, the "Islamic State of Iraq and the Levant"—that had recently come to control considerable territory and the loyalties of heavily armed militias, including many foreign fighters who had filtered into Syria from nearby lands. After long inaction, the United States and its Western allies were gearing up to launch an aerial bombing campaign, aimed at punishing Assad's forces for their use of sarin gas in chemical weapon attacks against defenseless civilians in an opposition-controlled area just outside Damascus.

While the Vatican shared the revulsion expressed that August by U.S. President Barack Obama for such egregious violations of the Geneva Conventions, Pope Francis spoke out with an appeal for restraint. Not only would the proposed airstrikes surely cause numerous casualties, even if civilians were not the intended targets, but only "collateral damage," but they would likely exacerbate instability by further weakening the Assad regime's hold on power and handing ISIS a strategic boost. In the ongoing battle between several unsavory rivals for supremacy in Syria, little good would come out of this proposed application of lethal force by the Western allies. Indeed, much further damage could come from likely escalations of hostilities unleashed by the planned aerial assaults.

Just six months into his papacy, Francis had yet to make his voice heard in a significant way on the global political scene. He knew that popes ultimately do not command much raw power on the world scene; Stalin had made a valid point with this mischievous question, "How many divisions has the pope?" What a pope *can* do is to employ what political scientists refer to as the "soft power" that comes from the application of subtle diplomatic pressure and moral appeals grounded in religious values. By the end of August, Francis had decided to engage the crisis in Syria with the only tools readily available to him: to offer spiritual resistance and to generate some pressure against the proposed escalatory bombings by swaying global public opinion.

Francis designated September 7 as a day of prayer and fasting for peace in Syria and encouraged Catholics around the world to join him however they could, including by tuning in to the electronic and media coverage of what would unfold that day at St. Peter's Square. He began to plan what would turn out to be a five-hour prayer vigil that evening—and Francis presided over every minute of it, thinking nothing of staying up past his accustomed bedtime. The service, somber and penitential in tone, included a public recitation of the Rosary, scripture readings, and spoken reflections that focused on sorrow over the persistence of violent conflict in our world.[7] The homily offered by Francis highlighted the sharp contrast between the ways of "harmony, peace, good unity and true fraternity" on the one hand, and "violence, division, disagreement and war" on the other hand. Toward the end of the sermon, the pope posed the question, "Is it possible to walk the path to peace?" With hundreds of millions of believers watching from afar via televised coverage of the spectacle, the pope answered in the affirmative: "I say: Yes, it is possible for everyone! From every corner of the world tonight....Yes, we want it!... Violence and war are never the way to peace."[8]

Assessing the effects of this public ritual event is no simple task. Without a doubt, this inaugural foray of Francis into applying the soft power of the papacy provided significant momentum for subsequent spiritual and diplomatic interventions in world affairs. One practical benefit was the establishment on this occasion of the Twitter hashtag #prayforpeace, which became an immediate global sensation and persisted as a prominent social media tool for many subsequent papal initiatives in support of peace. Somewhat harder to assess, for all the plaudits Francis received for conducting a powerful vigil that displayed both personal genuineness and media savvy, is the actual impact (in terms of persuasive power) of the pope's message that day. While the intended airstrikes were eventually called off, most of the credit probably belongs to political calculations rather than spiritual suasion. As it turned out, support for such retaliation was simultaneously drying up in London and Paris for reasons that had nothing to do with spiritual values or religious support for peacefulness, and the Obama administration was losing its appetite for escalation, no matter how many "red lines in the sand" may have been crossed by Assad. We will never know how much unintended harm or, for that matter, potential improvements in the situation, would have been caused by the proposed airstrikes, but we do know that Syria has remained a fratricidal mess for many years after this episode. The heroic leadership and communication skills of Pope Francis may have spared quite a few innocent lives in the short run, and perhaps that is reason enough to admire the prayer vigil that captured the world's attention on that occasion.

A Solemn Prayer Ritual during the Coronavirus Pandemic

An even greater number of eyeballs were fixed on Francis nearly seven years later when he conducted another prayer ritual, one that was even more dramatic, though less than half the length of the peace vigil in duration. The venue was the same—mostly outdoors in St. Peter's Square—but much else was different, for the world had changed suddenly and dramatically. In the weeks leading up to this event on March 27, 2020, the coronavirus pandemic had brought the world to a standstill, and brought the most affected regions and hotspots to their knees. It is worth noting that, as the head of state only of a microstate surrounded by Italy, Pope Francis did not really have to bear the heavy burdens placed upon public health authorities or even ordinary public officeholders elsewhere who faced hard decisions regarding mitigation strategies and lockdown policies. He was free to be a pastor of souls—the leadership role for which he was best suited and prepared in any case. What he could offer the world was a unique respite of spiritual reflection and a memorable blessing. Once he resolved to offer these simple bits of timely pastoral service, he engaged his communication skills to great effect.

Pope Francis responded to the COVID-19 pandemic in a variety of ways, of course, but the following paragraphs will describe only one key episode. Twice each year, at Christmas and Easter, popes in recent times have offered a blessing known as the *Urbi et Orbi* ("to the city [of Rome] and to the world"), usually preceded by a few paragraphs of prepared reflections on the state of the world, calling attention to any special needs judged worthy of prayerful consideration. When Francis decided to follow this same pattern, there was no question what these special needs consisted of. Even though the already planned Easter *Urbi et Orbi* was just over two weeks away, the world seemed desperately hungry for some communal pastoral care in this moment of acute trial. Francis scheduled an event for late in the day on that Friday in Lent, after the sun had set on one of the shortest and darkest days of the year. The ninety-minute event was billed as an "Extraordinary Moment of Prayer with an *Urbi et Orbi* Blessing."

The ritual foregrounded a nearly solitary Francis, clad in papal white and shuffling through a light drizzle between several locations in the court of St. Peter's Square. With a labored gait, the octogenarian pope mounted a canopied dais where cameras and microphones captured him reading (in Italian) the scripture and prayer texts he had chosen for the occasion. The square itself, with its capacity of eighty thousand spectators, was eerily empty, devoid of people because of the local ban on public gatherings of any size to prevent the spread of the virus. The ritual featured prolonged and poignant moments of silence. As Francis headed indoors for the ritual of divine benediction and adoration of the Blessed Sacrament, he paused at length before two particularly apt pieces of religious art that had been set up on display near the grand doors of St. Peter's Basilica. One was the image of Our Lady, Salvation of the Roman People (a painted canvas, with impressive dimensions of three by five feet); the other was the blackened wooden cross of St. Marcello Church. These historic icons of faith have been revered for centuries for miraculously delivering the city of Rome from plagues and public health crises, so the local population looked to them for protection once again. Francis had a long history of devotion to them, visiting each frequently in their usual locations in nearby churches.

The stunning visual effects and symbolic gestures on display were matched by the power of the words that Francis had written for the somber occasion. To acknowledge the fear and distress being felt by his millions of listeners, Francis reached back to the familiar story of Jesus calming the storm at sea in the fourth chapter of Mark's Gospel. Believers tuning in that day could surely relate to the vulnerability, disorientation, and sheer panic felt by the companions of Jesus as the storm tossed and threatened to capsize their boat. Francis broke open the words of that Gospel with skill, inviting his audience to appreciate the power and contemporary relevance of the metaphor. Just as the disciples' trust in Jesus was ultimately rewarded, like he promised, so our present experience of testing would culminate in ultimate deliverance if we now accept our own cross of hardship, including the isolation and suffering brought on by the pandemic.

The pope emphasized the centrality of the saving power of Jesus: "Embracing his cross means finding the courage to embrace all the hardships of the present time…and to allow new forms of hospitality, fraternity and solidarity….By his cross we have been saved in order to embrace hope and let it strengthen and sustain all measures…to protect ourselves and others." In a final appeal to his audience to grow beyond any temptation to despair, Francis continued, "The Lord asks us, and in the midst of the tempest, invites us, to reawaken and put into practice that solidarity and hope capable of giving strength, support and meaning to these hours when everything seems to be floundering." With rhetorical dexterity, the pope openly acknowledges the fear and apprehension prevalent among his hearers but beckons them to move beyond a place of doubt to a renewed trust in God. Redemption is always available, even amid a deadly pandemic striking fear into the hearts of billions. To paraphrase his final sentiments that expressed his own hope and confident resolve, there is no darkness that God will not dispel, no anxiety that God will not cast out.[9]

Space does not permit a comprehensive treatment of how Francis handled the global pandemic, from a pastoral perspective or even as a policy challenge for the worldwide church.[10] Suffice it to say that the pope consistently tailored his words and actions over many months to the needs of his global flock, even when he could only reach them through the constricted means of livestreams and virtual electronic contact. One close observer structured his entire book on this topic around the motifs of closeness and pastoral accompaniment, concluding that, during these challenging months, Francis was consistently holding up "the paramount importance of providing a consoling accompaniment embodied in poignant gestures and symbols that communicate compassion, mercy and hope in a time of crisis."[11] The solemn prayer service that Francis conducted just weeks into this global pandemic reflects especially clearly these achievements in effective communication and moral leadership.

Case Study #4: Convening Diverse Gatherings for Special Purposes

Almost all those who watched Francis preside over the two ritual events described in the previous case study were not present to participate in person; their viewership is a testament to the prevalence and newfound power of electronic communications, even for religious services. The next case study in effective communication focuses on a selection of in-person gatherings to which Francis summoned large numbers of people on occasions of great significance for him and his social justice priorities. Of course, popes routinely meet face-to-face with the many pilgrims who come to Rome for weekly general audiences or at least to attend the regular prayer rituals he leads at St. Peter's Square, such as the Angelus and the Regina Caeli addresses. Besides opportunities to be in the pope's presence for devotional events like these, occasional opportunities for more focused and intentional gatherings have, especially during the papacy of Francis, been extended to audiences for singular purposes. The efforts of Francis to convene these special assemblies are worth examining in detail, as they reveal much about his communication outreach and priorities.

Francis has sponsored four large gatherings called World Meetings of Popular Movements. These multiday assemblies are a novel Vatican initiative, for which Francis has repeatedly tapped the organizational capacity of the Pontifical Academy of Social Sciences and the Dicastery for Promoting Integral Human Development (and its predecessor until 2017, the Pontifical Council for Justice and Peace). Francis hosted two of these meetings in Vatican City in October of 2014 and November of 2016. The second in the series was held in July of 2015 in the Andean city of Santa Cruz, Bolivia, during the pope's visit to that landlocked South American nation. The fourth one was forced by the coronavirus pandemic into an online modality, and Francis participated in it virtually in October of 2021, offering a powerful thirty-eight-minute video message to delegates scattered across every continent. There have also been regional meetings connected to this series, including a prominent one held in Modesto, California, in February of 2017.[12]

On these occasions, hundreds of delegates throughout the world were invited (and their travel and lodging provided, at considerable expense) to deliberate on issues of social justice, particularly the protection of worker rights and the extension of economic opportunities to those currently excluded. The delegates are selected in such a way as to reflect the commitment of Francis to support grassroots organizations and to amplify the voices of local activists, especially in less developed nations. The representatives have included leaders of economic cooperatives and labor unions, hundreds of farmers working to implement land reform and community organizers striving for social change in their home countries. The goal of the meetings is to encourage grassroots movements, forge cross-sector solidarity, and energize social activism of many sorts. On each occasion, Francis offered his own keynote address tracing the contours of social justice struggles, challenging global capitalism and its labor practices, and advocating for measures that would better support human dignity and overcome barriers to the advancement of the marginalized. Chapter 4 will address the substantive content of these speeches of Francis, as we examine his advocacy for economic justice.

In line with present purposes, it is easy to recognize how these gatherings reflect the considerable communication skills and aspirations of Pope Francis. His keen desire to convene such meetings hearkens back to some of his trademark initiatives in Argentina, where he earned a reputation as an advocate for exploited workers, the unemployed, even the *cartoneros* (garbage pickers), who scratch out a living collecting recyclable materials and who repeatedly struggle to organize into cooperatives. As auxiliary bishop and later even as cardinal archbishop, Bergoglio was known as *un obispo callero* (a bishop who walks the streets) ever eager to support downtrodden people struggling for social justice in the poorest neighborhoods (*villas miserias*) throughout Buenos Aires. It was representatives of such constituencies who were invited to the World Meetings of Popular Movements.

In convening these gatherings, then, Francis draws upon at least these two things: (1) his longstanding desires to stand in solidarity with the marginalized and (2) the skills he honed through his successful pastoral planning in Argentina, which often included concerted efforts to mobilize parishioners to push for social change through community organizing. If we were to identify a third resource in the hands of Francis, it would be his Jesuit heritage. The pope appears to be tapping into a certain Jesuit genius for convening diverse groups creatively, a ministerial skill that the Society of Jesus has been perfecting for centuries. Bringing people together from diverse places and backgrounds has long been a strength of the religious order that formed Francis. By founding and administering schools that draw from many social strata, by sponsoring devotional sodalities (pious organizations for prayer and service), by undertaking missionary activities with extraordinarily broad reach, and by serving as chaplains to professional groups of all sorts, Jesuits have long displayed a knack for the art of convening people in an intentional way.

One excellent example of such Jesuit-sponsored organizations is the network of "labor schools" that American Jesuits established in the early decades of the twentieth century. They were organized by Jesuits in most major cities across the United States and operated primarily as night schools, on a model similar to continuing education classes. With the ostensible purpose of building up the repertoire of practical skills—such as public speaking, shop stewardship, and promoting workplace equity—necessary for members of trade unions, the several dozen labor schools offered the additional service of providing an informal network of companionship, advocacy, and job opportunities for millions of blue-collar workers, including Catholics and others.[13]

As an heir to this Jesuit tradition of creatively bringing diverse people together, Francis is naturally eager to take advantage of potential opportunities to convene gatherings of people for the purpose of community-building and pursuing social justice. The series of World Meetings of Popular Movements that he initiated is a premiere instance, but not the only one. For example, on January 17, 2016, to mark the annual World Day of Migrants and Refugees, Francis convened a remarkable gathering of "people on the move" for a Mass and outdoor Sunday audience. He welcomed to St. Peter's Square an amazingly diverse group of five thousand migrants and refugees representing thirty nations. On this exuberant occasion, Francis offered a rousing speech that encouraged his assembled guests to defend their dignity against the many forces that might hinder their progress on the way to what they most hoped for: a successful resettlement process that would lead them to a better life for their families.[14]

Taking the agenda of convening large groups to its logical conclusion on the largest of scales, in October of 2021, the Catholic Church inaugurated an extended three-year synod process focused on the theme "For a Synodal Church."[15] Although some have spoofed the seemingly redundant notion of a "synod on synodality," the image of "walking or journeying together" (following the Greek roots of the word *synod*) lies at the very heart of what it means to be church, with a style of proceeding that is inclusive and participatory. It comes as no surprise that Pope Francis is highly enthusiastic about this multistage worldwide synod process that is now well underway and represents an extension of his ardent desire to "convene the faithful" in ever wider circles, as we have glimpsed above. He has long emphasized the themes of dialogue and participation that support a synodal way and that challenge the church to listen closely to the voices of all, especially those at the grassroots and on the peripheries.

Ultimately, for Francis and others who support a more synodal church, the goal is to move beyond a model of church that is top-down and domineering in nature toward a model that embraces broad consultation and greater empowerment for those currently struggling to be heard. What Francis seems to have in mind in designing and leading this synodal process is the inauguration of a more Spirit-led church, one characterized by flexibility, pluralism, co-responsibility, and respect for local initiative. Many consider this "the unfinished work of Vatican II" and, as such, it emerges as a worthy topic for an extended synodal process at this point in the church's history. Not to be confused with simple democracy, a church that encourages broad participation becomes more sustainable precisely because agents of constructive change need not wait for permission from authorities at higher levels to apply their energies to the task of addressing pressing social problems and injustices. The energetic in-person gatherings that Francis so loves to convene may be a harbinger of a renewed church capable of gathering its members ever more creatively and effectively.

Case Study #5: Healing Wounds Caused by the Church

Previous case studies have considered the communication efforts of Francis when faced with two kinds of challenges: (1)

social concerns that arise and seek resolution well beyond the church; and (2) efforts to improve situations within the church itself. We now consider an important display of communication skills on the part of Francis that is neither strictly internal nor strictly external to the life of the church. The sad fact is that we will be examining how the pope is responding to a great injustice perpetuated by the church itself against a community of Indigenous people, threatening to erase an entire culture and inflicting serious damage upon thousands of lives.

For well over a century, in a practice that finally ended only in 1996, the Roman Catholic Church operated residential schools in various parts of Canada where children were forcibly separated from their Indigenous families and educated during their formative years in a style that amounted to forced conversion and assimilation into Western (primarily Eurocentric) ways. Tens of thousands never returned home to their families. This practice, mandated at the time by the Canadian government and contracted out to Christian denominations—two-thirds of the roughly 130 schools were run by the Roman Catholic Church—has been called "Canada's national shame." Over 150,000 children were subjected to harsh treatment in the schools, including physical, sexual, and mental abuse that led to emotional trauma, permanent injuries, and even death. Only recently was it revealed that over a thousand schoolchildren had died in the boarding schools, from various causes, and been buried in unmarked mass graves on school grounds. Besides the suffering and ongoing trauma of individual victims lies the larger offense against an entire way of life. A 2015 report of Canada's Truth and Reconciliation Commission declared the schools a form of "cultural genocide" displaying an undeniable intention to wipe out Indigenous languages, religions, and identity.

To communicate his sorrow for this shameful past, in late July of 2022, Francis embarked on a six-day visit to three parts of Canada, visiting several communities in Alberta, Québec, and remote Iqaluit in the far northern territory of Nunavut, in what he himself called a "penitential pilgrimage." His main purpose was to issue a long-awaited apology to Indigenous people affected by the harms inflicted by the Catholic Church during those decades. The process of reconciliation was long in the making and had actually taken a dramatic leap forward four months earlier, when several sizable delegations of these First Nations peoples, visiting Rome from several parts of Canada, met for three hours-long listening sessions with the pope in the course of a week.[16] Francis concluded that preliminary set of meetings with a verbal apology and expression of sorrow for the church's many past abuses at the final session on April 1, 2022. But it was widely understood that no words exchanged at the Apostolic Palace at the Vatican would complete the process of reconciliation satisfactorily. It was thus highly significant for the healing of so many festering wounds that Francis expended the great effort to travel to remote parts of Canada, as he had pledged to do, to meet Indigenous people face-to-face on their own land, as soon as pandemic precautions and his own health conditions allowed.

The pope's main public apology took place on July 25 in Alberta near the site of a former residential school, a place of spiritual significance to the Indigenous people present. In a heartfelt message delivered during a traditional powwow circle surrounded by teepees and campfires, the pope declared, "I humbly beg forgiveness for the evil committed by so many Christians against the Indigenous peoples." He went on to affirm that he was "deeply sorry" for the ways that "many Christians supported the colonizing mentality of the powers that oppressed the Indigenous peoples" and that he regretted the actions of "members of the church and of religious communities [who] cooperated with projects of cultural destruction and forced assimilation promoted by the government at the time."[17] After speaking these words, Francis accepted the invitation from a tribal elder to don a traditional feathered headdress of the local people, evidently eager to pursue any means available to signal his solidarity with the victims and their descendants who have suffered what amounts to intergenerational trauma.

This was by no means the first papal apology in history, nor even the first one regarding treatment of Indigenous peoples in the New World. John Paul II had issued a series of portmanteau apologies in 2000 expressing regret for centuries of offenses committed by church officials in many cultural settings around the world, including wrongdoing by missionaries in the colonization of the Americas. But the specificity of this new apology on the part of Francis for the harm perpetuated in this specific place and cultural setting added much value and poignancy. Francis earned high marks in the media for holding nothing back; he minced no words in Canada that week regarding his church's culpability. His words and gestures were direct and the scope of the sentiments of sorrow and regret he expressed was sweeping.

Still, a papal apology for the past sins of the church is always a complicated phenomenon; there is a vicarious or "proxy" aspect to this communicative act. Onlookers must surely appreciate that the man issuing the statement of apology is not the actual perpetrator of the regrettable acts, which occurred long before a given pope took office or was informed of the atrocities. Although he is not speaking for himself in the first instance, it is nevertheless fully appropriate for the person universally recognized as representing the entire institutional structure that perpetrated the oppressive and abusive behavior to issue a corporate acknowledgment of guilt and sorrow. However, just because Francis is standing in for the directly guilty parties does not diminish the importance of projecting a sense of sincerity and personal genuineness. The credibility of the man who is uttering the words of apology is crucial to the process of healing. He becomes the face of contrition for the entire institution, past and present, and must communicate utter transparency and a goodwill effort to acknowledge historic faults, assume the burden of guilt, and make sincere amends. On many counts, Pope Francis was the right man for this task.

As the media coverage of these events amply documented, on his sojourn to Canada, Francis required physical assistance at every turn, largely confined as he was to a wheelchair. He had relied upon it in public appearances for the preceding three months, hobbled as he was by the effects of a torn knee ligament. The eighty-five-year-old pope was also suffering from a recurrent sciatica condition that affected his back and was still recovering from serious intestinal surgery in 2021. He had canceled other planned travels to Lebanon, Congo, and South Sudan in the preceding two months, perhaps to save his strength for this imperative pilgrimage. For those who followed his travels in Canada that week, especially the photographs that augmented the coverage of the events in print and electronic media, it was striking to see a world leader so openly embracing his personal frailty and limitations. A *New York Times* story covering the final days of the pope's visit appeared on the newspaper's front page; it was laid out just beneath an above-the-fold photo of Francis being wheeled by two aides to the very lip of the shore of Alberta's Lac Ste. Anne, whose waters are considered by local communities to possess miraculous healing powers. The news story contained this perceptive reflection: "Seeing Francis in his increasing frailty and his advancing old age was very much a point of his visit."[18]

Whatever the level of premeditation behind such photo ops, it is beyond doubt that Francis was communicating most eloquently his embrace of his own personal fragility, indeed the existential vulnerability that is a universal feature of the human condition. The juxtaposition of this frank visual admission of weakness and the pope's mission of bringing to Canada an acknowledgment of the past sins of the church he leads is stunningly poignant. On neither count was there any attempt to hide unpleasant realities. Francis was showing his true colors, facing up with genuineness to the truth of the situation: this was a humble man bringing a message of sincere contrition from a church humbled by its faults and the growing collective awareness of a regrettable past.

For those of us eager to leverage the lessons of the past to forge a better future, an apology by itself is of course never sufficient, and it is certainly not the end of the narrative. To complete a genuine reconciliation, the process must include appropriate measures signifying accountability and offering some amends. The Truth and Reconciliation Commission set up by the Canadian government has already enacted a system of financial reparations to compensate survivors of the abuse and their descendants. The Canadian Conference of Catholic Bishops has authorized parallel arrangements called the Indigenous Reconciliation Fund to supply certain compensatory damage payments to victims but have received criticism for pledging only modest levels of support and for falling far short of the initial pledges. It goes without saying that nothing said or done today can fully heal the trauma or repair the egregious damage inflicted at the residential schools over several generations. But there is much to be said for extending as many good faith offerings as possible to the victims and their families. One creative suggestion is for Catholic agencies and religious congregations to open broader access to church archives that might allow the gathering of information that may somehow comfort some of the victims and their families.

Pope Francis did not delve into such details during that momentous visit to Canada, preferring to leave the task to appropriate local authorities to work out, but the messages he did communicate accomplished a great deal. By no means satisfied merely to generate some temporary good publicity, he committed the Catholic Church to a process of sincere grappling with its shameful past in a country where nearly 40 percent of the population currently professes the Roman Catholic faith.[19] At no point did he demonstrate any inclination toward ducking the blame or attributing the widespread abuse to "just a few bad apples." No, although the sins and crimes of individuals in this lamentable case are undeniable, the entire church rightly bears responsibility and must be acknowledged as blameworthy.

In this poignant case study, Francis displays his characteristic acute awareness of the salience of social structures and institutions in which we participate. Anyone who participates willingly in a structure or institution that turns out to be guilty of grave sins is culpable for the evil effects of any of its actions, even if this complicity is unintended on the personal level. This consciousness of systemic guilt is a prerequisite for facing up to collective responsibility for past wrongdoing in any part of the world. A profound and sincere apology is a worthy first step on the path of healing, and Francis served as a fitting messenger to communicate the sorrow and contrition of the entire church.

Case Study #6: Cultivating Personal Relationships with Diverse Partners

The final case study in this chapter is not really a single achievement or involvement of Pope Francis, but rather consists of a collection of his communicative performances with a variety of individuals. The pope has forged and maintained cordial, constructive, and fruitful relationships with many diverse personalities on the international stage. Space allows only brief treatment of a small selection of interactions between the pope and some of the prominent figures with whom he has rubbed shoulders during his papacy. The focus in the brief sketches that follow will remain on the lessons that emerge regarding leadership and communication skills; the specifics of the episodes described are only secondary. It is important to note at the outset that the collection of interactions presented here is slanted toward particularly difficult relationships—ones that have tested all the personal and communicative skills that Francis can muster. That the pope has persevered in managing these sometimes-fraught relationships with success and grace is very much to his credit, especially considering the plethora of challenges that a global religious leader like him is required to navigate on an ongoing basis.

The first relationship of note finds Francis walking a tightrope—but one of his own choosing. Eugenio Scalfari (1924–2022) was one of Italy's most famous and controversial journalists. He founded the liberal newspaper *La Repubblica*, which earned quite a reputation for "lobbing editorial salvos over the high walls of the Vatican" and which established Scalfari himself as an antireligious gadfly with a large megaphone.[20] The safest course of action for any new pope settling into life in Italy from abroad would be simply to ignore this aging militant atheist, but shortly after his election, Francis invited Scalfari to a series of one-on-one interviews that covered wide-ranging topics of considerable interest to the public. The pope even gave his interlocutor *carte blanche* to publish whatever version of their conversations he wished, without insisting on the usual protocols that include prior Vatican review of papal "on the record" quotations. Francis even trusted Scalfari's memory of the flow of the conversation, which was not recorded electronically nor through extensive or, as it turns out, reliable written notes. This procedure caused a bruhaha on more than one occasion, most notably in 2018 when Scalfari reported that the pope had professed doubts about the existence of hell as punishment for unrepented sins—in sharp contradiction of official Catholic teachings. An immediate sharp rejoinder from the Vatican doctrinal office challenged the journalist's account, claiming that the reconstruction of the conversation must have been faulty and that Scalfari had erroneously placed words in the unsuspecting pope's mouth—and not for the first time, either.[21]

Most likely, the pope stirred up considerable consternation among his red-faced coworkers, who repeatedly had to clean up the mess created whenever *La Repubblica* printed a new account of a conversation that did not accurately capture the sentiments of Francis. But somehow, Francis remained unfazed and kept inviting Scalfari back for further rounds of interviews, never insisting on a verifiable transcription or prior review of the journalist's accounts of what transpired between the two men. On the surface, this may look like a regrettable deficit of prudence on the part of the pope, but it is also possible to interpret these episodes as ultimately congruent with Francis's eagerness to maintain a cordial relationship with a prominent public intellectual and to conduct an ongoing freewheeling dialogue with a new friend, especially one who is a nonbeliever of evident goodwill.

Sure, Scalfari's accounts of the exchanges might be unreliable in some particulars, but the conversations remained valuable to Francis and his agenda, nonetheless. As the papal biographer Austen Ivereigh conjectures, "It was clear that to Francis the misuse or misunderstanding of what he might say weighed less than the relationship he had established with Scalfari, and the reaching-out beyond the Church's borders that it enabled. This missionary, pastoral approach, whose object is to speak to the heart of the other, lies deep in Jorge Bergoglio's Jesuit soul."[22]

These basic priorities of Francis explain his stance toward the media in general, such as his recurring practice of conducting long impromptu press conferences aboard the papal airplane on return flights from his international voyages. While previous popes limited their exposure to unscripted interchanges with the press, Francis upends such risk-averse policies by gladly embracing opportunities for frank and spontaneous give-and-take, even on sensitive topics. In keeping with his commitment to evangelization and open dialogue, he would clearly prefer to err on the side of greater access, trust, and transparency, rather than appearing to be closed, guarded, or controlling in any way. The easy path would be to grant interviews only to reporters who can be counted upon to provide favorable, even flattering publicity, but Francis's approach to communication policy is of a piece with his more general attitude of welcoming free dialogue, and especially cultivating relationships of mutual respect with people, like the late Eugenio Scalfari, who do not (at least for now) identify as members of the church that Francis leads.

If the journalist Scalfari turned out to be a challenging interlocutor for Francis, the religious leader Sheikh Ahmad Al-Tayyeb emerged as a most promising partner in dialogue. It might at first glance seem unlikely for a pope to cultivate a particularly close relationship with a top authority of another faith, and especially a leader of Islam given the centuries-long conflicts between it and Christianity, but Francis turned these normal expectations on their head. His overtures to the Muslim world have been enthusiastic and indefatigable. Perhaps he models his outreach to a Muslim leader on the famous episode in 1219 when St. Francis of Assisi, his chosen namesake and prototype for peacemaking initiatives, crossed the Mediterranean to conduct what turned out to be a historic three-week interreligious encounter with the Sultan Malik al-Kamel in Damietta, Egypt, to negotiate an easing of Islamic-Christian tensions at the perilous time of the bloody Fifth Crusade. Francis remarked explicitly about the historical parallels between his outreach to the Muslim world on the eight-hundredth anniversary of this encounter between the sultan and the saint. In any case, as the Grand Imam of Al-Azhar mosque in Egypt, the highest seat of learning of Sunni Islam, Tayyeb emerged as an especially significant figure with whom the pope might make an official overture, and it turned out that, during the exchanges and mutual visits over several years, the two men came to share a most warm friendship, far beyond the ambit of the common projects on which they worked.

The most consequential of these cooperative efforts was the cosigning of a groundbreaking agreement called, "Document on Human Fraternity for World Peace and Living Together." This document, drafted in advance by teams of advisors to both religious leaders, was formally ratified on February 5, 2019, when Francis was making his historic pastoral visit to Abu Dhabi in the United Arab Emirates. Francis and Tayyeb, representing the world's two largest religious communities, pledged common efforts to promote dialogue, mutual understanding, respect for human rights, and an end to intolerance and extremist violence.[23] In his historic visit to Iraq in March of 2021, Francis paid a most cordial visit to Grand Ayatollah Ali al-Sistani, the most revered authority in Shiite Islam that further contributed to the easing of tensions between Christianity and Islam in a sensitive region of the world.[24]

More than any previous pope, Francis has gone to great lengths to cultivate warm personal friendships with leaders of numerous other religious communities and traditions. Ecumenical Patriarch Bartholomew of Constantinople, head of the Orthodox Church, has become a close friend of the pope, appearing alongside him on many momentous occasions, including the visit to Lesbos in 2016 described above, as well as the groundbreaking day of prayer for peace in the Middle East—the two were joined by Israeli president Shimon Peres and Palestinian leader Abbas Mahmoud Abbas—that Francis hosted in the Vatican Gardens in June of 2014. Francis quoted Bartholomew favorably several times in his 2015 environmental encyclical *Laudato Si'*, praising him for his ecological leadership and commitment. Francis has repeatedly called Bartholomew "my brother" and even presented him with a precious relic believed to be a bone fragment of St. Peter.[25] The evident warm friendship between these two leaders has eclipsed the thousand years of tensions and even enmity, not to mention the mutual excommunications that followed the bitter eleventh-century schism, between these sibling churches, raising hopes of further progress toward eventual Christian unity on a model acceptable to these and perhaps other separated churches.

Similar observations apply to the relationships of the pope with heads of other Christian churches, such as the Coptic Orthodox Pope Tawadros II and the Archbishop of Canterbury Justin Welby, with whom Francis meets when travel schedules allow. Such encounters and joint public appearances are important supports for collaborative projects in the fields of diplomacy, peacebuilding, and interfaith dialogue. Even Christian churches with a less hierarchical structure, and therefore no single leader with whom Francis might approach personally, have received much positive attention from Francis. He reached out to Lutheran communities on many occasions, even making an unprecedented appearance on October 31, 2016, at the ecumenical ceremony in Sweden marking the approaching five-hundredth anniversary of the Protestant Reformation. He has received delegations of Lutheran and Evangelical leaders at the Vatican on several occasions as well.[26] The commitment of Francis to such endeavors is hardly surprising considering his remarkable efforts as the archbishop of Buenos Aires to reach out to the full range of religious communities in that capital city. The Argentinian Jewish leader Rabbi Abraham Skorka continues to be among his closest friends, with whom he wrote a well-received 2011 book on interfaith cooperation on ethical issues. The two religious leaders even appeared together on thirty-one episodes of a Buenos Aires television program, hosted by a Protestant theologian, where they discussed various social issues.[27]

Maintaining cordial relationships with leaders of many other organizations is a valuable leadership quality, but some such relationships inevitably come more easily than others. While Francis has displayed deep personal affection, mutual admiration, and enthusiasm for common projects with the religious leaders mentioned above, he has also reached out to certain more problematic leaders on occasion. Such relationships naturally require a somewhat different set of skills. One example is his fraught relationship with Patriarch Kirill of the Russian

Orthodox Church, which is the largest of the Eastern Orthodox churches. The churches represented by these two men have a centuries-long history of doctrinal and jurisdictional disputes, only exacerbated by Soviet-era tensions. In the sixty years since Vatican II, successive popes have courted Kirill and his predecessors to begin a dialogue to heal East-West wounds but to no avail.

It appeared that a breakthrough was in the offing when Francis arranged a meeting with Kirill at the airport in Havana, Cuba, on February 12, 2016, on the pope's journey to Mexico. It was the first-ever such meeting between a pope and a patriarch of the Russian Orthodox Church, and the possibility of future encounters were placed on the drawing board, perhaps even one in Moscow where no pope had ventured. On that occasion in the conveniently neutral venue of Cuba, the two leaders signed a thirty-point joint declaration pledging common aims and future cooperation, but the budding relationship with both Kirill personally and the Russian Orthodox Church more generally turned suddenly sour after the Russian invasion of Ukraine on February 24, 2022, given Kirill's unabashed support of Vladimir Putin and Russia's barbaric use of horrific and massive force. Communications between Kirill and Francis in the months after the start of the war, most notably in a March 19, 2022, videoconference, exposed the frosty quality of this new stage of the relationship, damaged so badly by Kirill's failure to distance himself from the Putin regime and its bloody aggression.

A set of more general lessons regarding successful communication are on display in this episode. As world leaders often do, Francis found himself walking a diplomatic tightrope—one that opened him up to sharp criticism from those who normally agree with him on issues of peace. The critics contend that Francis had not gone far enough in denouncing the Russian attack on Ukraine (something that, on the record, he had done repeatedly) or the attacker (something that Francis was careful not to do overtly by name). However, the decision of Francis not to explicitly name Putin or, for that matter, his apologist, Kirill, does not derive from cowardice, approval, acquiescence, or even capitulation to political expediency, all of which motives would be indefensible. Rather, the pope has pursued a strategy that prudently attempts to preserve his role as a potentially pivotal diplomatic player, and he is perhaps the only person who could imaginably provide a bridge of negotiation between the two sides in this protracted armed conflict.

Francis was taking meticulous care to act in ways that are less likely to be interpreted as creating a definitive break with the Russian side (that is, the church or the state). The pope was unusually forthright in public forums at the time about explaining his rhetorical strategy,[28] but this did not satisfy many voices eager for Francis to name names and issue a frank condemnation of Russia's political and religious leaders. Only time will tell if his gambit to "play the long game" of diplomacy will pay off and thereby offset the short-term discomfort, if not outrage, that many express at the sight of a pope ceding some of the moral high ground and holding his tongue against definitively denouncing an unjust aggressor.[29]

In considering the situation in Ukraine, we have already transitioned from the topic of relationships with other religious leaders to the next closely related topic: how Pope Francis manages difficult relationships with political leaders on the world stage. One illustrative episode involved President Abdel Fattah el-Sisi of Egypt, an authoritarian who had ascended to power in a 2013 military coup after a period of prolonged national instability. The pope's visit to Egypt in late April of 2017 gave Francis an opportunity to communicate his mixed assessment of the policies of Sisi. On the one hand, the strongman had been instrumental in opposing Islamic extremists and terrorists, such as those responsible for the deadly Palm Sunday bombings of Coptic Christian churches just weeks earlier. (In fact, lingering security concerns almost prompted Francis to cancel his visit.) But on the other hand, Francis was eager to stand up to Sisi for his appalling record of human rights abuses, especially against dissidents and prisoners of his regime. Although the pope agreed to meet with Sisi and even to stand beside him in a joint public appearance and photo opportunity, he nevertheless communicated his disapproval of the president's ruthless tactics and signaled by gestures and in words that the many rights violations in Egypt had not gone unnoticed.

The stakes in this specific episode were especially high. When confronted by an authoritarian political leader (more so than any religious leader) who has the power to make life even more difficult for religious minorities in each jurisdiction, popes must be extremely careful how they comport themselves. In this case, there is only a modest contingent of Catholics (or any Christian group beyond the local communities of Copts) in a Muslim-dominated Egypt, and fears of persecution and terrorist attacks are well founded. Mindful of every pastor's solemn responsibility to protect his own flock, Francis proceeded to walk a very fine line between two roles he was eager to play: that of a global voice of conscience on behalf of human rights, and that of a real-world diplomatic player mindful of the obligation not to provoke any harm to the safety of his own church members. This same dynamic of needing to strike a delicate balance was a factor in other pastoral visits of Francis to nations where Catholics are a distinct minority in an authoritarian state (for example, Myanmar), and likewise required the most delicate application of the communication skills of the pope.

Another political leader who has presented a consequential challenge to Francis's ability to manage relationships is Viktor Orbán, the right-wing populist leader of Hungary. Orbán has a history of blatant xenophobia and demagoguery, elevating illegitimate grievances, and appealing to exaggerated fears of the loss of Hungarian national identity to support the aggressive and punitive policies he favors. A frequent target of his anger are refugees seeking asylum, whom he has repeatedly likened to invading hordes threatening Christendom and its traditional values—a common trope in Orbán's idiosyncratic way of injecting religion into politics. It is hard to imagine a political leader whose extremist stance of defensive nationalism provides a sharper contrast to the ethic of universal love, solidarity, and caring support for refugees that Francis preaches. Dealing with pressures that Orbán had exerted upon his European neighbors to adopt restrictive policies against asylum-seeking refugees had long been a headache for the Vatican. While Francis urged merciful generosity and warm welcome to those fleeing war and poverty and seeking a place in Europe, Hungary promoted ever tighter control of borders and harsh management of detention centers—all geared to discouraging the flow of "people on the move" and punishing harshly those who did somehow arrive.[30]

Orbán's peculiar version of Christian values thus presented a significant communication challenge to Francis—one that came to a head when Francis was planning a quick stopover in Hungary on his way to a more extensive four-day pastoral visit to neighboring Slovenia to preside over the closing Mass of the 52nd Eucharistic Congress in Budapest. The seven hours the pope would spend in Hungary on September 12, 2021, were clearly not intended as an opportunity for a politically oriented visit, but it would be awkward to refuse outright the invitation that arrived from Hungary to meet with Prime Minister Orbán. Francis agreed reluctantly, but orchestrated the encounter carefully, limiting the time spent in the presence of the prime minister to forty minutes, insisting that the "courtesy meeting" include many other officials, and even arranging to sit far away from Orbán in the assembly space.[31] Orbán had to settle for a rather perfunctory handshake with Francis, which the Hungarian media—favorable to the strongman, perhaps out of fear more than anything else—immediately spun into an indication of blanket endorsement from the pope. Of course, anyone who had read the pope's October 2020 encyclical *Fratelli Tutti* championing universal solidarity appreciated the contrast of viewpoints in the room, but the words, gestures, and even the body language on display that day confirmed the pope's disapproval of the nationalistic brand of populism and xenophobia that his host represented.

This episode in Hungary prompts reflection on the wider task of forging a diplomatic strategy that walks the fine line between communicating disapproval of objectionable policies while still seeking constructive engagement with figures who support those policies. This situation hearkens back to the venerable Christian adage that one should "hate the sin but love the sinner." People are indeed capable of conversion and change, even if they currently act on wicked values that all should reject. In fact, it would be a contradiction for a religious leader promoting universal love and acceptance to ostracize permanently and reject out of hand all overtures from a political leader whose track record of practicing acceptance of others leaves something to be desired. The most effective communication strategy, then, is to combine two messages: to signal that the door of welcome remains open, but also that entering fully through that door is conditioned upon improved behavior, in this case through enacting humane public policies.

Francis does not allow policy disagreements to prevent him from engaging other leaders or treating them merely as pariahs; he has even met three times with Vladimir Putin and offered to visit him to foster peace even after the Russian invasion of Ukraine in 2022. Little is accomplished by simply berating a person whom you judge to be mistaken about human values. The priority is always to maintain a relationship even while expressing disapproval of the specific actions of another. Despite occasional criticism on this score, there is ultimately little danger that this strategy of constructive engagement practiced by Francis could credibly be interpreted as appeasement of dictators or as condoning violations of human rights. More important than forestalling such accusations is avoiding a bluntly confrontational approach that cuts off all future opportunities to dialogue, to challenge an interlocutor to change approaches, and to take the next good step toward reconciliation. What started out as a prudent *pastoral* strategy (often referred to as gradualism) turns out to be an effective *diplomatic* strategy as well. Such an approach prioritizes the paving of a path to future cooperation and refuses to give up even on those who offend humane values.

In this final case study, then, we have seen several faces of the priority of Pope Francis to maintain a dialogue with the diverse cast of characters he has encountered on the world stage. In some cases, the stakes are especially high, especially when global peace itself is on the line. As one reporter reflected, while covering the pope's meeting with President Sisi during his 2017 visit to Egypt: "The pope…[has] repeatedly made the case that he will meet anyone, anywhere to establish dialogue and deliver his inclusive message."[32]

Francis, then, may be seen as ascribing to the venerable adage that peace is the product of many personal relationships. The trust required to dialogue successfully with others in pursuit of peace and justice does not come all at once, of course, but must be built up over time in repeated efforts at respectful communications. Some might wonder where Francis derives his skills and his intense commitment to engaging with such challenging dialogue partners, including the ones we saw in the episodes of this case study and many beyond. Part of the answer surely lies in the spiritual well from which Francis has found nourishment his entire adult life: the *Spiritual Exercises of Saint Ignatius Loyola*. Early in the text of this handbook for prayer, Ignatius includes a paragraph (usually called the "Presupposition") containing a piece of advice especially valuable for guiding relations with difficult interlocutors. This Ignatian spiritual principle affirms the wisdom of giving the other person the benefit of the doubt in communications. It constitutes a reliable rule of thumb to place the most favorable interpretation on the initial utterance of another and then working out through dialogue the precise way that the interlocutor intends any statement that might initially offend or befuddle.[33]

Not only is this practice prudent, but it is also irenic, for it favors peaceable relations that might be threatened by overly hasty judgments drawn from first impressions. Never satisfied to allow relationships to hit an impasse, Francis seeks forward momentum in dialogue, as the instances described above illustrate, based on the kind of mutual respect that the Presupposition advocates. Those searching for answers to the question "What makes Francis tick?" when it comes to his commendable communication skills and strategies do well to consider this pearl from his Jesuit background and spiritual heritage. Along with his seemingly instinctive possession of an open mind and the Ignatian aspiration for genuine spiritual freedom, the Presupposition appears to guide Francis in his interactions with diverse partners in dialogue.

Conclusion

Many books and articles have already been published analyzing (sometimes in baffling technical terms drawn from the academic fields of linguistics and semiotics) the rhetorical and communication strategies of Pope Francis. Some authors openly speculate about the level of intentionality guiding the pope's interactions with the public and the media.[34] Is Francis "playing to the gallery" and projecting a premeditated and hyper-polished image, only revealing what will be most flattering to him and useful for his purposes? Is the public somehow being manipulated when they see Francis performing certain gestures or hear him employing verbal tropes to promote his messages? Even when such questions are posed by authors who are ultimately highly complimentary to the pope, it might make the casual observer wonder about a gap between the seeming genuineness of the humble Francis we feel that we know, on the one hand, and a more calculating and image-conscious Francis who lurks just offstage, on the other hand.

Considering all we have witnessed in this chapter and elsewhere, it seems far-fetched to imagine Francis as a slick schemer who indulges in crass manipulation or self-serving image-burnishing in pursuit of shady objectives. Yes, he does have a sizable staff of public relations professionals working for him in the Vatican Press Office whose job it is to place the best spin on the pope's words and activities; his social media presence (such as his @pontifex twitter handle) is indeed curated with notable deliberateness.[35] Certainly, Francis does display an eye for dramatic symbolic gestures and appears mindful of the optics of what he does and where he travels, but there is no dishonor in deliberately adopting a savvy communication strategy. We all do this instinctively in our daily lives whenever we decide on a message worth sending and employ pragmatic approaches to delivering that message to the right people. What may prove helpful in the case of the pope is to work more at deciphering his words and actions to determine the overarching message he is attempting to send and to assess the genuineness of that message. That is the task of these final paragraphs of this chapter.

This task turns out not to be very hard, principally because Francis possesses a genius for directness of communication and even, most of the time, at least, an economy of words. He speaks and writes in a pastoral or devotional style, employing accessible prose and clever turns of phrases that catch the ear, engage the imagination, and prove easy to remember. The linguist Christopher Oldenburg calls these "pope tropes"—particular phrases that Francis repeats from time to time because they seem to work effectively in appealing to a broad audience.[36] One recurring example, first heard widely in his addresses to the World Meetings of Popular Movements, is the triad of *tierra, trabajo, techo* (those three "T words" in the original Spanish of his addresses may felicitously be rendered in three similarly alliterative words in English, namely, "land, labor, lodging"). This memorable phrase tends to appear whenever Francis reaches for words to describe the legitimate aspirations of the excluded for access to the means for a better material life.[37]

This example also illustrates Francis's general aversion to abstractions. Experienced pastor that he is, the pope clearly prefers to deal in the vivid and concrete, especially when communicating with a broad audience. In *Evangelii Gaudium*, the first major teaching document he wrote that was published in November of 2013, he professed the wisdom of four axioms that have long guided his thought; perhaps the most emblematic of the four is, "Realities are more important than ideas" (no. 231). By no means does this imply that Francis is uninterested in speculative theology or the life of the mind, but it does place him on record as prioritizing the kinds of practical things that make an observable difference in the lives of the people about whom he cares so much.

Whether or not Francis is employing a deliberate rhetorical strategy, he displays a genius for selecting rich and appealing images that capture his priorities in a nutshell. He has repeatedly invoked the vivid image of "pastors with the smell of the sheep" to describe the best ministers of the gospel and "a field hospital after battle" to portray the type of service the church aspires to provide for vulnerable people today. Perhaps the most employed and effective trope of Francis is to describe patterns of thought and activity as "a culture of" something or other. Commentators have referred to this tendency as "a verbal tic" of the pope, one that leads him to couch his praise for certain things as a culture of care or mercy or accompaniment, and alternately to criticize other things as reflecting a culture of callousness or selfishness or, most ominously of all, "the throwaway." Sometimes, Francis presents paired items to help his audiences appreciate the sharp contrasts of human attitudes and ethical values at stake in the stances we choose to adopt. So, we hear from the pope's lips of the moral superiority *of a culture of inclusion* over *one of exclusion*, and of *a culture of care* over *one of indifference*. Note how these phrases are not intended to present novel or unfamiliar ideas to listeners, but rather to express in highly accessible and memorable terms the moral dangers and rewards of daily human decisions that form patterns and shape our world.

If there is one recurring phrase of this sort that runs like a red thread through the discourse of Pope Francis, it is "the culture of encounter." This phrase appears seven times in his 2020 encyclical, *Fratelli Tutti*, a document that includes forty further appearances of the noun or the verb encounter. Along with the themes of mercy, joy, and dialogue, it constitutes a central motif of his entire papacy. Repeatedly in his published documents and spoken addresses, the pope exhorts us to "work for a culture of encounter" wherever we find ourselves. Like the somewhat folksier and more relatable recurring image he invokes of "keeping the doors of the church wide open," this memorable phrase appeals to us to retain a welcoming stance toward all newcomers and constitutes an endorsement of an entire approach to evangelization. If the Christian community's accustomed ways of doing things does not include an enthusiastic embrace of such new encounters, then the church is not living up to its mission to spread the gospel to the entire world. Of course, no pope sitting in Rome can provide a detailed program to guide local evangelization efforts in all settings and parts of the world, but a visionary leader can exhort church personnel working in all contexts to adopt the attitudes, mission priorities, and even the culture that may inspire effective work for evangelization. Because there is no substitute for the kind of face-to-face engagement that Francis endorses for the healthy life of the church, the phrase "culture of encounter" says everything the pope seeks to communicate about this essential topic.

This chapter on the pope as communicator would not be complete without a final note on the themes of diversity and reconciliation. Like the motif of culture of encounter to which each is closely related, Francis appeals to these notions frequently in exhorting members of the church to carry out their missions in service of all. The pope is keenly aware that the task of evangelization can never proceed on a one-size-fits-all basis. It is crucial to take seriously the historical particularities of diverse peoples of many cultures, even while preserving the principle of unity that holds that all human beings have key things in common: inherent dignity, legitimate aspirations, openness to the divine, and a common spiritual destiny. Sensitive religious engagement with a complex world never erases differences but affirms both unity and diversity simultaneously.

Francis's use of the polyhedron, a geometrical figure that expresses the values relating to "unity in diversity" and that he proposes in *Evangelii Gaudium* (no. 236), surely baffled many readers at first. Unlike a sphere where all points are equidistant from the center and display no marks of individuality, the pope explains, a polyhedron consists of many surfaces and points that preserve their distinctness and particularity. This complex shape presents an exemplary model for ministry and social relations exquisitely. There is a place for all, everyone has something to offer and the contributions of each are readily recognized and honored. Inspired by the model of a polyhedron, we can resist tendencies toward totalization and cultural homogenization in pursuit of truly ethical ends, such as fashioning "a globalization with a human face." Engaging complexity, respecting differences, and preserving diversity are the paradigms that Francis has pursued in his communications with so many interlocutors and groups around the world, as the case studies in this chapter illustrate so vividly.

A final theme worth recognizing in this context is that of reconciliation, a concept for guiding human relations with rich resonance in scripture and many Christian theological sources. All things are ultimately to be reconciled in Christ alone, of course, but we all have parts to play, even now. If the church is to fulfill its appointed role worthily as a peacemaker and as an agent of personal and social reconciliation, Christians must rededicate themselves to many of the principles that Francis addresses so often: generous hospitality, welcoming the stranger, outreach to the marginalized, and promoting dialogue and broad participation in truly just social structures. Only then will we veritably be taking up the central challenge that guides the ethical teachings and moral leadership of Pope Francis: discovering creative ways to build bridges rather than walls between the diverse people who share our wondrous world. To have a top leader so fluent in these central idioms of the Christian proclamation and so eager to communicate them with his persuasive skill is a great asset to the Catholic Church.

CHAPTER 4

FRANCIS, ADVOCATE FOR SOCIAL JUSTICE

THE OPENING PARAGRAPHS of the introduction to this volume divided the noteworthy accomplishments of Pope Francis into two categories: (1) those that pertain to the inner life of the church, such as its doctrines, internal practices, policies, and organizational management; and (2) those that focus on the intersection of the church and the wider world, dealing with issues that affect all people in the pluralistic global society with its many publics. As noted at the outset, the former fall under the category of *ad intra* leadership and may be likened to the domestic policies of any civil government. The later, conversely, involve what is termed *ad extra* leadership and may be compared to the foreign policy of a country. Of all the chapters of this book, the present one focuses most squarely on this second set of concerns, in an attempt to evaluate both the content and the style of the social teachings of Pope Francis and his advocacy for peace and social justice.

An Unfolding Vision of Proper Social Order

Christianity has, of course, always featured commitments to healthy social order, including advocacy for the advancement of values in line with its core doctrines: the promotion of human life, conditions ensuring a dignified existence for all, duties to the common good, care for God's common gift of creation, and the pursuit of peace within and among communities of people, to name just a few social values. The past 130 years witnessed the development of a specific set of Roman Catholic teachings that applied these general principles to the complex social and economic order of a newly industrialized society. With the 1891 social encyclical, *Rerum Novarum* ("Of New Things") of Pope Leo XIII, the Catholic Church went on record with its concerns about the conditions confronting exploited workers in a rapidly industrializing economy. Every pope since that pivotal moment has reaffirmed the basic directions of modern Catholic social teachings and played the role of advocate for peace, social responsibility, and economic justice.

However, that sturdy generalization in the preceding sentence requires some nuance. While it is easy to trace the basic continuity in Catholic social teaching over the past century and a third, it is also obvious that each successive pope has placed his own personal stamp upon the expression of those teachings. Each leader has emphasized certain themes or priorities that match especially closely the contours of his own social vision and the pressing needs of the specific historical moment. Thus, we witness certain papacies dedicating words and diplomatic efforts especially prominently to peacemaking (Benedict XV during World War I, Pius XII during World War II, and John XXIII at the most dangerous juncture of the Cold War), and others to economic development and worker justice (Pius XI addressing the Great Depression, Paul VI analyzing global development amid rapid decolonization, and Benedict

XVI diagnosing the causes of the economic crisis in 2008–9). It is probably fair to say that John Paul II, dealing as he did with the fall of Communism, which held momentous implications for both politics and economics, and Francis, dealing with a bewildering range of crises that include threats to peace, economic order, and environmental sustainability, are the recent popes who faced the widest array of simultaneous crises unfolding during their reigns. Because the challenges were so numerous, these two popes encountered an especially great opportunity to exert moral leadership as advocates for peace and social justice.

Of course, the point here is not to compare or to rank the popes, but to set the stage for the analysis to follow of how Francis has risen to the challenge of addressing the points of intersection between church and world in the current challenging times. The scrutiny provided in this chapter will document the firm continuity on display with previous papal social teachings and also propose that, under Francis, the church has witnessed a significant renewal in its social teachings. This is the type of revitalization that adds urgently needed updating and creativity without in any way disavowing what has been handed on by one's predecessors. Still, to be true to a rich heritage (as Francis has been) does not mean simply to repeat previous formulations without variation or enhancement. In both style and substance, Francis has renewed the tradition he inherited and forged an energetic revival in church social teachings, one that rises to the pressing challenges of today's world, including its grinding poverty, escalating inequality, a global refugee crisis, and numerous threats to peace as well as to the integrity of creation. His advocacy for the materially poor and vulnerable, his insistence on the inclusion of all in social development, and his prodigious attentiveness to the health of the natural environment—all these and further accomplishments described below constitute bold advocacy for peace and social justice in a way that stamps his papacy with an originality the world desperately requires today.

The Social Justice Commitments of Pope Francis

While no summary could possibly capture the full range of the social justice positions and commitments of Pope Francis, any accurate evaluation begins with the obvious continuity with existing Catholic social teaching. The pope hastens to emphasize this point himself. On many occasions, when the topic of church social teachings arises, Francis has been quick to affirm his high regard for the rich tradition of reflection on social order inherited from previous popes and councils, and especially notably from national and regional episcopal conferences when those meetings of bishops deliberate on matters of social justice.[1] He routinely acknowledges the brilliance of previous Catholic social thought and somewhat coyly steers those who inquire about the originality of his own social insights to previous works.[2]

Among these inherited principles reaffirmed by Francis is the dignity of human labor, universal solidarity, the value of subsidiarity, respect for private property, the promotion of the common good, the importance of free human associations starting with family life, and the full array of human rights and accompanying duties including making a preferential option for the poor. These and other themes guiding constructive social order are found throughout the social encyclicals and other documents of official Catholic social teaching, as well as in such nonofficial sources as the writings of saints, theologians, and the leaders of Catholic-inspired social movements and ministries, for example, Mother Teresa, Lech Walesa, Dorothy Day, César Chávez, and Monsignor George Higgins.

Helpful insights into the positions of Francis on proper social order will arise from analyzing the following two emblematic statements of the pope on social justice issues as they relate to the mission of the church. While many other selections could be offered, this pair of passages serves well the present purpose of glimpsing the overall social vision of the pope. Each provides helpful contextualization for the social priorities that Francis eagerly wishes to promote as the Catholic Church engages with the wider society. Furthermore, each selection recalls aspects of previous chapters of this present work, which described the leadership roles Francis routinely plays as ethicist, discerner, and communicator. To that formidable list, we now add his role as advocate for social justice—and one with a distinctive contribution to offer.

First, in his address to the second World Meeting of Popular Movements that was held in Bolivia during the papal visit in July of 2015, Francis delivered these prophetic words:

> Working for a just distribution of the fruits of the earth and human labor is not mere philanthropy. It is a moral obligation. For Christians, the responsibility is even greater: it is a commandment. It is about giving to the poor and to peoples what is theirs by right. The universal destination of goods is not a figure of speech found in the Church's social teaching. It is a reality prior to private property....It is not enough to let a few drops fall whenever the poor shake a cup which never runs over by itself. Welfare programs geared to certain emergencies can only be considered temporary and incidental responses. They could never replace true inclusion, an inclusion which provides worthy, free, creative, participatory, and solidary work.[3]

Second, chapter 3 of the 2020 social encyclical, *Fratelli Tutti* (nos. 116–17), includes these admonitions:

> Solidarity means much more than engaging in sporadic acts of generosity. It means thinking and acting in terms of community. It means that the lives of all are prior to the appropriation of goods by a few. It also means combatting the structural causes of poverty, inequality, the lack of work, land and housing, the denial of social and labor rights. It means confronting the destructive effects of the empire of money....When we speak of the need to care for our common home, our planet, we appeal to the spark of universal consciousness and mutual concern that

> may still be present in people's hearts. Those who enjoy a surplus of water yet choose to conserve it for the sake of the greater human family have attained a moral stature that allows them to look beyond themselves....The same attitude is demanded if we are to recognize the rights of all people, even those born beyond our borders.[4]

These two passages occasion many helpful observations about Francis's social agenda. To begin, each is clearly in marked continuity with the central themes of modern Catholic social teaching as it has developed over the course of thirteen decades. We readily see here typical concerns about the just distribution of wealth, the social responsibility that accompanies private property, the importance of available work opportunities and dignified work arrangements, solidarity, and commitment to the common good, even to the point of making significant sacrifices of one's own interests.

Perhaps the most prominent theme common to these two passages is the necessity of a commitment to social justice, above and beyond the perennial Christian commitment to practicing charity. From the beginning of the church, believers have been exhorted to perform charitable activities such as the corporal works of mercy: feed the hungry, offer shelter to the homeless, and so on. Francis follows a long line of Christian leaders who look approvingly on such generous responses to human needs; in the first passage, he commends the "welfare programs geared to certain emergencies" and in the second, he lauds "acts of generosity." But he is also eager to characterize these voluntary and occasional responses to immediate needs of the poor as insufficient in the long run.

For all its merit, the generous giving of philanthropy has the shortcoming of being "sporadic" and "temporary," to cite his words here. Such works of mercy are unreliable and thus inadequate to the long-term goal of supporting human dignity. While band-aids may need to be applied to cover short-term needs, a deeper surgery (to continue the analogy related to social wounds) must be performed to set wounded and vulnerable members of society on a promising path to healing and to guarantee all people a secure and dignified existence. Beyond performing works of mercy, persons of social conscience seek sustainable solutions to the needs of the materially poor, and these involve providing economic opportunities to all and empowering all to assume their rightful place in society.

By employing vivid phrases, such as "the empire of money," and images, such as invoking the shaking of a beggar's cup for coins, Francis is summing up a centuries-long development within Catholic social thought: the augmentation of a "charity alone" approach to alleviating dire material needs with a "social justice" orientation to social amelioration. In its truest form, such a commitment to social justice never disavows the works of mercy but rather supplements them with an awareness of the crucial project of transforming social and economic structures to empower the most vulnerable to become agents of their own history.

With laudable economy of expression, Francis is inviting his listeners and readers to recapitulate the remarkable growth of a movement known as "Social Catholicism" throughout the nineteenth century—a century that witnessed a growing realization among church leaders that the dawning age of the industrial revolution required a sophisticated response to the needs of the exploited workers in a new order of mass production and factory work that was both dangerous and inhumanely low paid. The church's initial reply to these changed economic conditions started as a theological response, reflecting on God's will that all be treated with dignity, and developed into an impulse toward social advocacy for enlightened policies to be adopted by leaders of industry and public authorities. The fundamental instinct to protect struggling employees was of course commendable, if at first vague and indeterminate. The earliest contributors to Social Catholicism knew that something had to be done to protect workers from an exploitative industrial order, but they groped about for suggestions. However, by the time these proposals had "trickled up" into the circles of influence around Pope Leo XIII, church advocacy for the poor included rather specific recommendations for adequate minimum wages, support for labor unions, and a range of workplace protections.

The full flowering of Catholicism's social justice perspective required many decades for it to unfold fully, but by the time Francis became pope, he could cite well-developed social doctrines in his own calls for the social responsibility that must accompany the holding of private property and political power. Both selections cited above include summary phrases that capture key elements of the social teachings of previous popes, upon which Francis is eager to build. Thus, we hear in just a few densely packed lines of text about "just distribution of the fruits of the earth," "universal destination of goods," "the denial of labor rights," and "solidarity."

The latter two were themes close to the heart, and often on the pen, of Pope John Paul II, who championed the dignity of human labor in his 1981 encyclical *Laborem Exercens* and held up solidarity as a key value guiding his opposition to the communist regimes that brought oppression to his homeland and its region for decades. The Polish pope also introduced into the papal lexicon another key notion of church social thought: structural evil. In his 1987 social encyclical, *Sollicitudo Rei Socialis*, John Paul II referred, in more than a dozen instances, to the pernicious effects of economic and social structures that not only originate in, and cause injury to, specific individuals but which somehow accumulate into self-replicating and accelerating patterns of injustices with systemic implications.

By labeling these, in alternating instances, as structures of sin, structural sin, social sin, or structural evil, John Paul II was calling attention to the perduring nature of such injustices as systemic racism, gender discrimination, crass consumerism, colonialism, and militarism. The harms we endure and the harms we do to others are often tangled up in the operations of large-scale institutions, such as corrupt political systems, skewed legal establishments, exclusionary social conventions, and exploitative economic organizations. Such forces have a distressing way of perpetuating themselves and making it more likely that individuals born into social systems affected by these distortions will be complicit in further social sin and systemic abuses.[5]

The remainder of this chapter highlights several areas of social justice advocacy where Francis applies the notions of structural evil and social sin—inherited from previous Catholic social teachings—to contemporary global challenge. The previous chapter already provided a glimpse at how Francis employs this thought pattern, as his communications frequently acknowledges the power of collective ways of operating—both institutional and cultural—over individuals and their decisions. When Francis analyzes world events in the terms described at the end of chapter 3 (recall his rhetorical device of attributing abiding patterns of both praiseworthy and blameworthy activity as "a culture of…"), he is echoing the notion that his Polish predecessor introduced to church social teachings. For better or worse, large and inherited structures exert power over the moral decisions of each of us.

The remaining sections of this chapter, then, will offer further commentary on how Francis fashions this insight regarding the importance of paying adequate attention to social structures into a set of tools to diagnose and combat various social injustices. But this present section would be incomplete without three observations regarding the foregoing analysis. First, Francis skillfully combines moral appeals that pertain to the level of the individual as well as the collective. In the two selections cited above and throughout the corpus of his ethical writings and addresses, he speaks of moral obligations in ways that appeal to both individual conscience and social responsibility. These two levels of ethical behavior and decision-making are inextricably linked; we are all obliged as individuals and as members of collectivities to obey the moral commandments of God and to discern practical implications of these inescapable principles of right behavior.

Second, Francis introduces into papal discourse a new emphasis on the importance of inclusion and, conversely, overcoming all manner of exclusions. As we will see below from the analysis of a key section of *Evangelii Gaudium*, inclusion and exclusion emerge as central categories in Francis's evaluation of the morality of any economic system. Third and finally, any perceptive observer will recognize that the pope's advocacy of social reform displays a sense of urgency rarely found in previous church social teachings.[6] More than just a rhetorical preference, the strong messages of Francis in this area assume a prophetic tone precisely because so much is at stake: the very lives of people struggling for, among other things, adequate land, work, and housing, whether or not we use the alliterative phrases he favors for these vital items in Spanish or alternative alliterative terms in English. If society fails, as he often exhorts, "to put the economy at the service of people,"[7] it will violate every vital aspect of economic justice. Especially if the church falls short in its advocacy for an inclusive and just achievement of integral human development, it will constitute a countersign to the proclamation of the gospel. Instead of releasing transformative energies that are deeply evangelical, a church that grows indifferent to social injustices is guilty of neglecting its mission and forfeiting its role as "light to the world."

The Structural Eye of Francis

The preceding section presented a summary of Pope Francis's core social justice commitments, culminating in the recognition that he is especially eager to apply the inherited insights of Catholic social teaching to contemporary challenges to justice. Related questions naturally arise: If a hundred years of gradual development of the tradition yielded an appreciation for the tools of social analysis of structural injustices, precisely how does Francis employ these tools? How do the well-developed convictions of Catholic social thought shape his practice of advocacy for justice in various areas of global social concern?

Regarding social justice advocacy, Francis is, as ever, a prudent moral leader who is keenly aware of both the possibilities and the limits of his potential contribution. No global religious authority can comprehend and address even a substantial fraction of all the justice challenges in every corner of the world, and no mortal being should pretend to possess all the insights and analysis that might prove helpful in all local contexts. The best any world leader can do is to promote a set of sound ethical principles and observations that might profitably be applied by local practitioners, whether they be other religious leaders, economic actors, public officeholders, or participants in civil society institutions eager for guidance on moral questions of the age. As noted above, one thing that contemporary popes are now well positioned to offer is a structural analysis of the moral dimensions of economic and social relations.

Earlier chapters have already treated two areas of social relations where Francis has applied his "structural eye" to social injustices. First, chapter 2 included a case study on the two synods on the family, including a summary of the concerns of the 2016 post-synodal exhortation *Amoris Laetitia* ("On Love in the Family"). In that document, Francis shared the fruits of an extended discernment, during which he invited broad global participation, regarding the many challenges to healthy family life today. Although the deliberations and final documents were mostly remembered for their treatment of just one issue—the neuralgic matter of the possible readmission to the sacraments of civilly divorced Catholics without benefit of an annulment—most of the exhortation displays a pope conducting a comprehensive social analysis of the cultural and economic structures that present severe challenges to families today. The reader of *Amoris Laetitia* witnesses Francis analyzing the pressures exerted on family life by such forces as unemployment, technology, poverty, addictions, and the "time squeeze" that together explain much of today's rampant family dissatisfaction and breakup, and even prevent many wary young people from making an initial commitment to family formation. Francis does not, of course, propose simple or tidy solutions to these deep-seated problems, but parts of the document present valuable ethical analysis of the structures and institutions that hold great importance for the desperately needed renewal of family life.

A second opportunity to observe Francis employing his structural perspective on a contemporary social problem arose in the first case study treated in chapter 3: his appearances on the Mediterranean islands of Lampedusa and Lesbos and other locales where he visited refugee camps and expressed his solidarity with hard-pressed "people on the move." Although the focus of that previous chapter was primarily on the communication practices of Pope Francis, much more was on display on those occasions than person-to-person empathy or even a pledge of institutional solidarity, although Francis himself and the church more generally have followed up admirably on the commitments expressed on each occasion. Rather, the ongoing involvement of Francis with the global refugee crisis is grounded in a structural analysis of the causes of the startling upsurge in migration and displaced people.

Evidence abounds of the pope's concern for refugees and deep insight into the causes of this global crisis. Although Francis has produced no lengthy teaching documents focusing exclusively on refugees, his annual messages for World Day of Migrants and Refugees[8] and the texts of his spoken addresses when visiting or even hosting[9] groups of refugees reveal especially deep analysis of the phenomenon of forced migration today. Francis has been bold in identifying the root causes of the refugee crisis, with its tens of millions seeking a safe haven abroad and others living as internally displaced persons within their shattered homelands. Some causes of this massive uprooting of people are as old as civilization: the desire to flee poverty and to seek greater economic opportunities—motives that impelled Francis's own parents and grandparents to venture from Italy to Argentina about a century ago.

However, other causes of the refugee crisis are more tragic and more recent in prominence: families fleeing for their lives from civil wars, lawless failed states, religious persecution, terrorism, violent gangs and drug cartels that target unfortunate bystanders who then seek escape and asylum abroad. Especially desperate are the millions of forced migrants who qualify as trafficked persons—lured or coerced across borders by those who would profit off their forced labor or sexual enslavement. A newer and growing category of involuntary migrants are climate change refugees, such as ranchers, herders, and farmers whose formerly arable lands have been swallowed by growing deserts or ruined by salt water from rising seas. Rendering service that transcends what a sociologist or political scientist might be able to document about global migration, Francis often offers ethical insights into the plight of refugees, treating the moral dimensions of the conditions that are causing the unprecedented crisis and the tragedy of global indifference to the widespread suffering. Not satisfied only to point a finger of blame at bad actors, Francis urges us all to cease being merely bystanders or onlookers to an unfolding tragedy and become "inlookers" who provide insight regarding root causes of human suffering and promising paths to a better future for all.

Pope Francis's credibility as an advocate for refugees is based on several pillars. One of these is surely the sincerity of his personal witness to these people on the move. The authenticity of his concern was on full display in the poignant moments of lament on the islands of Lampedusa and Lesbos described in chapter 3. Another is the excellent and accurate information he has at his fingertips, thanks to the efforts of the Pontifical Academy of Social Sciences, a professional society of top experts maintained by the Holy See to render advice on such weighty human affairs. Perhaps the greatest source of papal credibility on issues of migration is the immense contribution to the well-being of refugees offered by the global network of Catholic agencies, which labor on the frontlines to promote the safety and well-being of people on the move, including those in transit countries awaiting resettlement. While much of the credit for delivery of vital services belongs to donors, frontline workers, volunteers, and local church-affiliated agencies around the world, the pope's own curial offices play a vital role in coordinating these global efforts. The Dicastery for Promoting Integral Human Development includes a division—recently upgraded in personnel, resources, and on the Vatican's organizational chart—for the care and support of refugees, especially new arrivals in refugee camps. This acknowledgment of credit is a useful reminder that social justice advocacy always relies on a combination of gathering accurate information, producing insightful ethical analysis, and mustering adequate organizational capacity to make a real difference in the lives of people. As a matter of moral leadership, maintaining a commitment to serve the neediest people on earth requires all three of these factors and more.

This section has expanded on the findings of two case studies (on family life and refugees) from earlier chapters, identifying how Pope Francis's advocacy on each set of issues demonstrates his reliance on structural analysis into the root causes of social dysfunction, human suffering, and moral evil. The following sections of this chapter provide somewhat more detailed descriptions of three areas where Pope Francis employs his structural eye to good effect in his advocacy for social change: (1) in pursuit of peace and disarmament; (2) in dealing with threats to the natural environment; and (3) regarding economic justice for workers and those marginalized in society.

A Structural Approach to Peace and Disarmament

Francis inherited an impressive papal playbook of peace advocacy that has long included strenuous efforts and sophisticated strategies to advance the cause of peaceful resolution of conflicts. Observers throughout the world are no longer surprised to see the head of the Roman Catholic Church employing an array of strategies that encourage peace over war. When Francis condemned in rousing terms the 2022 Russian invasion of Ukraine, for example, he echoes his predecessor Benedict XV's prophetic denunciation of the disastrous resort to force that produced the fratricidal bloodbath of World War I. In working behind the scenes to broker a breakthrough—one that was admittedly partial and temporary—in U.S.–Cuba relations near the end of the Obama administration, Francis was channeling the momentous role played by Pope John XXIII in offering a diplomatic backchannel that may just have prevented the Cuban Missile Crisis from obliterating the entire world in October of 1962. When Francis appears at the United Nations to plead for continued efforts to support the peaceful resolution of grievances and conflicts across the globe, he is recapitulating the heartfelt efforts of all his recent predecessors who appeared in that same space with an identical purpose: to say no to war-making and bloodshed and yes to diplomacy and dialogue aimed at reconciliation.

We have already glimpsed a few further activities of Francis in support of peace. Two of the case studies in chapter 3 included descriptions of "Francis, the diplomat," meeting heads of state in conflicted regions or global hotspots, and "Francis, the leader of prayer for peace," presiding over the momentous outdoor prayer vigil for peace in Syria in September of 2013. These episodes represent just a small fraction of the peace-supporting implements in the toolkit of any pope. The most routinely employed of these tools is the written or spoken word, where Francis has excelled in producing original and challenging interventions. He has used his annual Messages for World Day of Peace (documents typically of five to ten pages in length, issued each December in anticipation of that January 1 celebration) to invite reflection on peace dimensions of many global issues and to promote nonviolence in stirring ways. Francis has similarly employed shorter spoken addresses, for example, the semi-annual *Urbi et Orbi* speeches and weekly Angelus messages, to promote peaceful attitudes in general, but also to call attention to specific violations of peace where innocent life is most threatened but where the dangers are often overlooked—witness the ongoing armed conflicts in Yemen, Congo, and Ethiopia that Francis has frequently highlighted.

Supplementing these regularly scheduled opportunities to promote peace are the extraordinary efforts the pope has made to travel to conflicted areas to deliver a message related to peace. A surprisingly large number of Francis's more than three dozen international voyages fit into the category of peace-themed visits. For example, in September of 2017, he traveled to make a firsthand appeal that all contending factions in the war-torn nation of Colombia, located on his own home continent, no less, abide by the terms agreed to in recently concluded peace negotiations—accords to which he had personally lent considerable diplomatic support.[10] Two years earlier (in November of 2015), he had visited the struggling landlocked nation of Central African Republic on a similar mission to signal his support for an ongoing peace process; only in this case, the temporary ceasefire between the warring factions was so fragile that Francis had to overrule the stern warnings of his security advisors to appear on the streets of the divided capital city of Bangui to mingle with throngs of well-wishers and even to visit the city's main mosque. Contemporary accounts speculated that this was the first papal visit to an active war zone.[11] The astonishing fearlessness demonstrated by the pope on that occasion provided encouraging reassurance to the bitterly divided Christian and Muslim populations of that poor country that risking their own security to engage their counterparts in daily interchange, not to mention trusting their rivals to abide by the terms of ceasefires and the larger peace process, was a real possibility as the country sought to return to an elusive normalcy.

Francis's first post-pandemic travel was to Iraq, a war-torn nation that also presented serious security concerns for papal travel but that had long been a priority destination for a pope eager to bring encouragement to those who had endured prolonged factional violence and terrorism. Being in Iraq also occasioned the visit of Francis with the most highly revered Shiite leaders (as described in chapter 3) that also promoted a message regarding peaceful interfaith relations. By way of chronological symmetry, the very last papal travels (November of 2019) before the onset of the COVID-19 pandemic included a four-day stay in Japan, where Francis engaged in much fruitful dialogue regarding, not a current violent conflict but an older though still painful national memory: the dropping of the atomic bombs on Hiroshima and Nagasaki in August of 1945. The speeches given by Francis at events hosted by those two rebuilt cities and during his emotional visit to Japan presented an opportunity for the pope to reaffirm his conviction that "a world without nuclear weapons is possible and necessary."[12]

Occasionally, papal advocacy for peace allows Francis to remain at home and conduct business as a host. Two such examples stand out, each representing papal support for longstanding but incomplete peace processes. First, on June 8, 2014, Francis hosted the leaders of Israel (Prime Minister Shimon Peres) and Palestine (President Mahmoud Abbas) for a joint day of prayer in the Vatican Gardens. Francis invited his close friend Patriarch Bartholomew of the Orthodox Church to join the experience of interfaith prayer, which was the pope's attempt at contributing to the eventual resolution of conflicts he had seen firsthand in his visit to both sides of the high wall dividing the Holy Land the previous month. By prior agreement, that day at the Vatican witnessed no attempt at formal negotiation of any sort, but rather simply the expectation that reflective time spent together might build up some measure of trust among the leaders of these two sides contending over territory, water rights, and much else.

A second and very different episode when Francis played host involved South Sudan, the newest nation on earth, and one bitterly divided between Christian and Muslim political factions who have regularly engaged in armed confrontation since independence was achieved in 2011. For two days in April of 2019, Francis hosted the President, Salva Kiir (a Christian), and opposition leader, Riek Machar (a Muslim), in a retreat aimed at reaching a political settlement in a ghastly civil war that had dragged on for six years, killing nearly half a million and displacing an additional four million people. As the time for departure approached without ostensible diplomatic progress, Pope Francis appealed for the two leaders to remain longer at the bargaining table to give peace a chance, at one point kneeling down on the floor and kissing the boots of the two military leaders, in a gesture of supplication and begging lest the parties abandon the negotiations. Although further progress did not come immediately, the rich symbolic gesture of Francis had communicated his point about the value and urgency of peace. The completed power-sharing agreement was at last signed by the two sides some months later on January 13, 2020; since it was negotiated by the Rome-based Catholic lay peace community Sant'Egidio, the signing took place in Rome, although not in the presence of Francis. Nevertheless, representatives of both sides testified to the spiritual power of the pope and his witness to peace. The parties to the agreement issued a statement that they "were humbled by the relentless spiritual and moral appeal for peace, reconciliation and fraternity by Pope Francis." Furthermore, the head of the South Sudan government delegation told Vatican Radio that the leaders "could feel the spirit of Pope Francis in the room as the agreements were being discussed."[13]

Evidently, papal peace advocacy does sometimes pay off. While other highly encouraging results of papal or other church-based peace efforts over recent years could be documented here, what is most important to comprehend is the specific nature of the influence that a pope may wield in the sensitive areas of human social relations that involve peacemaking. As previously noted, in political science terms, Francis, or any pope or other religious leader, possesses exclusively "soft power" as opposed to the "hard power" that comes from the projection of military or geopolitical capabilities.[14] This realization has not in recent years been in any doubt, at least since Joseph Stalin (reportedly during World War II) posed the mischievous question "How many divisions has the pope?" In ethical terms, a religious leader campaigning for peace seeks to parlay moral and spiritual authority into support for an agenda of nonviolent approaches to conflict resolution. The currency of this influence is the set of persuasive words and effective gestures that a religious leader can enlist in this cause, and the foregoing sketches of a select number of the peace-related activities of Francis demonstrate some very powerful tools that he has indeed employed.

Lest this analysis place too much emphasis on the personal qualities that contribute to papal persuasiveness, however, the time has arrived to highlight the more specifically structural dimensions of papal peacemaking, in keeping with the themes related to social analysis and structural evil introduced in the previous section of this chapter. At this juncture, one may ask: Is it possible that the same pope, who places such great confidence in the power of nourishing personal relationships and building up trust "on the retail level" in pursuit of global peace, also subscribe to a structural approach to peacemaking? Does the application of soft power allow space for both face-to-face dealings at the grassroots and more generalized approaches that rely on structural analysis of conditions conducive to peace? The answer is resoundingly in the affirmative. To understand how the "Francis Doctrine" regarding peace can include both the artisanal cultivation of one-to-one relationships with world leaders, on the one hand, and attention to social structures and institutions, on the other hand, it is important first to introduce three insights related to the realities of war and peace today.

First, regarding the nature of contemporary violence, the great majority of armed conflicts today do not involve large-scale engagements of uniformed national armies arrayed on a battlefield. If that older model of warfare still prevailed, then a pope or other religious leader would be wise to focus simply on persuading heads of state to "call off the dogs of war." But the achievement of peace today is complicated by the proliferation of relatively new kinds of violent conflict, including civil wars between rival armed factions within a nation, low-intensity conflicts across ethnic or religious divides, guerrilla warfare, armed gangs, and drug cartels seeking regional dominance, terrorist groups wreaking havoc within and across borders, and separatist groups challenging the sovereignty of larger nations or failed states. Activities such as piracy, kidnapping, human trafficking, hijacking, extortion, black market dealing, smuggling, trading in conflict minerals, and large-scale livestock rustling—all these faces of violence challenge inherited conceptions of what is required to protect innocent people from harm, to stop war, and to halt armed conflict. In short, those seeking to employ soft power to good effect have more work to do than ever.

Second, and partly in response to this evolving profile of global violence, the very terms we employ to describe the pursuit of peace have shifted. While *peacemaking* and *peacekeeping* are surely still useful concepts in many ways, these venerable terms have, in recent years, given way to the descriptive terms *conflict transformation* and especially *peacebuilding*.[15] Each calls attention to the holistic nature of the task of pursuing peace. Establishing tranquility is not a matter of merely completing a one-time transaction, but rather of creating sustainable conditions that might satisfy the many potential parties to a given conflict. If we are to produce peaceful outcomes from the inevitable conflicts that are part of the human condition, we must pay close attention to the full range of underlying conditions that either produce peace or exacerbate conflict.[16] Francis even labeled a section of his encyclical, *Fratelli Tutti*, "Inevitable Conflict" (see nos. 237–40), thereby signaling his awareness that the resolution of human discord requires more than good will; peaceful outcomes also require deep grappling with underlying factors that exacerbate preexisting tensions. Recognizing the deep-seated causes and wellsprings of violent conflict is one application of the structural approach we have already seen as key to the social justice advocacy of Pope Francis.

Third, while we might identify many factors that qualify as emerging root causes of escalating global conflict today (for example, the climate change stressors that may lead to resource wars due to conflicting claims to water supplies), no phenomenon is a more direct and disturbing cause of senseless bloodshed today than the global arms trade. The production and sale of deadly weapons fuels regional arms races among nations as well as placing dangerous tools of death into the wrong hands at local levels everywhere. The easy availability of both large weapon systems and small arms supplies oxygen to the flames of simmering ethnic rivalries and territorial disputes around the world, encouraging individuals and groups with grievances of many sorts to prolong antagonisms and turn them into violent rampages. The persistence of the arms trade within and between nations frustrates the goals of conflict transformation directly. Instead of constructively deescalating disputes, the wide availability of weapons encourages the illusion that the application of brutal force will resolve disagreements to the imagined benefit of the holders of those weapons. Under these conditions, the cycle of violence spirals further and further out of control, unchecked in its force and with the bloodiest of consequences.

To his credit, Pope Francis has campaigned long and hard against what he calls the "global bazaar" in large and small arms that claim countless lives each year and work systemically against peace.[17] In the course of insistent appeals throughout his writings and addresses on peace,[18] he explicitly acknowledges the structural dimensions of this threat to peace, tracing the horrific consequences of war and terrorism to the availability of weapons that are all too readily for sale. He frequently refers to those who sell weapons indiscriminately as "merchants of death" whose "hands are drenched with blood." Two and a half years into his papacy, Francis chose two high-profile occasions to share with audiences of influential policymakers his structural analysis of the damage done by arms sales. First, on September 24, 2015, speaking before a joint session of the U.S. Congress (the first ever convened to hear a pope), Francis inserted a plea for the end of the arms race and indiscriminate arms sales in his address to the legislative body with the most power of all to act on these issues—since the United States is by far the top manufacturer and exporter of arms in the world. Speaking in belabored English, Francis used one of the final paragraphs of his address to appeal for peace and disarmament with these words:

> Being at the service of dialogue and peace also means being truly determined to minimize and, in the long term, to end the many armed conflicts throughout the world. Here we have to ask ourselves: Why are deadly weapons being sold to those who plan to inflict untold suffering on individuals and society? Sadly, the answer, as we all know, is for money: money that is drenched in blood, often innocent blood. In the face of this shameful and culpable silence, it is our duty to confront the problem and to stop the arms trade.[19]

The next day, speaking to the General Assembly of the United Nations in New York City, Francis again leveraged the opportunity to shine a light on the structural evil of the indiscriminate global trade in arms. After sharing words of praise and congratulations for the achievements of the United Nations—"the resolution of numerous conflicts, operations of peacekeeping and reconciliation"—as it marked its seventieth anniversary, Francis challenged the organization to do even more to advance peace. He listed the proliferation of nuclear and conventional weapons as among the most urgent issues facing the global community. Early in the address, he lamented how "the weapons trade…[exacts a] toll in innocent lives" and later urged greater multilateral efforts to restrain the global arms trade. A paragraph near the end of his speech begins with an expression of the pope's great admiration for the ideals contained in the Charter of the United Nations, and proceeds to berate "the constant tendency to the proliferation of arms, especially weapons of mass destruction such as nuclear weapons….There is urgent need to work for a world free of nuclear weapons."[20]

In exercising moral leadership on issues of peace, then, Francis weaves together two idioms of ethical discourse, each aimed at motivating constructive change in its own way. One is a discourse of personal conscience, as the pope appeals to notions such as moral obligations, virtuous restraint, and the ethical conversion of the hearts and minds of individuals to the ways of peace and reconciliation. The second language addresses structural dimensions of peacebuilding, as humanity gropes its way toward creating conditions that foster peace rather than violence. This discourse addresses the level of large institutions, such as governments, industries, even the United Nations, where policy decisions hold life-or-death consequences for millions of potential victims. When he takes up this larger tableau, Francis readily shares his diagnosis that the global arms trade is a major cause of needless bloodshed, as well as his prescription that curtailing the proliferation of all sorts of weapons will mitigate this scourge.

It goes without saying that restricting or banning weapons sales entirely should be a priority for all who possess the power to do so. The officials Francis was peering at during his speeches at the United Nations and in the U.S. Congress were fully aware that arms nonproliferation proposals had been introduced to each deliberative body in the months preceding the papal visit, and that they might well be shamed into acknowledging the slow and incomplete progress of all such measures in the years since the visits of Francis in 2015. To identify a structure of evil in clear terms is difficult enough, but to move people and large institutions to end their complicity with a sinful structure is a further challenge.

A Structural Approach to Protecting the Natural Environment

Francis's leadership on environmental issues is so extraordinary that it may come as a surprise that so few references have been made to it thus far. Apart from possibly the Swedish teenage activist, Greta Thunberg, Francis has emerged as the most prominent global voice decrying the disastrous effects of climate change and promoting measures to support the ecological sustainability that humanity urgently needs to adopt. While entire volumes have been written describing the profound contributions of Francis in this area, the brief treatment here will focus on the structural approach the pope has adopted in treating the escalating environmental degradation facing the earth, which he habitually refers to as "our common home."

As with the tasks of peacebuilding treated above and of establishing greater economic justice discussed in the next section, the social advocacy exercised by Francis regarding ecology exhibits a keen sensitivity to structural dimensions of a contemporary crisis. The pope's activism in all three areas proceeds on the assumption that identifying and addressing the causal roots of a problem are keys to any adequate resolution. If we are collectively to rise to the challenge and make real progress against climate change and other faces of environmental degradation, our approach must consist of much more than mere short-term crisis management. Any program that will truly transform human awareness of these weighty matters and embrace substantial reforms to meet this existential threat will involve engagement at the causal roots of the ecological crisis. Pope Francis exhorts us to undertake a thorough revision of our approach to our common home, far beyond the superficial patches with which some commentators seem satisfied. Forging a path to a sustainable future—really, any future at all—will require a commitment first to truth-telling about our past abuses and patterns of exploitation, then careful planning to create more adequate institutional structures for interacting with the environment, and finally, an ongoing commitment to fulfilling our obligations to future generations. The structural eye of Francis is at work as he advocates for urgent attention to each of these tasks.

The major vehicle Francis employs for teaching about the environment is the encyclical *Laudato Si'*, released in June of 2015[21] with much fanfare and to heightened expectation from a global audience eager to see precisely how the pope would contribute to the debate leading up to a momentous climate change summit at year's end.[22] The forty-thousand-word encyclical was the first major papal teaching document dedicated in its entirety to the natural environment, although it built upon a solid framework of ecological concerns laid out over the previous quarter-century in briefer treatments by John Paul II and Benedict XVI. Reflecting the approach of much previous Catholic social teaching, the implicit methodology of the document follows the see-judge-act pattern; Francis reviews the state of the ecological crisis, then leads readers through an extended evaluation of what has gone wrong in human attitudes and practices that contributed to the crisis, and finally, recommends numerous thoroughgoing changes to address the problematic behaviors and reorient humanity toward our common home on a sustainable basis.

From the moment of his election, Francis has placed environmental concern front and center for the church. In media interviews, he has repeatedly explained his choice of the name Francis in terms of the three things that the revered saint from Assisi was famed for protecting and maintaining close relationships with: peace, the poor, and the environment. The very title of the encyclical, representing a rare departure from the convention of using Latin phrases, consists of two Italian words associated with Francis of Assisi, whose Canticle of the Creatures repeats "Praise be to you, my Lord." Invoking Franciscan spirituality in this prominent way, the pope sets the tone for the entire document, which felicitously remains in touch with the attitudes of awe, humility, wonder, and gratitude for the beauty of the created world even when the text delves into rather practical matters with considerable detail.

While it would be accurate to characterize the overall tone of *Laudato Si'* as inspirational, aspirational, and even devotional or mystical at times, the text also includes some harsh words about the human folly and distorted social priorities that led us to the precipice of environmental disaster. The pope scolds both greedy individuals and distorted social structures, such as corrupt governments and predatory corporations that extract exorbitant profits from nonrenewable resources, and that have contributed to unconscionable pollution and harmful greenhouse emissions. He identifies the pursuit of high-consumption lifestyles as a major causal factor in polluting and degrading the earth's ecosystems, and particularly in releasing the ruinous greenhouse gases that threaten all with rising sea levels and severe weather events. Francis readily affirms the consensus of climate scientists that short-sighted human activity has caused massive global warming[23] and that only drastic alterations of our patterns of energy and resource usage will suffice to prevent the worst calamity in human history.

Like any savvy proponent of broad and urgent change, Francis combines in his recommendations some small-scale local changes, in which all may readily participate directly and without delay, and other broader society-wide reforms, which hinge on the accumulation of patient efforts by many parties and institutions. In the former category are familiar recommendations for reducing waste in our use of food, water, energy, and other resources of the earth. The pope shares his own personal discomfort at witnessing gross overuse of disposable plastic and the prodigious waste of paper that never gets recycled; he shares such practical (even folksy) advice for reducing energy use as carpooling and donning a sweater before turning up the heat in winter (no. 211 feature many of these suggestions). On a higher level of analysis, he urges the adoption of public policies and corporate practices that genuinely respect the constraints of fragile ecosystems and respond to the climate crisis with much greater sensitivity and effectiveness than the world has witnessed thus far—an entire section of chapter 1 of the document is titled "Weak Responses" and chides systemic myopic inaction.

That this sharply challenging encyclical was not met with universal praise is hardly surprising, but the shape of the earliest criticism of the pope's message was at once unanticipated and highly instructive. Immediately upon its release, several public policy-minded commentators seized on two brief spots in the book-length text where Francis appears to dismiss or at least downplay the value of "the strategy of buying and selling 'carbon credits'" (primarily no. 171; see also no. 26). These critics took him to task for not endorsing the specific "cap-and-trade" carbon tax policies that had demonstrably succeeded in reducing carbon emissions in certain nations and locales.[24] While these critics may have a valid point or two to offer regarding the merits of specific market-oriented interventions and incentive-based mechanisms in carbon dioxide reduction strategies, their demurral ultimately missed the forest for the trees. As a close examination of the text surrounding these brief observations of Francis about these policies reveals, the pope was primarily interested in calling attention to the comprehensive change in attitudes that would be required before climate change could ever be reversed.[25] His was a *culture-based* call to comprehensive action, deliberately not a *market-based* set of proposals for a quick technical fix to a specific facet of a vast problem.

Fighting climate change and ecological damage in general is an example of urgent attitudinal change, where replacing a "throwaway culture" with a "culture of care" would make all the difference (both these phrases indeed appear in the text of *Laudato Si'*; see, for example, nos. 16 and 22). As a spiritual leader tapping into his soft power once again in this controversial field of human inquiry, Francis was fully aware that his contribution would remain primarily on the level of motivating people to walk in the ways of conscience and virtue regarding ecology, not to settle disputed scientific or policy matters in a polarized environment. Economic incentives may surely play a constructive role in progressive climate policy, but hardly exhausted the full range of the concerns of Francis. In any case, climate change deniers and those with already calcified policy opinions were never the primary audience of this encyclical. In the end, Francis was not writing to reject this specific policy or to propose any other carbon reduction strategy, but rather to relativize the value of any technical solutions that did not pay adequate attention to the "big picture" to which he sought primarily to call attention: the need for a thoroughgoing and society-wide ecological conversion that alone would be the game-changer humanity desperately needs today.

The broad range of topics covered in *Laudato Si'* further testifies to the comprehensiveness of the pope's ambit of ecological concern. There are entire sections on the right to clean water (nos. 27–31), the loss of biodiversity (nos. 32–42), global pollution (nos. 20–22), and the fascinating theme of obligations of intergenerational solidarity (nos. 159–62). The last is an innovative topic within Catholic social teaching, proposing a broadening of our understanding of the common good now to include justice between generations. If it is unjust to harm anyone living today, it is also incumbent on us to prevent harm to future generations of human beings and, by implication, any living being who will share our common home with our descendants. We indeed have a positive moral duty, Francis contends, to preserve the environment as a hospitable place where they may thrive and flourish, enjoying all the resources they will need to achieve their full potential.

Francis thus emerges as an advocate not only for social justice in the context of the contemporary human community, but a proponent of our duties in justice to anyone or any creatures who will make their home on this planet any time in the future. The stunning breadth of this vision unpacks the signature phrase by which he titles the fourth chapter of *Laudato Si'*: "integral ecology." Here, he places a series of descriptors before the word ecology, including the adjectives environmental, economic, social, and cultural. If ecology is to be authentic, it must exclude none of these dimensions of human life, and our vision of the good life gains acuity when we recognize these rich connections. Over a dozen times throughout the 246 paragraphs of *Laudato Si'*, the reader encounters the claim that "everything is interconnected" or "all things are interrelated" or that "nothing can be considered in isolation" (all three phrases appear in no. 138, among other places). These constitute reminders from the pope that the forces that might seem to alienate us from God, estrange us from one another, and separate us from the natural world can indeed be overcome, if only we embrace a truth that lies at the heart of our universe: that it retains an essential unity even in all its great diversity and complexity. The attention that Francis pays to the structural dimensions of specific issues like carbon footprints and renewable energy resources, and especially his frequent highlighting of the effects of standard practices on the lives of the poorest and most vulnerable on earth, may be attributed to his keen appreciation for the causal factors that shape our world, but which we ultimately retain the power to shape, if we can muster, the social and political will.

The moral leadership of Francis regarding the environment certainly did not stop with the publication of *Laudato Si'* in June of 2015. He continued to foreground ecological concern on many occasions, including in his high-profile speeches to the U.S. Congress and the General Assembly of the United Nations three months later. Three months after that, the delegation he sent to the 2015 Paris Climate Change Conference made consequential interventions in the course of the proceedings, buoyed by the highly favorable reception the encyclical enjoyed around the globe. In the years since 2015, to keep ecological issues ever before the eyes of the Catholic community (and many others) worldwide, Francis established an annual "Season of Creation" that began with the observance of a new "World Day of Prayer for the Care of Creation" on September 1 and continued, fittingly, to October 4, the feast day of St. Francis of Assisi.[26]

In 2022, the Vatican rolled out the ambitious "*Laudato Si'* Action Platform," a seven-year initiative to operationalize these teachings, raise awareness of their content, and implement practical steps for change on a personal, local, and society-wide level simultaneously. The agenda of transforming the encyclical's words into action proceeds quite prominently at the parish and diocesan levels in the form of many practical programs to recycle, conserve energy, introduce sustainable alternatives to fossil fuels, and to reduce carbon footprints in every way possible. Francis seems especially eager to empower youth to address the ecological crisis, to undertake green initiatives, to reject crass consumerism, and to seek creative solutions as they engage their prodigious energies for environmental care. Considering all these ongoing efforts to consolidate environmental progress and to follow up on the breakthrough of *Laudato Si'*, observers of "Francis, the ecological activist" would have a hard time finding evidence of any diminution of his commitment to urgent change to protect our common home.

A Structural Approach to Economic Justice, Worker Rights, and Challenging Inequality

Pope Francis sprinkled calls for economic justice throughout the text of the ecological encyclical *Laudato Si'*. He linked environmental degradation with the exploitation of vulnerable people most explicitly by concluding one section with the observation that "a true ecological approach always becomes a social approach; it must integrate questions of justice in debates on the environment, so as to hear both the cry of the earth and the cry of the poor" (no. 49). Global economic inequality plays a significant role in the pope's diagnosis of the interconnected dysfunctions that degrade the environment and the human community simultaneously.

We have already seen Francis's abiding concern for vulnerable people such as refugees, migrants, and workers exploited in the workings of the global economy in several episodes and case studies in earlier chapters as well as in two paradigmatic texts on economic justice presented at the start of this chapter. This section highlights further analysis of the pope's advocacy for economic justice. It starts with a review of his core ethical commitments regarding the economy and concludes by presenting several incidents when these concerns were on full display in some of his most colorful personal interactions with victims of economic injustice. Once again, structural causes of injustices garner much of Francis's attention as he advocates for reforms that will improve the lives of people who have been deprived of access to economic opportunities and the means to a truly fulfilling life.

The first major teaching document written by Francis, the apostolic exhortation, *Evangelii Gaudium* ("The Joy of the Gospel"), cited several times in previous chapters, contains the most extensive treatment of the topic of economic justice yet offered by the pope. Although it goes without saying that neither this nor any document of Francis functions as a free-standing treatise on economic matters, we nevertheless find here substantive guidance on moral issues relating to economic relations. Two sections of that long letter, "Some Challenges of Today's World" (nos. 52–60) and "The Inclusion of the Poor in Society" (nos. 186–216), focus directly on the causes and consequences of economic injustice. It is also here that we glimpse Francis at his most prophetic—some have even characterized these texts as his most scolding—as he denounces a callous global economy that disadvantages the materially poor and ultimately deprives them of a dignified life. Although his analysis of the deep social injustices that contribute to the oppression of the most vulnerable people on earth is in strong continuity with teachings of previous popes, Francis's excoriation of the forces that bring "exclusion and inequality" is especially pointed here. After describing the warped nature and distorted priorities of an economy that concentrates wealth in too few hands and dooms many of the rest to intolerable material insecurity, he concludes his doleful survey with the blunt conclusion: "Such an economy kills" (no. 53).

Expanding on this soundbite (one that garnered much attention in news coverage of this early document, and even became the title of the first major book on the economic teachings of Francis),[27] the pope proceeds to outline four features of "business as usual" in the global economy that must be rejected. The titles of consecutive sections of this part of *Evangelii Gaudium* capture his judgments about the causal roots of these injustices very pointedly: "No to an economy of exclusion; No to the new idolatry of money; No to a financial system which rules rather than serves; No to the inequality which spawns violence" (nos. 53–59). Similarly instructive is another attention-grabbing soundbite later in the document: "Inequality is the root of social ills" (no. 202). Note the sustained emphasis here upon the pernicious social effects of great divides in wealth and income; Francis is once again employing a structural lens to focus the gaze of all upon serious root causes of social dysfunctions that, if left unchecked, threaten not only the lives of the poor but the entire project of integral human development and the possibility of social harmony itself.[28]

With this analysis, Francis is issuing a direct moral challenge to the prevailing practices of the regnant neoliberal system of global capitalism, in the process calling for a rejection of its "trickle-down theories...which [have] never been confirmed by the facts" (no. 54). Are these excessively radical economic judgments and proposals for a pope? Do they expose Francis as a political revolutionary of some sort? Has he violated the contours of the Catholic social teaching tradition by transgressing the convention by which popes assiduously maintain strong continuity with their predecessors? The negative answer that seems warranted to each of these questions is supported by an appreciation for the very nature of modern church social teachings, which always seek to read and interpret the latest "signs of the times." When great injustices become endemic in society, church leaders rightly invoke their teaching authority to identify and propose solutions to such temporal concerns. Previous popes have indeed weighed in on the same range of social injustices that Francis takes up, and the heightened rhetoric that he employs, especially around the notion of exclusion, reflects the enhanced threat that spiraling inequality and stratification present in our time.[29] Because the stakes are so high—stakes measured in peril to human lives and prospects for social cohesion and peace itself—Francis denounces injustices in the global economy with the same level of urgency he employs in his structural analysis of the ecological crisis. The potential consequences of inaction are simply too dire to risk ignoring or postponing a wholehearted response on the part of all who possess the power to make a difference.

In the address that Francis delivered in Bolivia in 2015 to the second World Meeting of Popular Movements, excerpted at the outset of this chapter, the pope encouraged his energized audience to join him with these rousing words: "I would insist, let us not be afraid to say it: we want change, real change, structural change. This system is by now intolerable….Global interdependence calls for global answers to local problems. The globalization of hope…must replace the globalization of exclusion and indifference."[30] The realization that the economic status quo is unjust and unsustainable and requires deep reform has shaped many of the words and actions of Francis. His commitment to publicizing the need for deep structural change has brought him physically to many communities of the marginalized—out-of-the-way locales that find their way onto his chosen travel itineraries that consistently defy ordinary expectations for papal visits and leave many veteran Vatican watchers scratching their heads in disbelief. But it is here that the realities of economic exploitation, victimization, oppression, and inequity take on flesh and blood.

Francis's first overseas trip was the voyage to Brazil, in July of 2013, to attend the World Youth Day, but the pope made sure to visit parts of the host city, Rio de Janeiro, that tourists rarely seek out. The favela of Varginha is one of the poorest neighborhoods on the pope's native continent. As home to many thousands of people who are either unemployed or scraping by through gig work or day labor in the informal economy, Varginha is much like the *villas miserias* (or neighborhoods of ramshackle dwellings) to which the young Fr. Bergoglio, and later as Bishop and Cardinal Bergoglio, paid frequent pastoral visits, even when such direct service to the poor of Buenos Aires went far beyond his assigned or expected work. It was in Brazil, experiencing the proximity to humble people that had been his trademark in Argentina and which clearly energized him once again, that he started working into his less formal papal addresses one of his signature themes. Looking out over a throng of people with the most modest of economic prospects, he declared, "We must never allow the throw-away culture to enter our hearts, because we are brothers and sisters. No one is disposable!"[31]

This pattern whereby Francis schedules visits to neighborhoods of economically struggling people would repeat itself in many subsequent travels, but a few examples are especially illustrative of his special concern for worker justice and his use of structural analysis of economic realities. Each of the following three episodes displays a distinctive feature of his structural eye.

The Scampia District of Naples

On March 21, 2015, Francis visited the Scampia district of Naples, a hardscrabble neighborhood with a particularly challenging economic profile. Meeting with the large and demographically diverse audience he had invited to join him outdoors in a piazza named for the predecessor he had recently canonized, John Paul II, Francis began his remarks by naming and then analyzing the economic problem his audience knew all too well:

> ...the lack of employment for young people. Think: over 40 percent of young people aged 25 and younger are unemployed! This is serious! What does a young person do without a job? What future does he/she have? What path of life does he/she choose? This is a responsibility not only of the city, not only of the country, but of the world. Why? Because the economic system discards people....This lack of work robs us of dignity....We have to fight for...our dignity as citizens....This is the tragedy of our time. We must not remain silent.[32]

Providing a vivid illustration of his points, Francis proceeded to share the anecdote of his recent encounter with a young woman whose desperate search for any paying job she might find led her to accept a supposedly part-time position for a tourist agency—one in which the employer paid her at an unacceptably low level considering the long hours required (as many as eleven per day) and "without contributions for retirement or health care." Francis steps back from relating the details of the interchange to pin some revealing labels upon the plight of this woman. He refers to it as "partial-pay employment" and corruption, and further registers his exasperation by fulminating: "This is called slavery, this is called exploitation, this is not human, this is not Christian."

Ultimately, the structural diagnosis Francis offered during his visit to Scampia that morning is captured in a key word he inserted into his first sentence on that occasion: "I wanted to begin my visit to Naples here on the periphery." To be on the periphery of the modern economy transcends any merely geographical designation. The focus is not on location but on status, social standing, and resources. People on the periphery find themselves lacking in power in various ways. Their economic desperation often leads them to accept terms of employment that do not honor their human dignity, as Francis described vividly with the anecdote he shared. The goal of any genuine advocate of labor justice is to encourage the institutional reforms that might balance the scales of power; this explains the longstanding support of the Catholic Church and its leaders for labor unions and public policies that secure a living wage for all workers. As Francis suggested that day, institutions at all levels share the solemn responsibility to ensure fair work arrangements, so structural reform must be supported by all with a stake in the economy at the local, national, or global level.[33]

The Island of Sardinia

The part of Italy with the highest rates of unemployment in recent years is the island of Sardinia. Like Scampia, it is only a short distance from Rome, the cosmopolitan world capital of a prosperous and highly developed nation, but Sardinia is nonetheless accurately described as very much on the periphery of the world economy. Sardinia's top industry for many decades was bauxite mining, but a recent downturn in the market for that ore has thrown thousands of miners out of work and devasted the overall economy of the island. Francis surprised many with his resolve to visit this economically distressed corner of Italy so early in his papacy—it was his third voyage beyond Rome and transpired during just the sixth month of his papacy.

On September 22, 2013, Pope Francis began his pastoral visit in Cagliari, the principal city of Sardinia, by meeting with local workers, thereby signaling his ardent intent to direct the world's attention to work-related hardships on the island. He began his remarks on that occasion thus: "I want above all to express my closeness to you, especially to the situations of suffering; to the many young people out of work, to people on unemployment benefits." Global media coverage of his prolonged mingling with out-of-work miners that morning featured images of a splendid photo opportunity: in an eloquent gesture of solidarity, the pope donned the distinctive yellow protective helmet worn by bauxite miners on the job. The pope clearly identified very closely with the plight of those whose jobs were eliminated when mining corporations scaled back or ceased operations there and moved their jobs to lower-cost sites abroad. His remarks included an acknowledgment of the afront to the dignity of laid-off workers and an insightful, if compact, structural analysis of their plight. It was through no shortcoming of their own that these workers were suffering, he declared, but rather "it is the result of a global decision, of an economic system which leads to this tragedy; an economic system centered on an idol called 'money.'"[34]

Dhaka, Bangladesh

A third episode that displayed the structural eye of Francis regarding labor justice also unfolded in the early months of his papacy but involved even more imminent threats to the lives of workers. While the previous episodes gave Francis an opportunity to express his concerns about the availability of employment and the terms of unemployment, this one relates to the deadly consequences that ensue when working conditions become dangerous for laborers who are deprived of a voice in protecting their own safety. A tragic industrial accident took place on April 24, 2013, in Dhaka, Bangladesh, where an eight-story garment factory complex collapsed, killing over eleven hundred people and seriously injuring twice that number. The catastrophic structural failure of the Rama Plaza turned out to be no mere mishap of an unanticipated nature, but rather was caused by negligence on the part of factory owners who had ignored repeated advance warnings of cracked support beams and sagging building infrastructure.

This tragedy struck a mere six weeks after the election of Pope Francis and, although it occurred thousands of miles from Rome and in a nation with very few Catholics, it provoked in the new pope a most heartfelt reaction. While many world leaders sent perfunctory words of condolence to that traumatized South Asian nation, Francis exceeded ordinary protocols by extending especially heartfelt and repeated messages to the grieving members of the affected communities. He returned to the topic of the tragedy on multiple occasions, expressing his enduring personal sorrow, imploring people around the world to pray for the victims and pledging to visit the site of the horrible industrial accident to comfort the survivors when he could. Francis made sure that an eventual papal visit to South Asia in December of 2017 did indeed include a two-day stay in Bangladesh; when Francis addressed an interreligious peace meeting in Dhaka, he reminded his audience of "the common outpouring of grief, prayer and solidarity that accompanied the tragic collapse of Rama Plaza, which remains fresh in the minds of all."[35]

Most significant for present purposes was how the tragic turn of events prompted not only an expression of pastoral concern on the part of Francis but provided a poignant teaching moment regarding the callous structures of the global economy and indifference to the well-being of workers. Whenever he brought up the topic of the building disaster, for example, in his homily on the Feast of St. Joseph the Worker on May 1, 2013, exactly one week after the collapse, Francis shared his judgment that the workers were victims of more than the laws of physics.

Those killed and injured were victims of larger economic structures of exploitation that treated them as slaves whose lives were deemed less valuable than the prospect of squeezing out higher profits from their drudge work, which Francis referred to repeatedly as slave labor. When measures to prevent industrial accidents are judged too costly for penny-pinching owners and managers to bear, then the deadly risks of unsafe working conditions are tolerated without comment or second thought. The structural perspective informing the pope's assessment of the Rama Plaza disaster was clearly appreciated by a Catholic bishop from nearby India who attested:

> The pope's statement on the crash was widely acclaimed all over the world, particularly by economists and social activists. He called the job given to them 'modern-day slavery,' paying only a dollar or two a day. It was a hard-hitting critique of the management responsible for such practices.[36]

These three episodes by no means exhaust Francis's advocacy for the well-being of workers or for economic justice in general. The pope frequently expresses his solidarity with many groups of people who are victimized by adverse economic conditions, as general features of an inhospitable landscape, and greedy actors, more specifically, who engage in exploitative labor practices for their own benefit. But these three episodes are emblematic of Francis's commitment to the promotion of social change by publicizing great injustices and shedding abundant light upon situations that require redress and transformation. Francis does not present such advocacy as merely a personal project of his own. In *Evangelii Gaudium*, he commits the entire church to doing its part collectively "to eliminate the structural causes of poverty and to promote the integral development of the poor," specifically by fostering the "convictions and habits of solidarity [that], when they are put into practice, open the way to other structural transformations and make them possible" (nos. 188–89).

Conclusion

Francis's advocacy for social justice is a major component of his moral leadership of the Catholic Church. His words and actions in support of the disadvantaged are grounded in an overarching vision of social order—a picture of the universe that underscores the urgency of establishing not only economic justice but also peace and environmental sustainability, as the final three sections of this chapter describe. While the pope inherits the key elements of this social vision from previous Catholic social teaching, he also renews the tradition by adding updated lines of analysis, astute diagnoses of contemporary problems, and bold prescriptions for needed reforms—all with his own unique style and rhetoric infused with urgency and sensitive pastoral concern. His contributions to faith-based advocacy for justice consistently call attention to structural dimensions of the economy in ways that global audiences can hardly miss. Without pretending to possess all the answers to the bewildering complex problems of contemporary society, Francis displays a genius for encouraging and empowering people of all sorts to address injustices at the crucial level of root causes. By modeling astute social analysis and critique of distorted values and skewed structures, the pope inspires ever broader advocacy in pursuit of the social justice that has proved so elusive in our troubled world.

CONCLUSION

EXERCISING LEADERSHIP IN TURBULENT TIMES

THIS FINAL SECTION of our study of the moral leadership of Pope Francis affords an opportunity to step back somewhat from the "thick descriptions" of the pope's activities covered in the preceding chapters and to draw some pointed conclusions about the ethical significance of what he has accomplished and how. While previous chapters proposed certain sturdy generalizations about the leadership style and priorities of Francis, most of their content consisted of full portraits of the pope's initiatives, teachings, and activities. We observed in vivid detail many ways that the Argentinian pope has, with inspiring energy and shrewd strategy, placed his personal imprint on important developments in the Catholic Church throughout his papacy.

While genuine moral leaders—in religious organizations, business, government, and so on—invariably possess and advance a specific moral vision of their choosing, they rarely enjoy the prerogative of selecting the circumstances under which they come to exercise that leadership. Indeed, none of us exerts even a modicum of control over the historical moment into which we are born and participate in society. Ultimately, we can only play the hand of cards dealt to us. Note the phrase "turbulent times" that appears in the title of this concluding section. If Francis had his way, he surely would prefer to lead the church in a time characterized by harmony and stability, both within Catholicism and in the wider secular world. But, as we have seen, as pope he has found himself thrust into many crises and controversies—external ones such as an escalating environmental crisis, a time of heightened armed conflict, and a global economy replete with injustice, on the one hand, and internal church challenges that include the fallout from horrific clergy sex abuse, financial scandals, and the need for many urgent organizational reforms, on the other hand.

The point, however, is not to pity Francis for inheriting so many impossible situations over which he must preside, but rather to understand and assess how he has managed these many challenges. How well has the pope leveraged the available opportunities to exercise effective moral leadership? Has he taken advantage of the resources at his disposal to point the way successfully to a future of enhanced ethical attainments for the church he leads? How well has he navigated the challenges and opportunities to fulfill his mission as universal pastor, and even as Pontifex Maximus? While the jury is, of course, still out on each question, these closing pages of our study sketch a few of the most important items relevant to understanding the moral leadership of Francis that were not fully covered in the preceding chapters.

Facing Up to Stiff Opposition with Equanimity

In examining Francis, the ethicist, discerner, communicator, and advocate for social justice, the preceding chapters only occasionally noted opposition to Francis, within the church and beyond the Catholic community. Leaving aside for now secular political leaders who have sometimes presented the pope with significant diplomatic challenges (a few were indeed treated in chapter 3), it is no secret that Francis has consistently encountered staunch opposition from certain highly placed figures within his own religion. Chapter 1 noted the existence of detractors within the central bureaucracy of the church, where certain functionaries have issued objections—sometimes openly, but often in the form of anonymous gossip and whispers of disapproval—to his initiatives to reform and restructure the Roman Curia. The Italian journalist Marco Politi produced a book-length account of the opposition to Francis in the early months of his papacy—a potboiler of an ecclesiastical exposé with the provocative title *Pope Francis among the Wolves.*[1] With chapter titles like "The Enemies of Francis" and "The War of the Cardinals," Politi's account emphasizes the tenacious resistance to change in internal church practices and procedures that the reform-minded pope encountered immediately upon assuming office and signaling his intent to upend the status quo.

While none of this narrative is at all encouraging (nor should it surprise attentive readers of this study), a focus on Vatican "palace intrigue" reveals only a small fraction of what observers of the moral leadership of Francis most desire to know. Far more significant than the response of the pope to narrowly institutional opposition is his engagement with broader criticism within global Catholic culture, primarily on the level of theology and intellectual life. From within certain theological circles, detractors of the pope have taken Francis to task for specific positions he has voiced, for his support of certain mission priorities, frequently those most redolent of themes associated with the Second Vatican Council, and especially often and vehemently for his directives on liturgical practices.[2] While documenting each of these three items fully would require multiple volumes, suffice it to say that Francis has found himself in the crosshairs of a coterie of critics, most of whom fit the description of religious traditionalists.

Temperamentally given to nostalgia for previous cultural forms associated with Catholicism and ideologically aligned with forces that are suspicious of social reforms that would challenge the neoliberal economic order, the traditionalist opposition to Francis is concentrated in certain parts of the world. In his volume *Catholic Discordance: Neoconservatism vs. the Field Hospital Church of Pope Francis*, the scholar Massimo Borghesi identifies the United States and Italy as the hotbeds of the most fervent "poisonous backlash" against Francis and his initiatives.[3] Borghesi documents the recent rise of a movement of Catholic neoconservatives ("theocons"), who champion economic, social, and even military policies at sharp variance with inherited Catholic social teachings on peace, social justice, and global solidarity. Favoring sharply individualistic and radically free-market (even libertarian) values rather than authentic concern for the excluded and the common good in general, these neoconservatives assume the stance of "culture warriors," who present a combative social vision that clashes with the agenda of Francis in obvious ways. In their publications, journals, and think tanks, these commentators are quite open in their sharp criticism of the pope and other church leaders with whom they disagree with marked animosity and deliberate divisiveness.[4]

There is, of course, room for legitimate disagreement within church circles regarding which secular public policies advance the core values of neighbor love and constructive social outreach that are the starting points of any Christian response to the need for proper social order. Those who find the "theocon" movement objectionable point to both the polarizing ideologically driven content and the excessively harsh tone of these Catholic intellectuals. Defenders of Francis fault this combative movement for its misplaced nostalgia for an order, both within Catholicism and in the wider arena of secular society, that long ignored such enduring injustices as racial and gender exclusions, unconscionable economic disparities, and the perpetuation of unaccountable power in a sharply stratified society. The neoconservatives in this movement are certainly more eager to assert a particular version of Catholic identity they favor than they are to engage a pluralistic global society with the values of mercy, inclusion, and dialogue that we have seen Francis consistently advancing.

Regardless of the precise contours and long-term implications of these disagreements, the noteworthy takeaway regarding key qualities of moral leadership is the remarkable equanimity Francis displays in the face of such sharp opposition, whether in Italy, the United States, or elsewhere. On many occasions, Francis has assured interviewers that he is not at all worried about the possibility of schism or civil war within the church due to the opposition of traditionalists, whether based on their ideological objections to his leadership or on matters relating to allowable liturgical forms or even doctrinal disagreements.[5] While nobody relishes a place in the crosshairs of detractors or having a veritable target on one's back, Francis seems genuinely unfazed by the opposition, or at least so well adjusted to the challenges that he does not grant his opponents much space within his brain. Perhaps this display of equanimity can be attributed to the future pope's experience in handling prior tests and controversies, some of which involved life-or-death stakes. Recall that Fr. Bergoglio served as provincial superior of the Jesuits in Argentina (1973–79) while his nation was going through severe political upheavals that included the "Dirty War" that killed thousands in a spasm of brutal repression after a military coup. Bergoglio faced excruciatingly difficult circumstances throughout these years, witnessing violence firsthand and enduring the assassinations of colleagues. An especially trying episode unfolded when some Jesuits under his care were captured and jailed because their pastoral work among the poor was deemed subversive. The future pope eventually negotiated their release from prison by appealing to the military junta, for which good deed he was accused of collaboration and complicity with the generals.

Francis is thus familiar with the experience of being a leader placed in a political vice and facing up to divisive forces. He knows that the work of a true leader is not a popularity contest, and that some criticism may even be a sign indicating a leader's effectiveness and successful engagement with weighty issues. Francis is neither oblivious to the divisiveness around him nor indifferent to the regrettable acrimony but has somehow found a way to proceed with his leadership agenda, nonetheless. While he never sought to become a lightning rod for opposition, neither will he be deterred from his goals by the mere existence of a coterie of detractors.

Among his other leadership skills, then, the pope has clearly appropriated a lesson identified near the end of chapter 2 of this study: avoiding distractions is a valuable principle of discernment in the Ignatian tradition. Francis simply refuses to be distracted from the pursuit of his papal priorities. Opposition is surely a stressor but has not been a serious drag on the success of his papacy. Even the best leaders seldom enjoy universal acclaim or a unanimous consensus of support, so they invariably learn how to endure, without undue upset, challenges to their authority from followers with split (or absent) loyalties. The opposition to Francis may not be (or perdure as) a situation of utter impasse, but even if the tensions between Francis and certain traditionalists remain a matter of unbridgeable differences, the mission of the church must go on regardless.

Perennial Leadership Tasks That Present Additional Challenges

If the opposition of Catholic traditionalists represents an across-the-board rejection by some of Francis's leadership on ideological and theological grounds, other critics have objected on occasion to rather more specific actions and discrete strategies pursued by the pope. Many of the most fraught controversies involve the diplomatic interactions between Francis and heads of state and their governments. This pattern whereby criticism of this religious leader arises when he deals with political leaders is most pronounced when those rulers are authoritarians who wield unaccountable dictatorial power. Such interactions raise recurring ethical dilemmas for moral leaders like Pope Francis. Should he shun all heads of state whose regimes are credibly accused of human rights violations? Is it perhaps preferable to engage them in constructive ways that might foster better behavior and superior ethical outcomes in the long term?

Vatican watchers have witnessed several high-profile occasions when Francis was subjected to sharp criticism when he visited or hosted strongmen with a reputation for abusing minority groups within their borders. Chapter 3 mentioned his closely scrutinized encounters with authoritarians such as Abdel Fattah el-Sisi in Egypt and Viktor Orbán in Hungary. Furthermore, we may ask whether Francis should have visited Myanmar in 2017, given that government's well-documented oppression of the Rohingya minority. If the visit itself was morally acceptable, should Francis have spoken more forthrightly and frequently during that visit about the government's human rights violations, or would that perhaps have exceeded the bounds of prudence and potentially endangered both the Rohingya and that nation's small Catholic community? Should Francis more often signal his opposition to oppressive regimes by meeting with dissident groups? (He was accused of snubbing a Cuban dissident group while visiting Havana in 2015 and of failing to support Nicaraguan dissidents against the Ortega regime, which has conducted a crackdown that borders on wholesale persecution of the Catholic Church.)[6] The complexities of situations like these are daunting indeed; it is seldom clear when assuming a confrontational position is the best course of action for any religious leader.

Of course, wartime raises the stakes even higher regarding papal strategy for dealing with bloodthirsty dictators. One reliable observation looms over any analysis of the possibilities and constraints of moral leadership in such cases: history has not been kind to popes who maintained a general policy of silence when military aggression comes into play. Pius XI has been roundly criticized for turning a blind eye to the growing Nazi threat during the late 1930s that would eventually blossom into the full-blown horrors of the Holocaust. Pope Pius XII, who succeeded him in 1939, has even been called "Hitler's Pope" for his alleged complicity in the atrocities of the World War II era. Even though historians readily document a highly nuanced picture—both popes countered the Nazis in numerous ways, covert and overt in nature.[7]—these and other historical episodes constitute cautionary tales for any religious leader claiming the mantle of moral leader.

The actions of Francis since the Russian invasion of Ukraine in February of 2022 present the latest round of ethical challenges and potential second-guessing regarding the responses of Catholic leaders. Is the highest priority for the pope to seize the moral high ground, brook no compromises and denounce aggressors forthrightly by name? Or is the more valuable contribution of a pope who is aspiring to provide global moral leadership to position himself to play a potential role as an eventual mediator of conflict (the path Francis has taken up to the point of this writing by denouncing the invasion but not the invader by name)? Recall the final case study of chapter 3, situating the dealings of Francis with Russia's Vladimir Putin as among the most difficult of diplomatic relationships that the pope must manage. Criticism of this, or any, pope for his chosen diplomatic strategy is certainly understandable but not necessarily always justified. Such delicate dilemmas that vex the practice of religious leadership reprise the perennial debate between the merits of idealism and pragmatic realism, each of which may be employed to preserve certain important values, but neither of which guarantees the attainment of all such values in an imperfect world.

It is no surprise that outsiders second-guess popes on many such occasions; it is quite remarkable that Francis has been that rare global leader willing to admit that some of his earlier actions were mistaken. The premier occasion of such a reversal involves Francis's dealings with the bishops of Chile, a nation that was roiled by an extended series of allegations of clergy sex abuse and cover up at the very time that Francis visited in January of 2018. At first, Francis issued a defense of a bishop (Juan Barros of Osorno), who had been accused of covering up the offenses of a notorious abuser (Fr. Fernando Karadima). But when a fuller and more accurate account of the situation eventually reached the pope, he issued a sweeping apology and even demanded resignation letters from all Chile's bishops, in the end accepting the resignations of several bishops proven to be complicit in the cover up and disinformation campaign.[8]

It is, of course, much to the credit of any leader to be willing to admit and face up to mistakes, especially when "coming clean" in this way necessitates admitting such systemic corruption within one's own organization. The deportment of Francis during the

Chile episode confirms what we have already seen in the coverage within our first chapter of the apologies to the Indigenous peoples of Canada: that the moral leadership of Francis includes a willingness to face up forthrightly to the past failures of the church. Rather than hiding behind such excuses as "only a few bad apples are responsible for all the trouble," Francis acknowledges the deep structural dimensions of such abuses and acts with firm resolve to root out and correct the corruption, however uncomfortable that process may make other participants and observers.

Distinctive Aspects of Papal Moral Leadership

As acknowledged at the outset of this chapter, it is the rare leader who has much say about the circumstances and contexts they inherit when they assume leadership of any organization. Most who come into high office must settle for navigating through conditions they did not select or determine. Men elected pope fit this pattern: they find themselves muddling through challenges and situations that are by no means of their own choosing. A new pope is not like the typical political candidate (who actively campaigned for the support of voters) or corporate executive (who applied for a leadership post in a business firm) regarding how he arrives in office or even how he starts off. There is no provision before or after a papal election for the winner to receive supervised on-the-job training; it is unlikely that a newly elected pope has enjoyed the opportunity to develop an elaborate agenda for leadership before assuming office. So, in evaluating the moral leadership of any pope, it is wise to keep in mind at least these three distinctive elements of this particular leadership position: (1) the new pope is a man who assumes the top office in his organization later in life than most leaders; (2) often to his great surprise; and (3) usually without the benefit of the usual advance planning to develop a detailed leadership agenda.

The content of these reminders may seem like serious handicaps to effectiveness and may even lower our expectations of what any pope can ever accomplish. But these conditions need not constitute grave drags on papal efficacy. Rather, these distinctive conditions of papal office simply introduce a certain structure to the enterprise of papal moral leadership, a process that includes at least three stages. First, a newly elected pope must spend the early months of his papacy *developing* his moral agenda; second, he must make strenuous efforts to *communicate* his agenda of key initiatives to the worldwide Catholic community; and third, sometime later in his papacy he must deliberately return to each item to *consolidate* the achievement of the agenda.

The attentive reader will recognize in the activities of Francis (as described in the foregoing chapters of this study) evidence of each of these stages. Recall that Francis spent months after his election in March of 2013 largely confined to Rome, as he studied closely the ethical challenges facing him, planned his detailed response, and designed his core proposals. Those were valuable months during which the ideas of Francis were percolating with intensity, as he sorted out all the relevant considerations and needs of the church in prayerful discernment. His deliberately infrequent travels that year, especially the July visits to Lampedusa and then to World Youth Day in Brazil, afforded him valuable opportunities to hone and rehearse his message of various social concerns, as described throughout this study. The second stage, the announcement of the moral agenda, was accomplished with the publication of *Evangelii Gaudium* in November of 2013, the key initial teaching document that Francis wrote and promulgated to communicate his overall agenda of evangelization and church reform. Much of this study has been devoted to documenting the "rollout phase" of the various initiatives that flowed from the vision articulated in that programmatic early document. Subsequent teaching documents, papal travels, the convening of worldwide synods, and organizational reform and updating were all part of the unfolding of further aspects of this moral agenda, with elements that fit into the *ad intra* and *ad extra* categories we have seen.

It is, of course, hard to pinpoint with precision when the rollout phase gave way to the consolidation phrase in Francis's papacy, but certain signs of this transition have cropped up from time to time.[9] One plausible interpretation identifies the start of the global pandemic in March of 2020 as the moment when Francis became conscious of the need to consolidate the many initiatives that he had introduced piecemeal thus far. In a variety of deliberate ways, he acted upon this impulse to formalize the changes he had long sought and pursued with tenaciousness. For example, the publication of the social encyclical *Fratelli Tutti* in October of 2020 gave Francis the opportunity to pull together many strands of his social teachings over the previous seven years and to weave together such signature themes as mercy, dialogue, encounter, and reconciliation into a unified whole. Scholars evaluating that text noted a "greatest hits of the pope" feature to its succession of topics and analysis.

Several of the contentious internal church reforms (regarding finances, liturgy, organizational structures, and so on) that Francis had initiated in earlier years were formalized in the course of 2022, through the promulgation of important ecclesiastical documents, such as *Praedicate Evangelium*, *Pascite Gregem Dei*, and two apostolic letters on the liturgy, *Desiderio Desideravi* and *Traditionis Custodes*.[10] This is precisely what the stage of consolidation looks like, as a reform-minded pope "fills in the details" regarding the implementation of his agenda and equips the church with the resources and guidelines it will need to carry forward important reforms into a future of promise. For Francis, one capstone of these forward-looking developments is his supervision of a multiyear synod process, to run through the end of 2024, to focus on the contours of a church that exhibits the quality of synodality itself.

This mention of the future of the church raises a final facet of moral leadership to consider in our study of Pope Francis: the value of succession planning. Here again, the situations facing popes who lead the Roman Catholic Church are markedly different from those encountered by leaders of most other organizations. A corporate leader or political officeholder approaching the end of a term in office is often expected to participate in a planning process that will select a successor, or at least identify promising candidates. Much advance legwork is expected, and the timelines are usually predetermined, but, of course, popes are elected to a life term and ordinarily hold office until their natural death. The voluntary resignation of Benedict XVI in February of 2013 was the first since that of Gregory XII in 1415. All potential successors (according to a pattern that stretches back even further) have been members of the College of Cardinals, that body of about 130 high church officials who are chosen by sitting popes and who vote (if they are under age eighty) in a conclave for the next pope.

The contours of papal succession, then, mean that Francis has a rather limited toolkit for providing future leadership resources to the church. His main contribution is the creation of cardinals, who will participate in a future conclave, whether this comes after the resignation or the death of Francis. The final pages of chapter 1 identified a desire for broader geographic representation in the College of Cardinals as one of the priorities of Francis to improve the governance of the church and to serve better its peripheries. But, of course, the identities and personal qualities of those cardinals are at least as important as where they happen to live and work. While Francis cannot determine his successor, he can at least continue to enrich the College of Cardinals with men who share much of his moral vision and dedication to excellent ethical leadership. All Catholics will join Francis in trusting the Holy Spirit to guide one of these worthy candidates into the Chair of St. Peter, where he may lead the church into a promising future of further moral achievements.

NOTES

Introduction

1. Chris Lowney, *Pope Francis: Why He Leads the Way He Leads: Lessons from the First Jesuit Pope* (Chicago: Loyola Press, 2013).

2. Chris Lowney, *Heroic Leadership: Best Practices from a 450-Year-Old Company that Changed the World* (Chicago: Loyola Press, 2003).

3. Chris Lowney, *Everyone Leads: How to Revitalize the Catholic Church* (Lanham, MD: Rowman & Littlefield, 2017).

4. As just one example: a widely recognized principle of excellent presiding at liturgies is that priest-presiders should communicate the quality of vulnerability while celebrating the holy Mass. This recommendation regarding optimal style of ministerial presence surely applies to all ministries, ordained as well as lay.

5. For details of the announcement of the postponement of this papal voyage, see Gerard O'Connell, "Pope Francis Apologizes for Cancelling Trips to Congo and South Sudan," *America Magazine*, June 12, 2022, https://www.americamagazine.org/faith/2022/06/12/pope-francis-congo-south-sudan-ukraine-243140.

6. All quotes from the homily of Pope Francis in St. Peter's Square on March 19, 2013, are taken from the text appearing on the website of the Holy See. See https://www.vatican.va/content/francesco/en/homilies/2013/documents/papa-francesco_20130319_omelia-inizio-pontificato.html.

7. One account of the inaugural Mass of Pope Francis that expands on this claim is Joshua J. McElwee, "Francis at Inaugural

Mass: Pope Must Be Servant, 'Inspired by Lowly.'" *National Catholic Reporter*, March 19, 2013, https://www.ncronline.org/news/vatican/francis-inaugural-mass-pope-must-be-servant-inspired-lowly.

Chapter 1

1. The three social encyclicals of John Paul II are *Laborem Exercens* (1981), *Sollicitudo Rei Socialis* (1987), and *Centesimus Annus* (1991).

2. It is true that Francis made a small alteration to no. 2367 of the *Catechism of the Catholic Church* to strengthen the church's opposition to capital punishment. The 2018 insertion deems the death penalty "inadmissible" now for various enumerated reasons. In addition, some observers have interpreted Francis's repeated gestures of welcome and pastoral encouragement to members of the LGBTQ community as constituting something of a doctrinal change. In the absence of a formal doctrinal statement regarding a new church stance toward matters of sexual identity, however, this remains a matter of reading between the lines. Pastoral strategies are not synonymous with doctrinal positions on moral matters.

3. Francis, *Amoris Laetitia*: Apostolic Exhortation on Love in the Family, March 19, 2016, no. 37, https://www.vatican.va/content/francesco/en/apost_exhortations/documents/papa-francesco_esortazione-ap_20160319_amoris-laetitia.html.

4. Part of the agenda taken up by Pope John Paul II in *Veritatis Splendor* was to uphold objective moral truths found in natural law. Toward this end, he registered serious concerns regarding certain aspects of the school of thought known as proportionalism. Here, John Paul concurs with the criticism that excessively consequentialist moral methodologies are objectionable.

5. See the volume containing the interview by Antonio Spadaro, SJ, *A Big Heart Open to God: A Conversation with Pope Francis* (New York: America Press and HarperCollins Publishers, 2013). The same English translation of the transcription of this twelve-thousand-word interview was published as the September 30, 2013, edition of *America Magazine* 209, no. 8.

6. Spadaro, *Big Heart*, 34.

7. All quotations in this paragraph are found in Spadaro, *Big Heart*, 35.

8. The quoted phrases appear throughout the section titled "The Church as Field Hospital," which can be found in Spadaro, *Big Heart*, 30–35. It is noteworthy that many of the phrases that Francis invoked in this interview would also appear in his first major teaching document, the apostolic exhortation *Evangelii Gaudium* ("The Joy of the Gospel"), November 24, 2013, https://www.vatican.va/content/francesco/en/apost_exhortations/documents/papa-francesco_esortazione-ap_20131124_evangelii-gaudium.html.

9. There is no dearth of prominent critics of Francis, both within and beyond the church community itself and in various parts of the world. For an informative account of who these detractors are and what motivates them, see "Mercy and Its Discontents," in Austen Ivereigh, *Wounded Shepherd: Pope Francis and His Struggle to Convert the Catholic Church* (New York: Henry Holt and Company, 2019), 277–314.

10. Christopher Lamb, *The Outsider: Pope Francis and His Battle to Reform the Church* (Maryknoll, NY: Orbis Books, 2020), 147–67.

11. Francis, *Laudato Si'*: Encyclical on Care for Our Common Home, May 24, 2015, https://www.vatican.va/content/francesco/en/encyclicals/documents/papa-francesco_20150524_enciclica-laudato-si.html.

12. See *Laudato Si'*, nos. 122–23 and *Evangelii Gaudium*, no. 80. The latter draws a distinction between two varieties of relativism, doctrinal and practical—each of which Francis calls his readers to resist. The latter goes further in lamenting the effects of the culture of relativism that is so prevalent today.

13. For details regarding this interview, see Austen Ivereigh, *The Great Reformer: Francis and the Making of a Radical Pope* (New York: Henry Holt and Company, 2014), 43.

14. The July 2013 press conference was widely reported in global media, even beyond the news outlets represented aboard the papal airplane that day. Francis elaborated on the thinking behind his airborne comments during his interview with Fr. Spadaro the following month.

15. This eighteen-minute TED talk, recorded privately in the pope's study and shared on video in late April of 2017, is in Italian but English subtitles are available in this version, accessed on June 27, 2022, https://www.youtube.com/watch?v=36zrJfAFcuc.

16. The quoted phrase is the subtitle of Decree 4 ("Our Mission Today") of the Documents of the 32nd General Congregation, a worldwide Jesuit legislative gathering attended by Bergoglio when he was Provincial Superior of the Jesuits of Argentina. See *Documents of the 31st and 32nd General Congregations of the Society of Jesus* (St. Louis: Institute of Jesuit Sources, 1977), 411.

17. The message of *Traditionis Custodes* was reaffirmed and expanded by Francis in his apostolic letter *Desiderio Desideravi*, a profound reflection on the underlying principles of the liturgical reform of Vatican II. For these two liturgical reform documents, see *Traditionis Custodes*: Apostolic Letter on the Use of the Liturgy Prior to the Reform of 1970, July 16, 2021, https://www.vatican.va/content/francesco/en/motu_proprio/documents/20210716-motu-proprio-traditionis-custodes.html; and *Desiderio Desideravi*: Apostolic Letter on the Liturgical Formation of the People of God, June 29, 2022, https://www.vatican.va/content/francesco/en/apost_letters/documents/20220629-lettera-ap-desiderio-desideravi.html.

18. Perhaps the most complete account of these events comes from veteran Vatican watcher Gerard O'Connell, *The Election of Pope Francis: An Inside Account of the Conclave that Changed History* (Maryknoll, NY: Orbis Books, 2019). In this volume, O'Connell registers some wonderment that his fellow journalists considered Bergoglio such a "dark horse" papal candidate in 2013, especially since he had reportedly received the second-most votes among the electors in the immediately previous (April 2005) conclave that elected Benedict XVI. On both occasions, however, Cardinal Bergoglio was considered the outsider who garnered support due to the expectation that he would bring greater energy for substantial church reform than other, initially more prominent candidates.

19. *Spiritual Exercises of St. Ignatius Loyola*, no. 230. Translations of this phrase vary slightly in the numerous available editions of this classic work of spirituality. This appears in the edition used throughout this volume: David L. Fleming SJ, *The Spiritual Exercises of St. Ignatius: A Literal Translation and A Contemporary Reading* (St. Louis: Institute of Jesuit Sources, 1978), 138.

20. Francis, apostolic letter *Vos Estis Lux Mundi*, May 7, 2019, https://www.vatican.va/content/francesco/en/motu_proprio/documents/papa-francesco-motu-proprio-20190507_vos-estis-lux-mundi.html.

21. Francis, apostolic constitution *Pascite Gregem Dei*, May 23, 2021, https://www.vatican.va/content/francesco/en/apost_constitutions/documents/papa-francesco_costituzione-ap_20210523_pascite-gregem-dei.html.

22. For details, see Ivereigh, "Epilogue: The Great Reform," in *Great Reformer*, especially 376; and John L. Allen Jr., "God and Mammon: Reforming the Vatican's Finances," in *The Francis Miracle: Inside the Transformation of the Pope and the Church* (New York: Time Books, 2015), 89–114.

23. The most prominent of these was the apostolic letter "Regarding Provisions on Transparency in the Management of Public Finances," April 26, 2021, https://www.vatican.va/content/francesco/en/motu_proprio/documents/papa-francesco-motu-proprio-20210426_trasparenza-finanzapubblica.html.

24. For one instance of typical coverage of this initiative in the secular media, see Elisabetta Povoledo, "Pope Issues Sweeping Decree Aimed at Fighting Corruption at Top Levels of the Church," *New York Times*, April 30, 2021, A12.

25. Pope Paul VI, in the wake of Vatican II, had introduced certain curial reforms with his 1967 apostolic constitution, *Regimini Ecclesia Universae*. John Paul II also tried his hand at modest curial reorganization with the 1988 apostolic constitution, *Pastor Bonus*. To find the only two previous episodes of formal curia reform attempted via apostolic constitutions, one needs to go back to 1908 (under Pius X) and 1588 (under Sixtus V).

26. Junno Arocho Esteves, "In New Interview, Pope Francis Says Becoming Pope Made Him Less Rigid and More Merciful," *America Magazine*, July 1, 2022, https://www.americamagazine.org/faith/2022/07/01/pope-francis-telam-interview-243290?utm.

27. This phrase appears in the preamble of Francis's apostolic constitution *Praedicate Evangelium* ("On the Roman Curia and Its Service to the Church in the World"), no. 4, March 19, 2022, https://www.vatican.va/content/francesco/en/apost_constitutions/documents/20220319-costituzione-ap-praedicate-evangelium.html.

28. One well-reasoned early assessment of the reorganization of the Roman Curia appears in Thomas Reese, "Pope Francis' Reforms to Church Governance Are Unlike Any Since Vatican II," *National Catholic Reporter*, July 15, 2022, https://www.ncronline.org/news/opinion/pope-francis-reforms-church-governance-are-unlike-any-vatican-ii.

29. See, for example, Francis's lofty praise for the irreplaceable church-supporting work of women in one important region (Amazonia) of his native continent of South America in the post-synodal apostolic exhortation *Querida Amazonia* ("The Beloved Amazon"), nos. 99–103, February 2, 2020, https://www.vatican.va/content/francesco/en/apost_exhortations/documents/papa-francesco_esortazione-ap_20200202_querida-amazonia.html.

30. For details of this progress as of mid-2022, see Cindy Wooden, "Pope Francis to Give Women a Role in Choosing Bishops," *America Magazine*, July 6, 2022, https://www.americamagazine.org/faith/2022/07/06/pope-francis-women-bishops-243306?utm.

31. Three examples (all from the early months of 2021) of Francis's appointments of women to posts previously held only by men: Sr. Nathalie Becquart to the position of Under Secretary at the Vatican's synod of bishops; Catia Summaria to the position of prosecutor in the Vatican Court of Appeal; and Sr. Nuria Calduch-Benages to the position of Secretary of the Pontifical Biblical Commission.

32. Gaia Pianigiani, "For the First Time, the Pope Names Women to the Office to Help Select Bishops," *New York Times*, July 14, 2022, A5.

33. Details of all these developments appear in Rita Ferrone, "A Wonderful Complexity: What Does Instituting Women in Ministries Really Mean?" *Commonweal*, April 2022, 10–13.

34. Quoted in Carol Glatz, "Abuse Survivor Says Pope Told Him God Loves Him the Way He Is," *National Catholic Reporter*, May 22, 2018, https://www.ncronline.org/news/vatican/abuse-survivor-says-pope-told-him-god-loves-him-way-he.

35. For details of several such episodes, see Claire Giangravé, "This Pride Month, Catholic Church Shows Clear, If Subtle, Shifts towards LGBTQ Welcome," *National Catholic Reporter*, June 28, 2022, https://www.ncronline.org/news/vatican/pride-month-catholic-church-shows-clear-if-subtle-shifts-toward-lgbtq-welcome.

36. James Martin, SJ, *Building a Bridge: How the Catholic Church and the LGBT Community Can Enter into a Relationship of Respect, Compassion, and Sensitivity*, rev. and exp. ed. (New York: HarperCollins Publishers, 2018). For details of the July 20, 2022, letter that Francis wrote to Fr. Martin commending the conference on LGBTQ ministries he had organized the previous month at Fordham University, see the unsigned news story "In New Letter to Outreach, Pope Francis Calls Catholics to Foster a Culture of Encounter," August 2,

2022, on the "Outreach" section of the website of *America Magazine*, https://outreach.faith/2022/08/in-new-letter-to-outreach-pope-francis-calls-catholics-to-foster-a-culture-of-encounter/.

37. Details of these events appear in Heidi Schlumpf, "The Pope's Openness to LGBT Catholics Hits a Wall," CNN.com, March 15, 2021, https://www.cnn.com/2021/03/15/opinions/pope-ruling-on-lgbtq-catholics-schlumpf.

38. Pope Paul VI set the target number at 120, but subsequent years have routinely witnessed numbers in the 130s.

39. For further details and statistics on the cardinal selections of Francis, see Tom Reese, SJ, "Pope Francis Is Remaking the College of Cardinals—and Setting the Stage for the Eventual Election of His Successor," *America Magazine*, May 31, 2022, https://www.americamagazine.org/faith/2022/05/31/pope-francis-cardinals-election-243083?utm.

40. Francis, *Gaudete et Exsultate*: Apostolic Exhortation on the Call to Holiness in Today's World, March 19, 2018, https://www.vatican.va/content/francesco/en/apost_exhortations/documents/papa-francesco_esortazione-ap_20180319_gaudete-et-exsultate.html.

41. Daniel J. Daly, *The Structures of Virtue and Vice* (Washington, DC: Georgetown University Press, 2021), 107–16.

Chapter 2

1. Indeed, the exchange that appears on the very first page of the August 2013 interview between Francis and Antonio Spadaro, SJ, referenced in the previous chapter, features precisely this admission. In response to Spadaro's initial question "Who is Jorge Mario Bergoglio?" the new pope responded, "I am a sinner. This is the most accurate definition. It is not a figure of speech, a literary genre. I am a sinner." Spadaro, *Big Heart*, 7.

2. Unfortunately, very few of Bergoglio's early writings on spirituality have been translated into English. For a sampling of these, and a comprehensive bibliographical listing through 2012, see these two consecutive issues of a premier spiritual resource sponsored by the Society of Jesus in North America: "Jorge Mario Bergoglio: Writings on Jesuit Spirituality I and II," ed. and trans.

Philip Endean, SJ, *Studies in the Spirituality of Jesuits* 45, nos. 3 and 4 (autumn and winter 2013).

3. John W. O'Malley, SJ, has written extensively about these developments in church history. For a recent and highly accessible account, from which the three quoted phrases in this paragraph are taken, see his "Papal Upgrades: How Popes Became So Powerful—and can Pope Francis Reverse the Trend?" *America Magazine*, July/August 2022, 38–41. The same article appears at https://www.americamagazine.org/faith/2022/06/30/papal-authority-omalley-pope-francis-243220.

4. Allan Figueroa Deck, SJ, analyzes Francis's preference for the more pastoral-sounding title in several sections of his aptly named volume *Francis, Bishop of Rome: The Gospel for the Third Millennium* (Mahwah, NJ: Paulist Press, 2016).

5. The analysis here relies on the highly regarded version of these texts appearing in Fleming, SJ, *Spiritual Exercises*.

6. For a report on one prominent example of the pope's tendency to attribute human (and especially ecclesial) discord to the devil, see Cindy Wooden, "Pope Francis: Liturgy Wars Are the Work of the Devil," May 9, 2022, *America Magazine*, https://www.americamagazine.org/faith/2022/05/09/pope-francis-latin-mass-242953.

7. The preliminary "annotations" (the first twenty short sections) of the *Spiritual Exercises* illustrate these tendencies of Ignatius to issue strong challenges to the retreatants who turn to him for spiritual guidance. One example is no. 13, where he issues a clear warning against temptations of several varieties, including laziness and self-deception. Pope Francis has issued similar stern admonitions (though in public, spoken forums) to groups of Vatican officials in the context of spiritual exhortations, most famously in a series of annual Advent reflections.

8. Among the many occasions when Francis treats discernment, a brief section of his apostolic letter *Gaudete et Exsultate* stands out as an extraordinarily straightforward and accessible account of the importance and dynamics of the process. He accomplishes much in just a few pages, boiling down the key elements of discernment to a handful of spiritual principles such as eliciting generous openness to divine promptings through prayer and even through close listening to the wise counsel of others. See nos. 166–75 of *Gaudete et Exsultate* (as above).

9. *Amoris Laetitia* is dated March 19, 2016, although it was not available until April 8, 2016.

10. The observations and characterizations in this and the preceding paragraph appear in an insightful feature-length assessment of the two synods: Michael J. O'Loughlin, "Walking with Peter: A Confident Pope Sets a New Example for Governing the Church," *America Magazine*, January 23, 2017, 27–33. Among those cited as a source of commentary is Cardinal Joseph Tobin, a veteran of five previous synod meetings.

11. The full text of each *relatio synodis* is available on the Vatican website, under documents of the Roman Curia. The 2015 report was posted on October 24, 2015, at https://www.vatican.va/roman_curia/synod/documents/rc_synod_doc_20151026_relazione-finale-xiv-assemblea_en.html.

12. Although it required six years to come to fruition, this proposal of Francis to improve the process of marriage preparation for engaged Catholic couples led to the announcement (by the Dicastery for Laity, the Family and Life) of a program called "Catechumenal Itineraries for Married Life," in a document released June 15, 2022. See Cindy Wooden, "Citing 'Superficial' Marriage Prep, Pope Francis Calls for Yearlong Marriage Program for Engaged Couples," June 16, 2022, *America Magazine*, https://www.americamagazine.org/faith/2022/06/16/marriage-prep-revamp-243173.

13. An insightful early survey of reactions to the document (including both some of these criticisms and much positive reception in several countries) appears in James F. Keenan, SJ, "Receiving *Amoris Laetitia*," *Theological Studies* 78, no. 1 (2017): 193–212.

14. In fact, the substance of this new approach to the pastoral applications described does not really appear in the main text of *Amoris Laetitia* but is "buried in the footnotes" to chapter 8. Footnote 351 is the main locus (where eventual admission to Eucharist is explicitly mentioned as a possibility), along with supporting treatment in footnotes 329, 336, 344, 348, and 364. Interestingly, of the document's 391 footnotes, these 6 are almost all the ones that contain commentary of any sort, beyond merely providing source information for citations.

15. Excellent analysis of the balance of continuity and newness of this document in light of previous teachings appears in Gerald O'Collins, SJ, "The Joy of Love (*Amoris Laetitia*): The Papal Exhortation in Its Context," *Theological Studies* 77, no. 4 (2016): 905–21.

16. Helpful commentary regarding these points on annulments (and about the reception of *Amoris Laetitia* in general) appears in Julie Hanlon Rubio, "The Newness of *Amoris Laetitia*: Mercy and Truth, Truth and Mercy," in *Amoris Laetitia: A New Momentum for Moral Formation and Pastoral Practice*, ed. Grant Gallicho and James F. Keenan, SJ (Mahwah, NJ: Paulist Press, 2018), 61–69.

17. The guiding principle of Francis in this regard is stated in footnote 351 of *Amoris Laetitia*, which quotes his earlier document *Evangelii Gaudium* to this effect: "The Eucharist is not a prize for the perfect, but a powerful medicine and nourishment for the weak."

18. For analysis of this distinction and how it relates to the notion of dissent in the church, see Peter Folan, SJ, "Can Catholics Dissent from Pope Francis's Teaching on the Family? Wrong Question," *America Magazine*, April 17, 2017, 36–37.

19. The post-synodal exhortation does, however, contain valuable material touching on leadership qualities. See *Christus Vivit* ("Christ Is Alive: To Young People and to the Entire People of God"), March 25, 2019, https://www.vatican.va/content/francesco/en/apost_exhortations/documents/papa-francesco_esortazione-ap_20190325_christus-vivit.html.

20. Francis, *Querida Amazonia*.

21. The brief "Synod Profile" document was posted on the Vatican website for the worldwide synod of bishops on March 14, 2019, https://www.vatican.va/roman_curia/synod/documents/rc_synod_doc_20190314_profilo_en.html.

22. This principle of avoiding distraction in prayer motivated Ignatius to include in the Jesuit *Constitutions* (see no. 583) certain recommendations for superiors to regulate aspects of the prayer of their charges, for example setting appropriate times and duration of prayer so that they will not exceed advisable limits or otherwise be distracted by too many potential foci. When the likelihood of distraction is not high, the "discretion of the individual" is the norm.

23. The full text of the *relatio synodi* of October 26, 2019, appears at https://www.vatican.va/roman_curia/synod/documents/rc_synod_doc_20191026_sinodo-amazzonia_en.html.

24. For this and other details of the final report of the synod, see Gerard O'Connell and Luke Hansen, SJ, "Synod Votes to Ordain Married Men, and to Protect Amazon's Indigenous Peoples and Rain Forests," *America Magazine*, October 26, 2019, https://www

.americamagazine.org/faith/2019/10/26/synod-votes-ordain-married-men-and-protect-amazons-indigenous-peoples-and.

25. It is important to note that the Catholic Church comprises twenty-three different rites, and that most of them (including several Eastern Rite Catholic communities, such as the Maronite Rite) make at least some provision for priests to be married. Still, by far the largest is the Latin Rite, which has, since the eleventh century, enforced the discipline of celibacy for ordained priests. Rare exceptions have been made, such as recent acceptance into Roman Catholic ordained ministry of Anglican or Episcopalian priests who were already married at the time of their conversion and application to serve in priestly ministry. Pope John Paul II introduced this pastoral provision to accommodate the special circumstances of such converts.

26. This detail, and much valuable further analysis of the Pan-Amazon Synod, appears in Austen Ivereigh, "Exposing the Spirits: What the Amazon Synod Decided and What It Revealed," *Commonweal* (December 2019): 18–23.

27. Ivereigh, "Exposing the Spirits," 18. This quote represents Ivereigh's paraphrasing of Francis's original sentences in Spanish on this occasion, while the phrases in the internal quotes are direct translations of the pope's literal words.

28. See Peter-Hans Kolvenbach, SJ, "*Discreta Caritas*," trans. Philip Endean, SJ, *Review of Ignatian Spirituality XXXVII*, no. 3 (issue 113, March 2006): 9–21 at 15. Also, at http://www.sjweb.info/documents/cis/pdfenglish/200611302en.pdf.

29. One prominent example, dating to an important teaching document published over four years before the synod on Amazonia, is no. 38 of the social encyclical *Laudato Si'* (May 24, 2015). Here, Francis identifies "the Amazon and Congo basins" as "those richly biodiverse lungs of our planet."

Chapter 3

1. The web address for Vatican News is https://www.vaticannews.va/en.html. The homepage for official documents of the Holy See is https://www.vatican.va/content/vatican/en.html. The URL specifically for the Press Office of the Holy See is https://www.vatican.va/news_services/press/index.htm.

2. As elsewhere in this volume, quotations from this classic work of spirituality are taken from Fleming, SJ, *Spiritual Exercises.* Page 139 of Fleming's translation contains no. 230 of Ignatius's text, which follows the longstanding convention of paragraph enumeration.

3. All quoted words in the preceding three paragraphs appear in Francis, "Homily during Visit to Lampedusa," July 8, 2013, https://www.vatican.va/content/francesco/en/homilies/2013/documents/papa-francesco_20130708_omelia-lampedusa.html.

4. Ivereigh, *Great Reformer*, 42.

5. Francis, "Homily at Holy Mass on the Solemnity of the Assumption," at World Cup Stadium in Daejeon, South Korea, August 15, 2015, https://www.vatican.va/content/francesco/en/homilies/2014/documents/papa-francesco_20140815_corea-omelia-assunzione.html.

6. The event was organized by the Hank Center at Loyola University in Chicago. Insightful coverage appears in Brian Fraga, "Pope Francis Takes Notes during Two-Hour Dialogue with Students across the Americas," *National Catholic Reporter*, February 24, 2022, https://www.ncronline.org/news/people/pope-francis-takes-notes-during-two-hour-dialogue-students-across-americas?utm_.

7. For further details of the peace vigil and the events that precipitated it, see Allen, *Francis Miracle*, 78–81.

8. Francis, "Homily at Vigil of Prayer for Peace," at St. Peter's Square, September 7, 2013, https://www.vatican.va/content/francesco/en/homilies/2013/documents/papa-francesco_20130907_veglia-pace.html.

9. The quoted words and general descriptions in these two paragraphs are found in "Extraordinary Moment of Prayer Presided Over by Pope Francis," at St. Peter's Square, March 27, 2020, https://www.vatican.va/content/francesco/en/messages/urbi/documents/papa-francesco_20200327_urbi-et-orbi-epidemia.html.

10. Perhaps the most comprehensive account of Francis's approach to the pandemic is the volume *Let Us Dream: The Path to a Better Future* (New York: Simon & Schuster, 2020). The words of that volume are those of Pope Francis, but the text is compiled and edited by Austen Ivereigh based on his notes and recordings from several long interviews with the pope between June and August 2020, during the early months of the COVID-19 pandemic.

11. Agbonkhianmeghe E. Orobator, SJ, *The Pope and the Pandemic: Lessons in Leadership in a Time of Crisis* (Maryknoll, NY: Orbis Books, 2021), xxiv. This work covers only the first six months of the pandemic, but it includes broad coverage of the words and deeds of Francis during that pivotal time.

12. The texts of all four addresses by Francis to these meetings are posted on the Vatican website. One instance of favorable press coverage of the fourth in this series is Gerard O'Connell, "Pope Francis's 9 Commandments for a Just Economy," *America Magazine*, October 16, 2021, https://www.americamagazine.org/faith/2021/10/16/pope-francis-universal-basic-income-george-floyd-241668?utm_.

13. A brief history of the labor schools is provided by the last Jesuit to direct one of them; see Edward Boyle, SJ, "At Work in the Vineyard: The Jesuit Labor Apostolate," in *A Worker Justice Reader: Essential Writings on Religion and Labor*, ed. Joy Heine (Maryknoll, NY: Orbis Books and Interfaith Worker Justice, 2010), 62–67. Fr. Boyle led the Labor Guild of Boston until his death in 2007; that Boston-area labor school survives as the last of the more than one hundred that existed across the United States in their heyday in the mid-twentieth century.

14. For further details of this gathering and the pope's warm welcome, see "Pope Welcomes 5,000 Migrants in Rome Prayers," unsigned news story, posted January 17, 2016, on the website of *The Times of India*, https://timesofindia.indiatimes.com/world/europe/pope-welcomes-5000-migrants-in-rome-prayers/articleshow/50615105.cms.

15. The main landing page on the Vatican website for numerous resources relating to this 2021–24 synod process is https://www.synod.va/en/resources.html.

16. For details, see two contemporary accounts co-authored by reporters Elisabetta Povoledo and Ian Austen: "Pope Hosts Canadians Who Request Apology for Indigenous Schools," *New York Times*, March 29, 2022, A9; "'I Feel Shame': Pope Apologizes to Indigenous People of Canada," *New York Times*, April 2, 2022, A4.

17. These quotations and translations from the original Spanish of the pope are taken from Jason Horowitz and Ian Austen, "Pope Expresses Grief in Alberta Over Brutality: Apologizes for Abuse of Indigenous Children," *New York Times*, July 26, 2022, A1, A12.

18. Jason Horowitz, "Pope Makes His Frailty a Lesson in Compassion," *New York Times*, July 29, 2022, A1, A8.

19. For helpful contextualization of Francis's visit to Canada, see the insightful analysis of the shifting demographics of the Catholic community in Canada contained in Ian Austen, "In Canada, Catholicism Maintains Its Stability," *New York Times*, July 30, 2022, A5.

20. See the lengthy obituary: Alan Cowell, "Eugenio Scalfari, Italian Journalist and Newspaper Founder, Dies at 98," *New York Times*, July 18, 2022, A20.

21. Cowell, *Scalfari*, A20. It is remarkable that this incident earned space in an obituary covering a long and consequential life. Scalfari's newspaper, *La Repubblica*, published a continuing series of these interviews, featuring loose characterizations of what the pope shared in their exchanges; the first two appeared on October 1, 2013, and July 13, 2014.

22. Ivereigh, *Great Reformer*, 383.

23. The text of this document, dated February 4, 2019, appears at https://www.vatican.va/content/francesco/en/travels/2019/outside/documents/papa-francesco_20190204_documento-fratellanza-umana.html.

24. See Jane Arraf and Jason Horowitz, "Iraq Finds Affirmation in Pope's Successful Visit at a Critical Moment," *New York Times*, March 9, 2021, A9.

25. See George E. Demacopoulos, "The Pope's Relic Diplomacy: Can a Bone Shard Mend a Schism?" *Commonweal*, August 9, 2019, 14–15.

26. For one example, see "Address of Francis to a Delegation of the Evangelical Lutheran Church of Germany," December 18, 2014, https://www.vatican.va/content/francesco/en/speeches/2014/december/documents/papa-francesco_20141218_chiesa-evangelica-luterana.html.

27. Details of the Skorka-Bergoglio relationship appear in Ivereigh, *Great Reformer*, 323–26.

28. See Elisabetta Povoledo, "Pope Condemns War, but Avoids Putin by Name," *New York Times*, April 23, 2022, A7.

29. Further analysis of the difficult diplomatic position occupied by Francis appears in Jason Horowitz, "Pope Denounces Invasion, but not Mastermind," *New York Times*, March 19, 2022, A1, A11.

30. See Jason Horowitz and Benjamin Novak, "Pope Treads Fine Line with Leader of Hungary," *New York Times*, September 12, 2021, 10.

31. Details appear in Jason Horowitz, "In an Increasingly Isolated Hungary, Francis Urges Diversity," *New York Times*, September 13, 2021, A8.

32. Jason Horowitz, "Pope Francis, in Egypt, Delivers a Blunt Message on Violence and Religion," *New York Times*, April 29, 2017, A6.

33. Fleming, SJ, *Spiritual Exercises*, 21. The Presupposition is no. 22 in the standard enumeration of paragraphs in this text. Fleming's "contemporary-style translation" of this principle begins with the phrase "For a good relationship to develop…" and proceeds to recommend that "a favorable interpretation…should always be given to the other's statements." Though originally intended to govern the relationship between a spiritual director and directee, this advice clearly applies to interlocutors of any sort, including potentially challenging ones as we have seen Francis engaging.

34. See, for example, Christopher J. Oldenburg, *The Rhetoric of Pope Francis: Critical Mercy and Conversion for the Twenty-First Century* (Lanham, MD: Lexington Books of Rowman and Littlefield, 2018).

35. For analysis of this aspect of the pope's social media presence, see Michael J. O'Loughlin, *The Tweetable Pope: A Spiritual Revolution in 140 Characters* (New York: HarperCollins, 2015).

36. Oldenburg, *Rhetoric of Francis*, xix.

37. See, for example, Francis, *Let us Dream*, 128–32.

Chapter 4

1. For example, *Laudato Si'* quotes (with evident approval and even admiration) documents from well over a dozen episcopal conferences, representing a notable departure from previous popes who rarely did so.

2. In interviews Francis granted after the release of *Evangelii Gaudium* in late 2013, including a prominent one that appeared in the Italian publication, *La Stampa*, Francis denied having introduced "anything not already in the teachings of the social doctrine of the Church." Indeed, in no. 184 of that document, Francis included an approving recommendation that readers in search of insight into social justice simply consult a 2004 Vatican-produced reference work *Compendium of the Social Doctrine of the Church*, calling this

resource "a most suitable tool…whose use and study I heartily recommend."

3. Francis, "Address to the Second World Meeting of Popular Movements" (section 3), Santa Cruz, Bolivia, July 9, 2015, https://www.vatican.va/content/francesco/en/speeches/2015/july/documents/papa-francesco_20150709_bolivia-movimenti-popolari.html.

4. Francis, *Fratelli Tutti* (Encyclical Letter on Fraternity and Social Friendship), October 3, 2020, https://www.vatican.va/content/francesco/en/encyclicals/documents/papa-francesco_20201003_enciclica-fratelli-tutti.html. The opening four sentences of this selection from nos. 116–17 consist of an internal citation from the pope's address in Rome on October 28, 2014, to the First World Meeting of Popular Movements.

5. The document "Justice in thc World" of the 1971 worldwide synod of bishops had pioneered the use of the related phrase "social sin," but John Paul II developed much further the notion of the social roots of injustices.

6. The one possible exception is the text of *Populorum Progressio*, the 1967 social encyclical treating global poverty and lamenting the barriers to economic development. Before its publication, Paul VI had been criticized for indulging in an excess of qualifications and caveats (he had been labeled derisively "the pope of buts"), but the soaring prophetic rhetoric of that encyclical altered his reputation, at least temporarily.

7. The phrase "Put the economy at the service of people" appears at the beginning of no. 3 of Francis's address to the Second World Meeting of Popular Movements in Bolivia, among other places in the corpus of his writings on ethics.

8. The landing page on the Vatican website for these annual messages of Francis is https://www.vatican.va/content/francesco/en/messages/migration.index.html.

9. Recall the coverage in chapter 3 of the exuberant January 17, 2016, festive event in St. Peter's Square marking World Day of Migrants and Refugees.

10. For two especially illuminating contemporary accounts of Francis's visit to Colombia see: Nicholas Casey and Susan Abad, "Pope Urges Colombians to Accept Peace Accord," *New York Times*, September 8, 2017, A6; Nicole Winfield and Alba Tobella, "Colombia:

Pope Seeking to Heal Long War's Wounds," *San Francisco Chronicle*, September 9, 2017, A2.

11. See Chris Stein and Somini Sengupta, "In Africa, Pope Makes First Visit to a War Zone," *New York Times*, November 30, 2015, A6.

12. These words appear in the address of Francis at Atomic Bomb Hypocenter Park in Nagasaki on November 24, 2019. See Pope Francis, *Against War: Building a Culture of Peace* (Maryknoll, NY: Orbis Books, 2022), 49. This excellent resource contains revealing excerpts from nearly one hundred addresses and writings of Francis on peace, including over ten pages of material from his visit to Japan and over twenty pages from his visit to Iraq. The full texts of his official writings and addresses on peace on all occasions, including his annual Messages for World Day of Peace, appear on the website of the Holy See.

13. These last two sentences—the first being a direct quote from the statement cited and the second appearing as the reporter's paraphrase of an interview—appear in an unsigned news story originating with Catholic News Service and appearing as "Rome-Brokered Peace Deal Increases Chances of Papal Visit to South Sudan," January 16, 2020, *America Magazine*, https://www.americamagazine.org/politics-society/2020/01/16/rome-brokered-peace-deal-increases-chances-papal-visit-south-sudan?utm_. For details of the original April 2019 encounter, see Jason Horowitz, "Pope Kisses Leaders' Feet as He Begs for Peace," *New York Times*, April 12, 2019, A12.

14. The most complete account of these concepts is Joseph S. Nye Jr., *Soft Power: The Means to Success in World Politics* (New York: PublicAffairs of the Perseus Books Group, 2004).

15. An impressive network of church-based activists and practitioners in the field of peace is the Catholic Peacebuilding Network. Its mission statement refers to the goal of "expanding the peacebuilding capacities of the Church in areas of conflict" by means of sharing and analyzing best practices, especially on the local level where peace is forged. Its central secretariat office, located at the University of Notre Dame, maintains a website at https://cpn.nd.edu.

16. These insights into the importance of focusing on the wider conditions that contribute to peaceful or violent outcomes are prominent in the school of thought called the Just Peacemaking Paradigm, of which the late American Protestant ethicist Glenn Stassen was a pioneer.

17. Francis was not the first pope to identify and oppose the arms trade as the scourge that it is. Pope John XXIII denounced the arms race and the proliferation and sale of armaments in his 1963 encyclical, *Pacem in Terris* (no.112). Pope Benedict XVI echoed these sentiments on many occasions, including his 2006 Message for World Day of Peace.

18. To cite just one example, Francis's 2019 World Day of Peace message contains a prominent call to halt "the uncontrolled proliferation of arms contrary to morality and the search for true peace."

19. Francis, "Address to the Joint Session of the United States Congress," September 24, 2015, https://www.vatican.va/content/francesco/en/speeches/2015/september/documents/papa-francesco_20150924_usa-us-congress.html.

20. Francis, "Address to the General Assembly of the United Nations," September 25, 2015, https://www.vatican.va/content/francesco/en/speeches/2015/september/documents/papa-francesco_20150925_onu-visita.html.

21. As often happens with papal documents, the actual release date (in this case June 18, 2015) differs from the date listed in the official text (Pentecost Sunday, which fell on May 24, 2015).

22. The Paris Climate Change Conference (officially, "COP 21 of the United Nations Framework Convention on Climate Change," where COP stands for "Conference of the Parties" to the Kyoto Protocol of 1997) had long been scheduled for December of 2015. Leaders of several other world religions (Judaism, Islam, and Buddhism among them) similarly released statements during these preceding months on the importance of addressing climate change from their own spiritual perspectives. The pope delegated supervision of this writing project to Cardinal Peter Turkson of Ghana, whose regular reports to the media regarding the progress of the document created considerable anticipation of its release.

23. The title of chapter 3 of the encyclical is "The Human Roots of the Ecological Crisis."

24. See, for example, two news articles published by major U.S. newspapers within hours of the release of *Laudato Si'* that covered the instant debate: David R. Baker, "Pope Blasts State Cap-and-Trade System," *San Francisco Chronicle*, June 19, 2015, A1, A14; Coral Davenport, "Francis Targets Economists' Favored Path to Change: Carbon Credits," *New York Times*, June 19, 2015, A8. The takeaway is that the several critics who weighed in so quickly were painting

various proposals that Francis was offering from a thoroughly nonideological perspective with a political- or economic-policy brush.

25. It is ironic that these critics, primarily economists and politicians whose agendas substantially overlap with social reforms often recommended by Francis, did not recognize themselves in the pope's explication of a central theme of chapter 3 of the encyclical. Here, the pope criticizes the incompleteness of "the technocratic paradigm [that] tends to dominate economic and political life.... Some circles maintain that current economics and technology will solve all environmental problems" (no. 109). He further writes, "The specialization which belongs to technology makes it difficult to see the larger picture" (no. 110).

26. The Orthodox Church had been marking a parallel observance since 1989, and today the Season of Creation is observed by many Christian denominations and the World Council of Churches. An ecumenical website featuring extensive resources and information is https://seasonofcreation.org/resources/.

27. Andrea Tornielli and Giacomo Galeazzi, *This Economy Kills: Pope Francis on Capitalism and Social Justice* (Collegeville, MN: Liturgical Press, 2015).

28. For a contemporary theological analysis of the importance of recent trends toward growing inequality, see Kate Ward and Kenneth R. Himes, "'Growing Apart': The Rise of Inequality," *Theological Studies* 75, no. 1 (2014): 118–32. For a parallel analysis of the dangers of sharp social stratification from the perspective of the discipline of public health, see Richard Wilkinson and Kate Pickett, *The Spirit Level: Why Greater Equality Makes Societies Stronger* (London: Bloomsbury Press, 2009).

29. Worth mentioning, beyond these precedents in papal teaching, are the many occasions when statements on social justice from national or regional conferences of bishops identified economic inequality as a key injustice. The 1986 pastoral letter of the United States Conference of Catholic Bishops, "Economic Justice for All," reflects many of the same concerns, as do successive documents of CELAM (the regional Conference of Latin American Bishops) in which Bergoglio often participated. Among other involvements over the decades, he served as chief redactor of the final documents of its 2007 meeting in Aparecida, Brazil.

30. Francis, "Address to the Second World Meeting of Popular Movements" (see no. 3 of this chapter), section 1.

31. Francis, "Visit to the Community of Varginha," Rio de Janeiro, Brazil, July 25, 2013, https://www.vatican.va/content/francesco/en/speeches/2013/july/documents/papa-francesco_20130725_gmg-comunita-varginha.html.

32. This quotation and the briefer citations in the following two paragraphs appear in Francis, "Address to People of Various Social Categories of the Neighborhood of Scampia," at Piazza Giovanni Paolo II, Naples, March 21, 2015, https://www.vatican.va/content/francesco/en/speeches/2015/march/documents/papa-francesco_20150321_napoli-pompei-popolazione-scampia.html.

33. John Paul II made a similar point in his 1981 social encyclical, *Laborem Exercens*, introducing the term "indirect employer" to signal these broad responsibilities to guarantee fair labor standards. Although rather imprecise, this notion implies obligatory efforts to shape the policies of governments as well as corporate employers to protect workers and promote their dignity.

34. Both quotes in this paragraph appear in "Address of the Holy Father Francis in His Meeting with Workers," Cagliari, Sardinia, September 22, 2013, https://www.vatican.va/content/francesco/en/speeches/2013/september/documents/papa-francesco_20130922_lavoratori-cagliari.html.

35. Francis, "Address to an Interreligious Meeting for Peace," Dhaka, Bangladesh, December 1, 2017, https://www.vatican.va/content/francesco/en/speeches/2017/december/documents/papa-francesco_20171201_viaggioapostolico-bangladesh-pace.html.

36. Bishop Thomas Dabre, "Not Just Admiration but Taking Steps unto Imitation," in *Unto the Margins: Pope Francis and His Challenges*, ed. John Chathanatt, SJ (Bangalore, India: Claretian Publications, 2013), 55–60 at 56.

Conclusion

1. Marco Politi, *Pope Francis among the Wolves: The Inside Story of a Revolution*, trans. William McCuaig (New York: Columbia University Press, 2015). The original version was published in Italian in 2014.

2. Controversies over the reform of liturgical practice tend to garner more attention in the Catholic media. It is surely no accident that the same traditionalists who resist the social implications of

the Second Vatican Council have often also opposed measures Francis has taken to curb the use of pre–Vatican II rituals such as the Tridentine Latin Mass. The promulgation of two documents (*Traditionis Custodes* and *Desiderio Desideravi*) in 2021–22, which further restricted the use of these older ritual forms angered traditionalists greatly. See two brief but especially revealing articles that appeared between the release dates of those two apostolic letters on the liturgy: Austen Ivereigh and Gregory Hillis, "Has the Pope Been Too Hard on Traditionalists? An Exchange," *Commonweal*, March 2022, 15–19; Cardinal Blase Cupich, "Securing the Legacy of Vatican II: Why Pope Francis' Latin Mass Reforms Are Necessary," *America Magazine*, January 2022, 38–41.

3. Massimo Borghesi, *Catholic Discordance: Neoconservatism vs. the Field Hospital Church of Pope Francis*, trans. Barry Hudock (Collegeville, MN: Liturgical Press Academic, 2021). This quoted phrase appears only in the text on the inside dust jacket of the hardcover edition of this book, but the book's introduction describes fully the origin and features of the startling backlash.

4. Borghesi analyzes the positions of many figures in this school; the most prominent Americans are George Weigel and the late Michael Novak and Richard John Neuhaus. Surely worth adding to this list is Catholic public intellectual Ross Douthat. See, for example, Douthat's sharp rebukes of Francis in these two writings: "The Slow Road to Catholic Schism," *New York Times*, September 15, 2019, 9; *To Change the Church: Pope Francis and the Future of Catholicism* (New York: Simon & Schuster, 2018).

5. Reporters pressed Francis on how he views his critics during an extended airborne interview in 2019 and were amazed at his words of appreciation for his detractors because he "had always found value in criticism, because it prompted self-reflection." Quote appears in Jason Horowitz, "Returning from Africa, Pope Reflects on Critics," *New York Times*, September 11, 2019, A10.

6. David Agren, "Popes Rarely Intervene in Authoritarian Politics. Nicaraguans Want Pope Francis to Make an Exception," *America Magazine*, August 25, 2022, at https://www.americamagazine.org/politics-society/2022/08/25/pope-francis-nicaragua-silence-243618?utm_.

7. For example, Pius XI published the March 1937 encyclical *Mit Brennender Sorge* (the original text, by way of great exception, is in German, no less) to put the Nazis on notice that the pope was

watching the growing abuses of power closely. In English, it translates as "With Burning Concern" with the subtitle, "On the Church and the German Reich." Pius XII is credited with working behind the scenes to save thousands of Jewish lives in Italy and elsewhere. His muted criticism of Hitler may be generously interpreted as an attempt to prevent wider bloodshed against Catholics in Germany and Italy, not to mention retaliation against the Vatican itself.

8. A full account of these events in the church in Chile appears in Ivereigh, *Wounded Shepherd*, 100–48.

9. One prominent journalist who subscribes to the view that Francis has entered a phrase of consolidation is Michael Sean Winters. See his "Pope Francis' Tenure Isn't Over. In Fact, Themes of His Pontificate Are Starting to Gel," *National Catholic Reporter*, September 2, 2022, https://www.ncronline.org/news/opinion/pope-francis-tenure-isnt-over-fact-themes-his-pontificate-are-now-starting-gel.

10. Insightful analysis of the apostolic letter *Traditionis Custodes* (July 16, 2021) appears in Michael Sean Winters, "On the Latin Mass, Francis Pulls Off the Band-Aid," *National Catholic Reporter*, July 16, 2021, https://www.ncronline.org/news/opinion/distinctly-catholic/latin-mass-pope-francis-pulls-band-aid.

SELECT BIBLIOGRAPHY

THIS LISTING INCLUDES the most important resources cited in the text of this volume. Excluded are a few church documents of lesser import for the topic at hand and most news stories and media accounts of developments in Francis's papacy.

Allen, Jr., John L. *The Francis Miracle: Inside the Transformation of the Pope and the Church*. New York: Time Books, 2015.

Borghesi, Massimo. *Catholic Discordance: Neoconservatism vs. the Field Hospital Church of Pope Francis*. Trans. Barry Hudock. Collegeville, MN: Liturgical Press Academic, 2021.

Boyle, SJ, Edward. "At Work in the Vineyard: The Jesuit Labor Apostolate." In *A Worker Justice Reader: Essential Writings on Religion and Labor*, ed. Joy Heine, 62–67. Maryknoll, NY: Orbis Books and Interfaith Worker Justice, 2010.

Cupich, Blase Cardinal. "Securing the Legacy of Vatican II: Why Pope Francis' Latin Mass Reforms Are Necessary." *America Magazine*, January 2022, 38–41.

Dabre, Bishop Thomas. "Not Just Admiration but Taking Steps unto Imitation." In *Unto the Margins: Pope Francis and His Challenges*, edited by John Chathanatt, SJ, 55–60. Bangalore, India: Claretian Publications, 2013.

Daly, Daniel J. *The Structures of Virtue and Vice*. Washington, DC: Georgetown University Press, 2021.

Deck, SJ, Allan Figueroa. *Francis, Bishop of Rome: The Gospel for the Third Millennium*. Mahwah, NJ: Paulist Press, 2016.

Demacopoulos, George E. "The Pope's Relic Diplomacy: Can a Bone Shard Mend a Schism?" *Commonweal*, August 9, 2019, 14–15.

Douthat, Ross. *To Change the Church: Pope Francis and the Future of Catholicism*. New York: Simon & Schuster, 2018.

Endean, SJ, Philip, ed. and trans. "Jorge Mario Bergoglio: Writings on Jesuit Spirituality I and II." *Studies in the Spirituality of Jesuits* 45, nos. 3 and 4 (Autumn/Winter 2013).

Folan, SJ, Peter. "Can Catholics Dissent from Pope Francis's Teaching on the Family? Wrong Question." *America Magazine*, April 17, 2017, 36–37.

Ferrone, Rita. "A Wonderful Complexity: What Does Instituting Women in Ministries Really Mean?" *Commonweal*, April 2022, 10–13.

Fleming, SJ, David L. *The Spiritual Exercises of St. Ignatius: A Literal Translation and a Contemporary Reading*. St. Louis: Institute of Jesuit Sources, 1978.

Ivereigh, Austen. "Exposing the Spirits: What the Amazon Synod Decided and What It Revealed." *Commonweal*, December 2019, 18–23.

———. *The Great Reformer: Francis and the Making of a Radical Pope*. New York: Henry Holt and Company, 2014.

———. *Wounded Shepherd: Pope Francis and His Struggle to Convert the Catholic Church*. New York: Henry Holt and Company, 2019.

Ivereigh, Austen, and Gregory Hillis. "Has the Pope Been Too Hard on Traditionalists? An Exchange." *Commonweal*, March 2022, 15–19.

Keenan, SJ, James F. "Receiving *Amoris Laetitia*." *Theological Studies* 78, no. 1 (2017): 193–212.

Kolvenbach, SJ, Peter-Hans. "Discreta Caritas." Translated by Philip Endean, SJ. *Review of Ignatian Spirituality* XXXVII, no. 3 (issue 113, March 2006): 9–21. Also available at http://www.sjweb.info/documents/cis/pdfenglish/200611302en.pdf.

Lamb, Christopher. *The Outsider: Pope Francis and His Battle to Reform the Church*. Maryknoll, NY: Orbis Books, 2020.

Lowney, Chris. *Everyone Leads: How to Revitalize the Catholic Church*. Lanham, MD: Rowman & Littlefield, 2017.

———. *Heroic Leadership: Best Practices from a 450-Year-Old Company that Changed the World*. Chicago: Loyola Press, 2003.

———. *Pope Francis: Why He Leads the Way He Leads; Lessons from the First Jesuit Pope*. Chicago: Loyola Press, 2013.

Martin, SJ, James. *Building a Bridge: How the Catholic Church and the LGBT Community Can Enter into a Relationship of Respect, Compassion, and Sensitivity*. Revised and expanded edition. New York: HarperCollins Publishers, 2018.

Nye, Jr., Joseph S. *Soft Power: The Means to Success in World Politics*. New York: PublicAffairs of the Perseus Books Group, 2004.

O'Collins, SJ, Gerald. "The Joy of Love (*Amoris Laetitia*): The Papal Exhortation in Its Context." *Theological Studies* 77, no. 4 (2016): 905–21.

O'Connell, Gerard. *The Election of Pope Francis: An Inside Account of the Conclave that Changed History*. Maryknoll, NY: Orbis Books, 2019.

O'Loughlin, Michael J. *The Tweetable Pope: A Spiritual Revolution in 140 Characters*. New York: HarperCollins, 2015.

———. "Walking with Peter: A Confident Pope Sets a New Example for Governing the Church." *America Magazine*, January 23, 2017, 27–33.

O'Malley, SJ, John W. "Papal Upgrades: How Popes Became So Powerful—and Can Pope Francis Reverse the Trend?" *America Magazine*, July/August 2022, 38–41.

Oldenburg, Christopher J. *The Rhetoric of Pope Francis: Critical Mercy and Conversion for the Twenty-First Century*. Lanham, MD: Lexington Books of Rowman and Littlefield, 2018.

Orobator, SJ, Agbonkhianmeghe E. *The Pope and the Pandemic: Lessons in Leadership in a Time of Crisis*. Maryknoll, NY: Orbis Books, 2021.

Politi, Marco. *Pope Francis among the Wolves: The Inside Story of a Revolution*. Translated by William McCuaig. New York: Columbia University Press, 2015.

Pope Francis. "Address of the Holy Father in His Meeting with Workers." Cagliari, Sardinia. September 22, 2013. https://www.vatican.va/content/francesco/en/speeches/2013/september/documents/papa-francesco_20130922_lavoratori-cagliari.html.

———. "Address to a Delegation of the Evangelical Lutheran Church of Germany." December 18, 2014. https://www.vatican.va/content/francesco/en/speeches/2014/december/documents/papa-francesco_20141218_chiesa-evangelica-luterana.html.

———. "Address to an Interreligious Meeting for Peace." Dhaka, Bangladesh. December 1, 2017. https://www.vatican.va/content/francesco/en/speeches/2017/december/documents/papa

-francesco_20171201_viaggioapostolico-bangladesh-pace .html.

———. "Address to People of Various Social Categories of the Neighborhood of Scampia." Piazza Giovanni Paolo II, Naples. March 21, 2015. https://www.vatican.va/content/francesco/en/speeches/2015/march/documents/papa-francesco_20150321_napoli-pompei-popolazione-scampia.html.

———. "Address to the General Assembly of the United Nations." September 25, 2015. https://www.vatican.va/content/francesco/en/speeches/2015/september/documents/papa-francesco_20150925_onu-visita.html.

———. "Address to the Joint Session of the United States Congress." September 24, 2015. https://www.vatican.va/content/francesco/en/speeches/2015/september/documents/papa-francesco_20150924_usa-us-congress.html.

———. "Address to the Second World Meeting of Popular Movements." Santa Cruz, Bolivia. July 9, 2015. https://www.vatican.va/content/francesco/en/speeches/2015/july/documents/papa-francesco_20150709_bolivia-movimenti-popolari.html.

———. *Against War: Building a Culture of Peace*. Maryknoll, NY: Orbis Books, 2022.

———. *Amoris Laetitia*: Apostolic Exhortation on Love in the Family. March 19, 2016. https://www.vatican.va/content/francesco/en/apost_exhortations/documents/papa-francesco_esortazione-ap_20160319_amoris-laetitia.html.

———. Apostolic Letter: Regarding Provisions on Transparency in the Management of Public Finances. April 26, 2021. https://www.vatican.va/content/francesco/en/motu_proprio/documents/papa-francesco-motu-proprio-20210426_trasparenza-finanzapubblica.html.

———. *Christus Vivit*: Apostolic Exhortation to Young People and to the Entire People of God. March 25, 2019. https://www.vatican.va/content/francesco/en/apost_exhortations/documents/papa-francesco_esortazione-ap_20190325_christus-vivit.html.

———. *Desiderio Desideravi*: Apostolic Letter on the Liturgical Formation of the People of God. June 29, 2022. https://www.vatican.va/content/francesco/en/apost_letters/documents/20220629-lettera-ap-desiderio-desideravi.html.

———. *Evangelii Gaudium*: Apostolic Exhortation on the Joy of the Gospel. November 24, 2013. https://www.vatican.va/content/

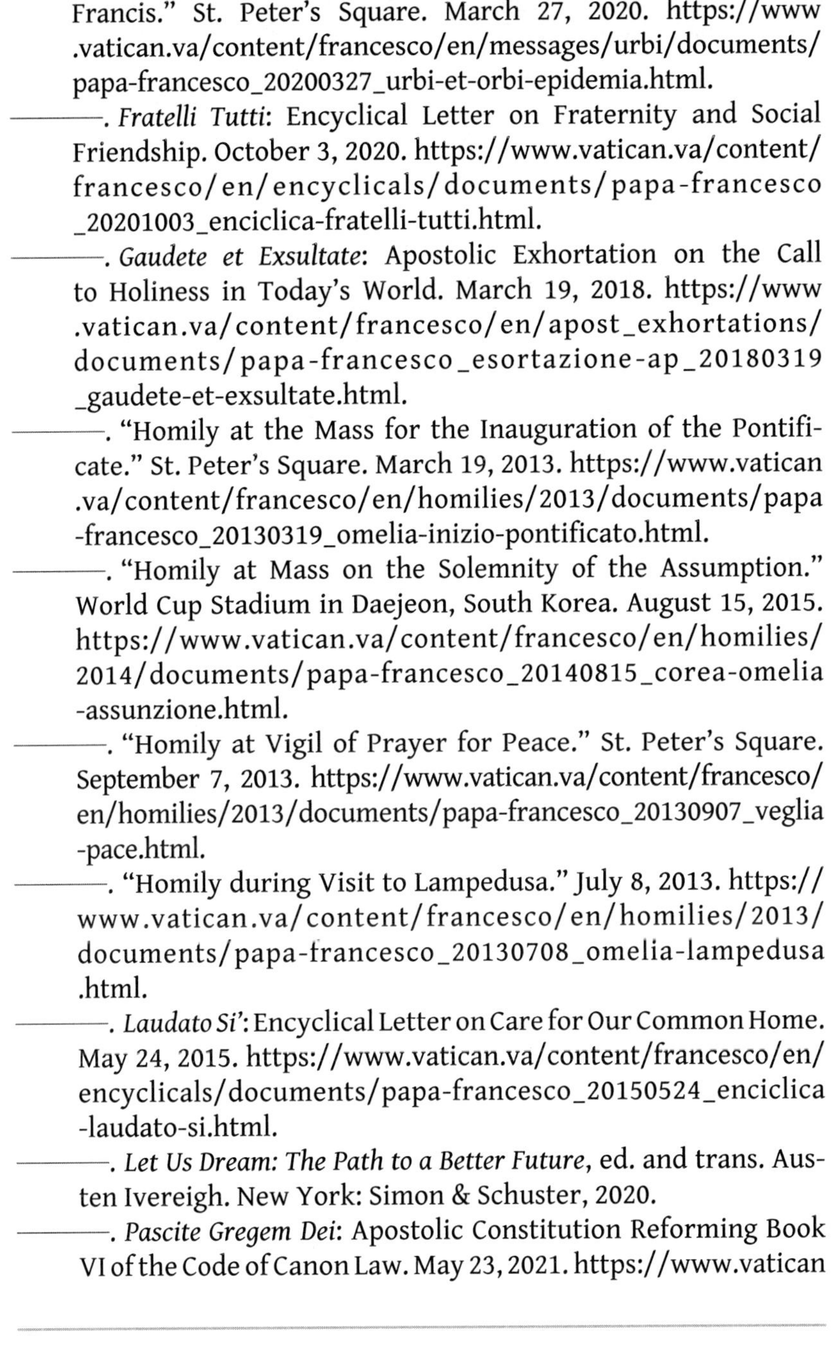

francesco/en/apost_exhortations/documents/papa-francesco_esortazione-ap_20131124_evangelii-gaudium.html.

———. "Extraordinary Moment of Prayer Presided over by Pope Francis." St. Peter's Square. March 27, 2020. https://www.vatican.va/content/francesco/en/messages/urbi/documents/papa-francesco_20200327_urbi-et-orbi-epidemia.html.

———. *Fratelli Tutti*: Encyclical Letter on Fraternity and Social Friendship. October 3, 2020. https://www.vatican.va/content/francesco/en/encyclicals/documents/papa-francesco_20201003_enciclica-fratelli-tutti.html.

———. *Gaudete et Exsultate*: Apostolic Exhortation on the Call to Holiness in Today's World. March 19, 2018. https://www.vatican.va/content/francesco/en/apost_exhortations/documents/papa-francesco_esortazione-ap_20180319_gaudete-et-exsultate.html.

———. "Homily at the Mass for the Inauguration of the Pontificate." St. Peter's Square. March 19, 2013. https://www.vatican.va/content/francesco/en/homilies/2013/documents/papa-francesco_20130319_omelia-inizio-pontificato.html.

———. "Homily at Mass on the Solemnity of the Assumption." World Cup Stadium in Daejeon, South Korea. August 15, 2015. https://www.vatican.va/content/francesco/en/homilies/2014/documents/papa-francesco_20140815_corea-omelia-assunzione.html.

———. "Homily at Vigil of Prayer for Peace." St. Peter's Square. September 7, 2013. https://www.vatican.va/content/francesco/en/homilies/2013/documents/papa-francesco_20130907_veglia-pace.html.

———. "Homily during Visit to Lampedusa." July 8, 2013. https://www.vatican.va/content/francesco/en/homilies/2013/documents/papa-francesco_20130708_omelia-lampedusa.html.

———. *Laudato Si'*: Encyclical Letter on Care for Our Common Home. May 24, 2015. https://www.vatican.va/content/francesco/en/encyclicals/documents/papa-francesco_20150524_enciclica-laudato-si.html.

———. *Let Us Dream: The Path to a Better Future*, ed. and trans. Austen Ivereigh. New York: Simon & Schuster, 2020.

———. *Pascite Gregem Dei*: Apostolic Constitution Reforming Book VI of the Code of Canon Law. May 23, 2021. https://www.vatican

.va/content/francesco/en/apost_constitutions/documents/papa-francesco_costituzione-ap_20210523_pascite-gregem-dei.html.

———. *Praedicate Evangelium:* Apostolic Constitution on the Roman Curia and Its Service to the Church in the World. March 19, 2022. https://www.vatican.va/content/francesco/en/apost_constitutions/documents/20220319-costituzione-ap-praedicate-evangelium.html.

———. *Querida Amazonia*: Apostolic Exhortation on the Beloved Amazon. February 2, 2020. https://www.vatican.va/content/francesco/en/apost_exhortations/documents/papa-francesco_esortazione-ap_20200202_querida-amazonia.html.

———. *Traditionis Custodes*: Apostolic Letter on the Use of the Roman Liturgy Prior to the Reform of 1970. July 16, 2021. https://www.vatican.va/content/francesco/en/motu_proprio/documents/20210716-motu-proprio-traditionis-custodes.html.

———. "Visit to the Community of Varginha." Rio de Janeiro, Brazil. July 25, 2013. https://www.vatican.va/content/francesco/en/speeches/2013/july/documents/papa-francesco_20130725_gmg-comunita-varginha.html.

———. *Vos Estis Lux Mundi*: Apostolic Letter "You Are the Light of the World." May 7, 2019. https://www.vatican.va/content/francesco/en/motu_proprio/documents/papa-francesco-motu-proprio-20190507_vos-estis-lux-mundi.html.

Pope Francis and Ahmad Al-Tayyeb (Grand Imam of Al-Azhar). "A Document on Human Fraternity for World Peace and Living Together." February 4, 2019. https://www.vatican.va/content/francesco/en/travels/2019/outside/documents/papa-francesco_20190204_documento-fratellanza-umana.html.

Rubio, Julie Hanlon. "The Newness of Amoris Laetitia: Mercy and Truth, Truth and Mercy." In *Amoris Laetitia: A New Momentum for Moral Formation and Pastoral Practice*, ed. Grant Gallicho and James F. Keenan, SJ, 61–69. Mahwah, NJ: Paulist Press, 2018.

Society of Jesus. *Documents of the 31st and 32nd General Congregations of the Society of Jesus*. St. Louis: Institute of Jesuit Sources, 1977.

Spadaro, SJ, Antonio. *A Big Heart Open to God: A Conversation with Pope Francis*. New York: America Press and HarperCollins Publishers, 2013.

Tornielli, Andrea, and Giacomo Galeazzi. *This Economy Kills: Pope Francis on Capitalism and Social Justice*. Collegeville, MN: Liturgical Press, 2015.

Ward, Kate, and Kenneth R. Himes. "'Growing Apart': The Rise of Inequality." *Theological Studies* 75, no. 1 (2014): 118–32.

Wilkinson, Richard, and Kate Pickett. *The Spirit Level: Why Greater Equality Makes Societies Stronger*. London: Bloomsbury Press, 2009.

INDEX

Books By and About Pope Francis

On Care for Our Common Home
Pope Francis
4980-3 $9.95
160 pp.

The Joy of Love: On Love in the Family
Pope Francis
5318-3 $11.95
256 pp.

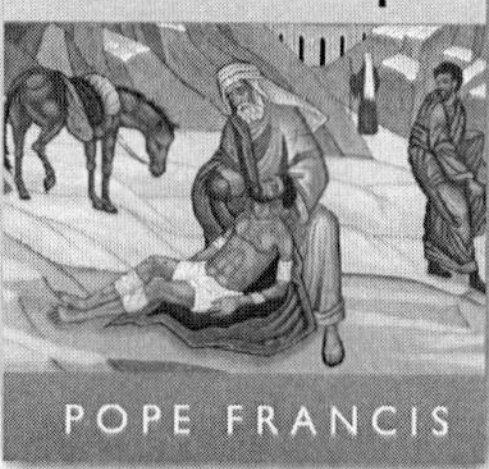

On Fraternity and Social Friendship
Pope Francis
5564-4 $9.95
160 pp.

On the Liturgical Formation of the People of God
Pope Francis
5660-3 $15.95
88 pp.

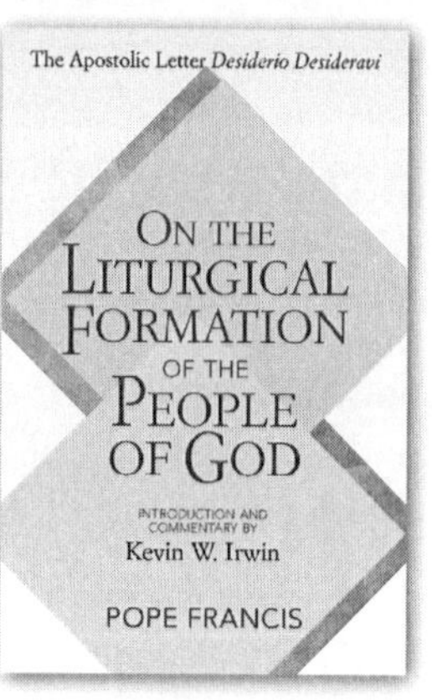

The Francis Project
Víctor Manuel Fernández
4963-6 $17.95
128 pp.

Go into the Streets!
Thomas Rausch, & Richard Gaillardetz
4951-3 $19.95
192 pp.

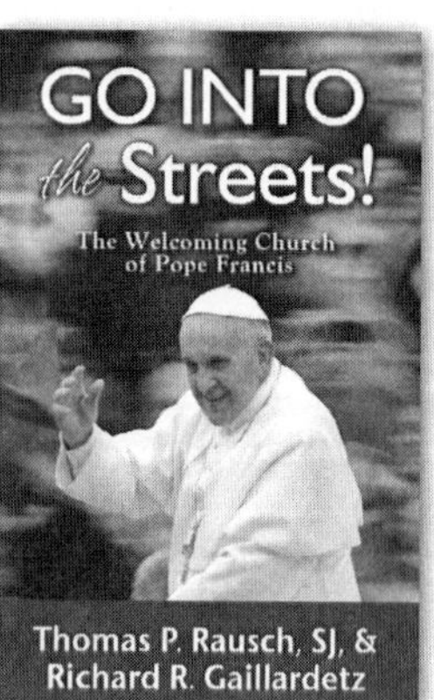

www.paulistpress.com

Books By and About Pope Francis

Pope Francis' Revolution of Tenderness and Love
Cardinal Walter Kasper
0623-3 $16.95
128 pp. HC

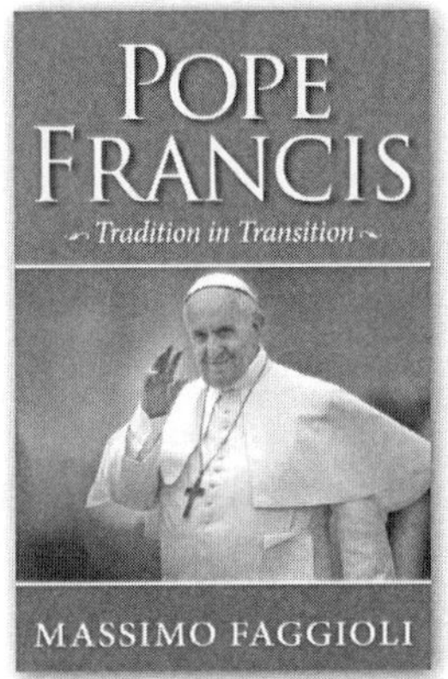

Pope Francis
Massimo Faggioli
4892-9 $14.95
128 pp.

Pope Francis and the Liturgy
Kevin W. Irwin
5471-5 $29.95
216 pp.

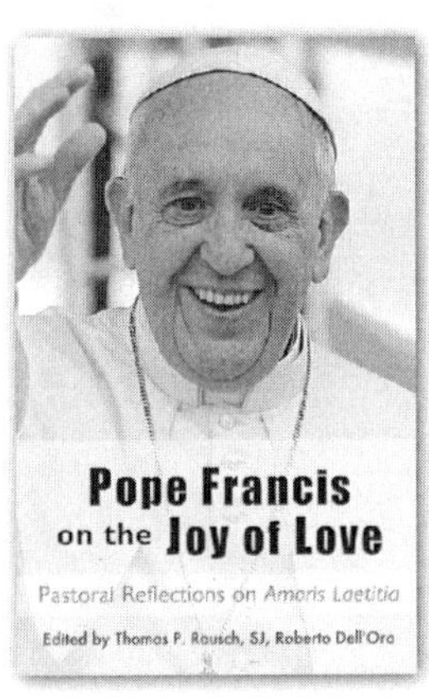

Pope Francis on the Joy of Love
Thomas Rausch & Roberto Dell'Oro
5418-0 $24.95
200 pp.

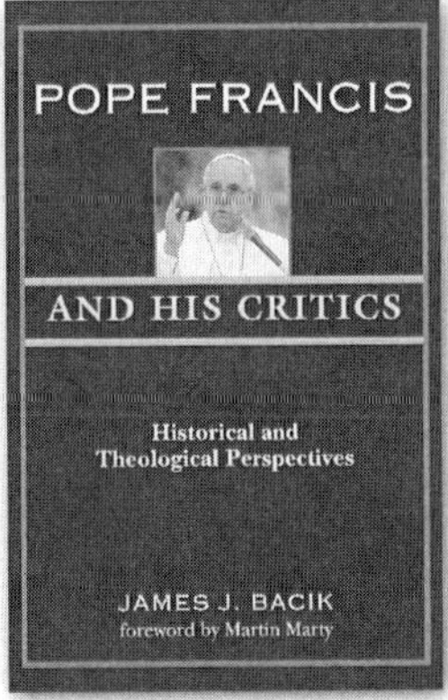

Pope Francis and His Critics
James J. Bacik
5453-1 $14.95
136 pp.

Pope Francis, *Evangelii Gaudium*, and the Renewal of the Churchy
Duncan Dormor & Alana Harris
5367-1 $39.95
352 pp.

www.paulistpress.com

Books By and About Pope Francis

Theology of the People
Juan Carlos Scannone, SJ
5475-3 $39.95
256 pp.

The Study Guide to the Encyclical Letter of Pope Francis
Marcus Mescher
5565-1 $19.95
224 pp.

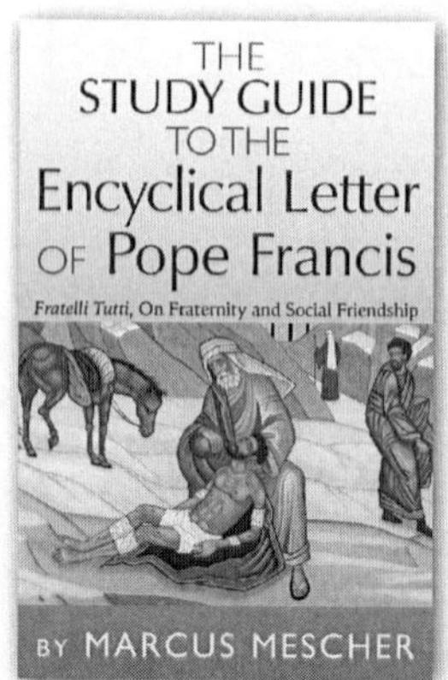

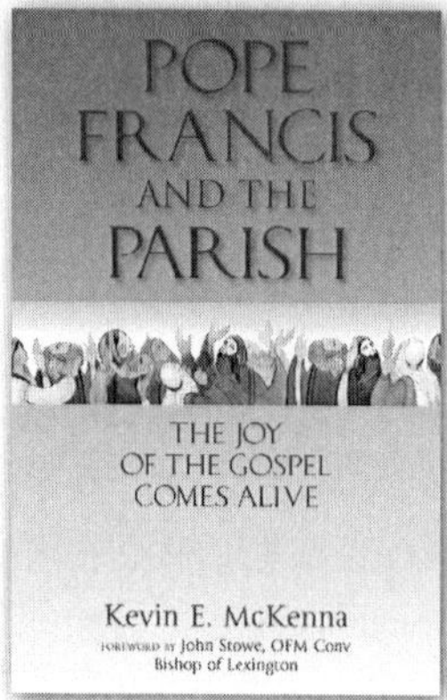

Pope Francis and the Parish
Kevin McKenna
5600-9 $19.95
112 pp.

Francis, Bishop of Rome
Allan Figueroa Deck
0622-6 $19.95
160 pp. HC

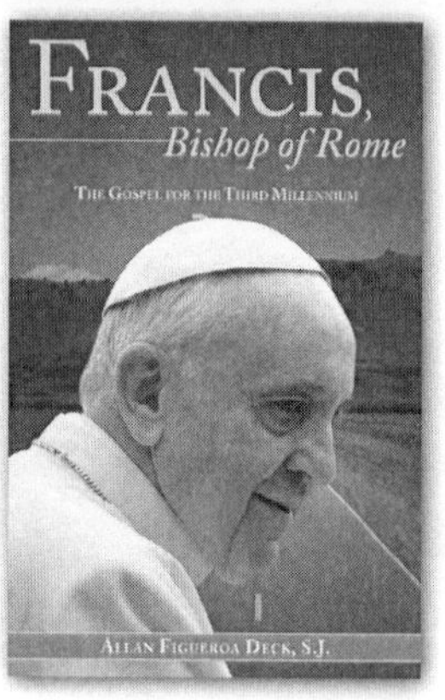

Pope Francis, the Family, and Divorce
Stephen Walford
5429-6 $19.95
232 pp.

You Are in My Heart
Pope Francis
5410-4 $4.95
336 pp.

www.paulistpress.com